"*Bow to Life* is ... ...book. The author opens readers to many positive attitudes that martial arts philosophy can inspire. With an interesting theme and simple exercise for each day, this book offers practical advice and accessible ways to apply it."
—C. Alexander Simpkins, PhD, & Annellen M. Simpkins, PhD, coauthors of the Simple series and *Taekwondo: Building on the Basics*

"Joseph Cardillo has done it again. *Bow to Life* is a clear and simple guide to living a fulfilling life—mentally, spiritually, and physically. The one-day-at-a-time format is very easy to understand and practice. I like this book very much."
—Fred L. Miller, author of *How to Calm Down* and *Yoga for Common Aches and Pains*

And praise for Joseph Cardillo's previous book,

Be Like Water

"A fascinating and helpful book for everyone trying to make sense of our crazy world."
—Joe Hyams, author of *Zen in the Martial Arts*

"Drawing from his basis in the martial arts, Joseph Cardillo guides the reader through an exciting passageway of new discoveries—ultimately leading to a more refined method of encountering and interacting with life."
—Scott Shaw, author of *Nirvana in a Nutshell* and *The Warrior Is Silent: Martial Arts and the Spiritual Path*

"A lovely little book that strikes its target perfectly."
—Nancy O'Hara, author of *Find a Quiet Corner* and *Serenity in Motion*

"Delivers ancient tools for living well. This book will teach you how to walk in the world like a martial arts master."
—Fred L. Miller, author of *How to Calm Down*

JOSEPH CARDILLO has held the post of head advisor and instructor for the Hudson Valley Community College Martial Arts Club for more than a decade. He is a black belt martial arts expert and longtime practitioner of several martial arts, including Kenpo karate, Wing Chun kung fu, Tai Chi Chuan, Kali, and Dumog. He has taught creative writing for twenty-seven years at several colleges, including the University of Albany, where he served as visiting professor in the School of Educational Theory and Practice. He is also the author of *Be Like Water: Practical Wisdom from the Martial Arts*. At present, Cardillo is a full professor of English and creative writing at Hudson Valley Community College of the State University of New York. He travels around the country regularly, giving seminars and workshops based on his writings.

Also by Joseph Cardillo

Be Like Water: Practical Wisdom from the Martial Arts

bow to life

365

SECRETS FROM THE MARTIAL ARTS *for* DAILY LIFE

JOSEPH CARDILLO

MARLOWE & COMPANY
NEW YORK

Bow to Life: *365 Secrets from the Martial Arts for Daily Life*

Copyright © 2006 by Joseph Cardillo

Published by
Marlowe & Company
An Imprint of Avalon Publishing Group, Incorporated
245 West 17th Street • 11th Floor
New York, NY 10011-5300

AVALON
publishing group incorporated

Library of Congress Cataloging-in-Publication Data

Cardillo, Joe.
Bow to life : 365 secrets from the martial arts for daily life / Joseph Cardillo.
p. cm.
ISBN 1-56924-308-5 (pbk.)
1. Martial arts. I. Title.
GV1101.C374 2006
796.801—dc22
2006008133

ISBN-13: 978-1-56924-308-4

9 8 7 6 5 4 3 2 1

Designed by Pauline Neuwirth, Neuwirth & Associates, Inc.

Printed in the United States of America

For our daughter,
Isabella
Whom we have loved since before she was born

A true warrior is armed with three things:
The radiant sword of pacification;
The mirror of bravery, wisdom, and friendship;
And the precious jewel of enlightenment

—MORIHEI UESHIBA

Contents

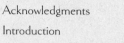

Acknowledgments

I WISH TO thank my immediate and extended family for their energies and guidance in helping to bring this project to completion. I further wish to express my gratitude to my friend and martial colleague Matthew Papa, as well as all my friends, martial arts associates, partners, and colleagues for their support, brotherhood, and sisterhood along this dazzling path of life.

Special thanks are extended to my wife, Elaine, for her understanding, joyfulness, and heartfelt support through this journey, and to our daughter, Isabella, for all of her magnificence, energy, and goodness.

It is with deep gratitude that I acknowledge my parents, Alfio and Josephine Cardillo, for their gifts of love, encouragement, and life.

Special thanks are also extended to Linda Konner and Matthew Lore for their excellent advice and terrific commitment to the vision of this project.

Introduction

IMAGINE HOW GOOD it feels to be able to power up your energy at will, to walk and act with confidence—to come and go in peace wherever you are. Imagine feeling and being stronger, healthier, and happier. Sometimes all it takes is a little glance in a different direction.

Bow to Life maps a direction rooted in the ancient traditions of martial arts. It invites you to explore a new and exciting tool to generate and tap in to tremendous inner power to achieve unparalleled successes wherever you wish—from dealing with relationships, family life, and the work world to managing emotional and health issues. It doesn't matter if you are a practicing martial artist or not; anyone and everyone can apply the principles in this text.

Martial arts from their inception have always been more about living than they ever were about fighting. Accordingly, *Bow to Life,* as my first book, *Be Like Water,* proceeds from the martial anthem that emphasizes, "A martial artist without philosophy is nothing more than a street fighter." In this spirit, *Bow to Life* threads martial ideals of self-actualization, courage, love, loyalty, sincerity, brotherhood, and sisterhood with techniques readers can immediately tap *and utilize* to access an energy source they may have never dreamed they possess.

Contemporary science and philosophy allude to this power as the *Universal Energy Field,* which they identify as the energy within everything in the universe. Interestingly, this concept has been the heart of martial teaching and development for more than three thousand years. Bowing to life is acknowledging this force as the energy behind all creative, free, spontaneous, peaceful, and enlightened living. Bowing to life is greeting the flow of Universal Energy through all nature, including yourself, and learning to move and grow gracefully with it—in thanks and humility. In bowing to the power and unity of life, you bow to yourself.

The philosophy of martial arts is meant to be experienced. It maps a journey in which you discover many incredible things. There are plenty of voices of knowledge: philosophical, theological, scientific, athletic, artistic, and more. Each voice tells us that there is more to life than we think. My aim in writing *Bow to Life,* however, is to share ancient wisdoms developed in the Shaolin Temple of China millenniums ago and passed down through generations of martial artists all over the world as *the most illuminating principles of creative, transformative energy we have in life.* In fact, history tells us these wisdoms were perceived as so life-strengthening that their practice was forbidden by warlords who saw them as threats to sovereign rule. Consequently, the temple itself was destroyed on three separate occasions. Thanks to the perseverance of these ancient teachers, who at times had to preserve their lessons in secret texts, such truths are available to us today.

As you journey through the pages of this book, you will begin to suspect that the word "dojo" can refer to more than just one specific place—and you're right. This is intentional as well as historical. *Dojo* is a word used to refer to the place where martial arts are learned and trained. However, as martial icon Joe Hyams says, "[The dojo] is an arena of confined conflict where we confront an opponent who is not an opponent but rather a partner engaged in helping us understand ourselves more fully." Indeed, we have an Earth dojo as well, where conflict, joy, and lessons ride side by side. Historically, the dojo evolves into a microuniverse—a place where you learn about who and what you are at your deepest and where life's biggest mysteries will unravel. There is a Zen saying, "Your dojo is everywhere." Indeed, when you bow to life you remind yourself that wherever you are is a place of enlightenment.

The process of learning to nurture yourself and others with the gift of life force energy is a riveting one. You will literally feel your body chemistry changing—cleansing. You will think more clearly. You will feel and know more deeply. Many amazing things are about to occur.

Welcome to your journey. I wish you many blessings!

How to Use This Book

Bow to Life is not a how-to guide for performing fighting techniques. It is, rather, an exploration of philosophies within the martial arts for the purpose of self-improvement and spiritual development. I have organized the book as a thorough yet simple journey straight through the heart of core martial principles. Each page presents a specific dojo secret, a martial concept, as well as how you can apply it in daily living. The book is designed to be read at your own pace. You can read through slowly, giving yourself time to absorb the techniques offered on each page. You can also read through quickly and return to those pages that are most applicable to your current life situations.

For readers who are unfamiliar with martial arts terminology, a glossary is included.

bow to life

1.

Bow to Life

TRADITIONALLY, BOWING IS the first thing you do when you enter a dojo and the last thing you do when you leave. It is a reminder that you come and go in peace. Bowing is a form of respect used in the martial arts, as well as throughout Asia. In a dojo the act of bowing is considered proper etiquette, equivalent to a handshake in Western cultures. In sparring the gesture sets an atmosphere of good sportsmanship, trust, and safety—implying that no one is there to hurt anyone else. There is hidden meaning to the bow—it is recognition of the Divine in another person. This notion is literal. Within each person and everything in our universe is a portion of Divine energy. This may sound blasphemous, but traditional martial arts teaches you to bow to another person because you see the Divinity in that person, because you are both directly connected to the Infinite and thus to each other. The study of martial concepts is a way to unlock this amazing power and to discover what can be done with it.

EXERCISE

SPEND A DAY looking for the good in everyone you encounter as if watching a sunrise over the ocean for the first time—no nitpicking. Shoot them a smile, even if just with your eyes. You are mentally bowing. You are showing respect and admiration for the good in life. Don't worry about if they do or do not see you. Do the same with other things in your environment: places you go, music you listen to, nature, whatever is in your path. At the end of the day, see how good you feel, how much better it is than to have gotten into a clash with a coworker or a cashier at the grocery store. A bow is Divine energy sent into the world. By bowing to someone, you actively choose what kind of energy comes back to you.

Follow the Hidden Meaning of Prayer Hands

THE PRACTICE OF *prayer hands*—where you position your palms to face each other and hold them together as if praying—reveals another hidden concept. The gesture is an ancient sign of humility and respect that is often combined with a bow as a greeting. Symbolically, the right hand represents the physical self, and the left hand represents the spiritual self. It reminds you that life is a composite of both body and spirit. And your mind is the pathway between the two. Ceremonially, martial artists form the right hand into a fist and cover it with the left. This represents your partnership to everything in the universe. It also signifies that you can always be entirely who you are, physically, mentally, and spiritually, and still be part of something bigger—what many call the Infinite or God. It marks your agreement with the world to be authentic at all times and to use your art to dissolve stress and conflict and to heighten joy. All life is physical and spiritual. Agree to honor both in everyone and everything.

EXERCISE

TAKE SOME TIME during your day to help alleviate someone else's stress. See how you feel at the end of the day. Energy flows with balance. It recycles. The best thing you can do while you are waiting to de-stress yourself (or make more money, make peace with somebody, make a good time better, and the like) is to help someone else accomplish the same thing. This is an easy way to connect body, mind, and spirit, as positive energy recycles itself from person to person.

3.

Act with Supreme, Ultimate Power

THE SUPREME, ULTIMATE power everyone seeks is inside us. You can learn to access it at will. In Chinese this energy is called *Tai Chi, Tai* translating to *supreme ultimate, Chi* to *power* (energy). In Japanese it is known as *Ki;* in Sanskrit, *Ka;* to the Greeks it was known as *Pneuma; Ruakh* in Hebrew; and *Spiritus* in Latin. People everywhere on the planet are aware of this energy and have tried to understand it. Martial arts, from the get-go, is all about harnessing and utilizing this spiritual elixir. Your job is to hook up and stay connected. Basketball superstar Kareem Abdul Jabbar, who studied martial arts with Bruce Lee, calls Chi an "incredibly powerful" force, "one of the very few willable miracles" life offers. But you don't have to be a martial artist or Kareem Abdul Jabbar to plug in to your Chi. A senior master once told me, "Anyone can summon Chi just by walking down the street." He was explaining how easily you can connect with this ultimate life force energy. Tap in. Feel restored. Use the energy of the universe to animate your life. Act with supreme, ultimate power.

EXERCISE

MAKE YOUR GOAL becoming attentive to the energy generated by your movement. Take a walk, play tennis, do lawn work, whatever you do for fun—but focus on where energy is welling up in your body. Chi generally first appears as a sensation of warmth or heat in the chest or abdominal areas. Turn up your awareness and feel it moving through you. If you don't experience this recognition right away, be patient. You will become more sensitive with practice. Be conscious of where the energy starts and the pathways it follows as it flows through your body.

4.

Channel Your Chi

THE CONCEPT OF an invisible life force inside us and everywhere around us is nothing new. Millenniums ago, the Shaolin monks developed a series of postures intended to build and channel Chi. These exercises were adapted from animal movements and natural elements. The movements, performed like a slow dance, kept the monks healthy and peaked their mental and spiritual powers. Stories abound with how the monks became so strong that they could turn stone columns into powder with their bare hands, collapse opponents with a fingertip, and heal themselves and others of great illnesses by the touch of a hand. They could even transport consciousness beyond their bodies. We are all born with such ability. To find your ability you must first learn to harness Chi. The Shaolin monks discovered that by combining meditation with movement, you can connect to the beauty, grace, Chi, and the knowledge of nature and the Divine. Moreover, you can use this technique to transform your life and the lives of others. Harnessing your Chi requires practice. I'm a big believer that most dojo concepts take time to master. But you *can* do it. The payback is immediate, even as you learn. New skills become part of life, and the benefits increase from there.

EXERCISE

ALL ENERGY IS magnetic. Make yourself aware of the energy your body generates through movements and draws from the environment around you. Visualize yourself as a magnet. Feel the energy coming to you. Feel yourself able to summon energy from all around. Remember this feeling. You will be doing a lot more with it.

5.

Find Your Center

MARTIAL ARTS TEACH you to find and strengthen your core. This process is called *centering*. To do this you have to pinpoint the major location of Chi in your body. Centering helps you develop more Chi and better issue it into your life. Such power can produce explosive attacks on the mats, just as it can help you lift a fifty-pound bag of topsoil from the trunk of your car and smoothly set it in the driveway. After breaking a series of boards, an upper-level student once smiled and said that learning to center was literally his first *religious experience*—and he was right. He was experiencing an internal power that he would later use to transform events in his life and create the future he desired. When you are centered, you are genuine, more spontaneous, and stress-free. You are in the best possible place from which to begin interrelating with the Divine.

EXERCISE

TO CENTER, find a quiet space and relax. Close your eyes and breathe evenly, inhaling through your nose and exhaling through your mouth. Then focus your attention on your breath. Follow it down like an elevator to your abdomen. The major location of Chi in your body is the lower *Dan Tien,* a space a few inches below the navel. This is also your body's exact center point of gravity. Visualize your energy as pure, nutritious white light. If necessary, hold your hand to that part of your body so that you can create a target and direct your breath. Feel your energy surge with each in-breath. Feel your core strengthening. Outer strength comes from inner strength. Always focus on inner strength in order to extend outer force.

6.

Achieve a Sense of Balance

YOU LEARN THE power of balance early on in all martial arts training. In martial philosophy this arises from a respect for the natural balance in all things. Imbalance results in weakness and can spoil an otherwise great action. It will ultimately lead to self-defeat. I've seen plenty of martial artists, including myself, lose their footing while executing an otherwise first-rate technique, winding up on the mats instead of on their opponent. Good balance results in a healthier body and quicker mind. It wards off conflict. It helps build Chi rather than run it down. It allows your spirit to flow smoothly and powerfully. It keeps you from tripping up. Martial arts teach that every movement needs to come from a point of balance. One way to accomplish this balance is to do as much as possible from your point of center (see the exercise on the previous page). This isn't easy and requires constant monitoring. The good news is that the more you live from such a vantage point, the easier and more desirable it becomes.

EXERCISE

FOR ONE WHOLE day, set your sights on achieving balance wherever you go. Begin your day by centering and boosting your positive energy. Imagine yourself with the same excitement you had when you were preparing for something that you were eagerly looking forward to. Use this image as an anchor whenever you need to recenter throughout the day.

Keep your good energy high. Subtly refocus often, even in mid-conversation, and consider the best response to keep you flowing in harmony with the people and situations you encounter. Pay attention to what happens when you go through your day refocusing in this manner. See how you feel about yourself and others.

7.

Practice Rooting

DURING THE EARLY stages of martial arts training, you are often required to freeze in mid-technique—holding a certain posture, usually a block or strike. The instructor then strikes at your arm or leg, testing to see if you can be knocked off balance. It comes as a bit of a surprise that even with the new techniques you have learned, you can still be pushed around the mats quite easily. Thus, most instructors introduce a stabilizing technique called *rooting*. Rooting is a way to strengthen your ability to balance. It is often taught with a variety of drills and visualizations to help you draw more energy from the environment and use that energy to fuel your actions. It helps you hold your ground both on the mats and in daily life, strengthens you physically, and quickens your mind.

EXERCISE

RELAX. REGULATE YOUR breathing by inhaling through your nose and exhaling through your mouth. Visualize a cord connected to your spine drawing energy up from the earth into your lower *Dan Tien*. Use your in-breaths to help direct the energy. Next, move your attention to the crown of your head. This area is your upper *Dan Tien* and is much smaller than the lower. Its function is to pull energy from the cosmos. Try drawing energy through this pathway down to your lower *Dan Tien*. Use your in-breaths to assist. Feel yourself filling with clean, positive power. With your arms extended to the sides, visualize your body being stable in the center of a circle, with the heavens above, the earth below. Radiate this energy as you approach whatever task is at hand. Practice rooting daily, especially whenever your balance is vulnerable or needs strengthening. It is your connection to Universal Energy.

8.

Harmonize

HARMONIZING WITH WHATEVER is around you is important on the mats and in the Earth dojo. In martial arts this harmony is known as *yin-yang*. The symbol for this concept consists of a circle with what looks like two fish, one white and the other black, swimming side by side yet in opposite directions. The circle symbolizes the cooperative nature of all things—the dark yin, representing female energy, and the light yang, male energy. In the dark there is a dot of light, and in the light there is a dot of darkness—showing the need for both in all life. Yin is reproductive energy; yang is productive. Most important, the idea is yin-yang, not yin *and* yang. You don't want all of one and none of the other. You don't want opposition. You need *both* for balance. Here's an image that helps. In the dojo we say that on the outside you are soft and relaxed. Yet inside, your will is iron. You can be soft, yet not yielding—a person of backbone; firm, yet not hardened—a person of flexibility and compassion. Harmony balances opposites just as day turns to night, and night to day, just as seasons change. There is no conflict or stagnation.

EXERCISE

FOR ONE WHOLE day, try to complement the actions of your environment, whether they are generated by a person, place, or circumstance. Don't barge into anything. If someone speaks, listen—relax when the traffic light turns red, don't gun through a yellow light, don't hand the clerk money until he or she is ready and shifts into "receive mode." Use your *passive* mode to build energy, your *active* mode to spend it. Be both soft and powerful. Be both firm and fluid.

9.

Go with the Flow

A MAJOR ANTHEM in martial arts is to *go with the flow*. In Chinese this is called *wu-wei* (non-striving), the guiding concept of both the *Tao Te Ching* and Zen. Wu-wei, or going with the flow, means the right action in any situation is the freest, easiest, and most fitting. Every particle in the universe functions this way. Science tells us this concept holds true even at the cellular level in that every cell contains within it the capability to build or rebuild any part of body it wants—knowing to build an eyeball, say, instead of a heart valve simply by paying attention to what is going on around it and joining in. A cell that insists on going against the flow, however, creates a tumor. On the mats, you learn to fit into actions. Going against the flow results in defeat. You don't let your attention overload anywhere, because once you do, you are vulnerable somewhere else. In fact, in sparring the oldest trick in the book is to congest your opponent's attention and then attack. Anybody who stops to analyze gets tagged. You must forget yourself and keep flowing.

EXERCISE

SPEND A DAY actively following people's actions without responding in any extremes. Decrease your effort to control people, places, and events. Don't go against the grain. Simply make yourself ready and alert and willing to participate. See what happens. See how you feel at the end of the day.

10.

Give Yourself Time

ALMOST EVERYONE WHO enters a dojo for the first time and watches a more advanced student perform thinks, "I'll *never* be able to do that." You think, "I'm not strong enough, flexible enough, coordinated enough, or graceful enough." Then experience shows you that given enough time, you *can* attain these skills—and pretty naturally. You look back and wonder how you could have had so little confidence. It doesn't take more than a few such accomplishments before you stop being so hard on yourself. You learn that unreasonable timelines decrease performance and increase anxiety. Giving yourself the time you need to reach your goals is like taking a hundred-pound weight off your back. In the end, you realize that you are capable of much more than you ever thought, and you can get there with less stress and a lot more fun—just by eliminating the restriction of time.

EXERCISE

IDENTIFY SOMETHING THAT you want to accomplish. List the skills, equipment, and anything else you need to reach your goal. Consider how you might acquire these. Then let the process flow. Allow your speed to be determined by what unravels along the way. Most of all, be present. Enjoy.

11.

Defeat Haste

IN THE DOJO, you learn that precision and mastery of movement is what counts, not how fast you can go through the list of requirements for your next belt. There is an old martial arts story that illuminates this lesson. An overeager student asks his teacher, "Can I test for my black belt soon? I practice for three hours daily. I am in great shape. I know all the required concepts and movements by heart." To this the teacher replies, "You must wait twice as long." The student waits a few weeks and asks again. The teacher replies, "You must wait twice as long as the last time you asked." Precision is what makes it possible for a small person to defeat a much larger opponent. More than knowing your lessons, you have to ingrain them into your every thought and movement, or the mats will call your bluff. If you have learned your lessons in haste, it doesn't matter what color belt you have, the skills you need to use your art effectively will not have sunk in. You are ready when you are ready. You don't need to announce it. It shows.

EXERCISE

TRY TO DO EVERYTHING with the best precision possible. Don't broadcast your effort, level, or rank. Just let it shine.

12.

Don't Waste Time, Spend It

IMAGINE A WALLET filled with money that you can spend any way you wish; however, once the money is spent, it is gone. What you do with your wealth is your choice. Watching the account deplete would make most of us pay more attention to which people, places, events, and activities we are forking money over to. When you come into the dojo, you are taught to enter with focus. You are taught not to waste time, but rather to spend it—doing the things you want and need to be doing to gain insight into concepts, techniques, yourself, and others. As Bruce Lee said, "We all have time to spend or waste, and it is our decision what to do with it." Time spent is used in a specified manner. Time wasted is used carelessly. Time is the most valuable commodity we have. Whenever you agree to devote time to someone or something, you are drawing on your account. Those who waste your time are stealing from you. Spend your life well.

EXERCISE

FOR ONE DAY, consciously pick what projects and situations are truly worthy of your time. Gracefully decline those that are not. Embrace those that are.

13.

Tap in to the Power
of Simplicity

A CENTRAL PRINCIPLE in martial arts is that *simplicity is best.*
You learn that the closer you live to the true martial Way, the easier
things get. In sparring you quickly discover that when an attack
comes, your simplest response is the right one. It is the most efficient.
It is the strongest. It gets the job done. You discover that showy, more
complicated moves may leave you vulnerable—or worse, out of
action. There's an old saying that asserts, "A punch is just a punch."
Some practitioners, however, bristle at that statement, thinking it suggests "anything goes"—an attitude that, unfortunately, some people *do*
apply to living. But the lesson contains a hidden message. There's a
time when we all just punch away, hoping to get our shots in any way
we can—though often this approach doesn't pan out. Then we learn
technique and suddenly find ourselves so restricted and self-conscious,
trying to get it right, that we still mess things up. Even so, after a while,
we start executing techniques effectively without thinking. Then we
perfect them. Knowledge and good skill become ingrained. Action
becomes free and functional. This is the power of simplicity.

EXERCISE

CHOOSE ANY OF the skills that we have been using in this book and start
to use it in a wide variety of circumstances and with a wide range of people.
Your goals are to be able to draw upon the technique in any situation and
to eventually make it so simple that it becomes automatic.

14.

Practice *Kimi*

KIMI IS FOCUSED, explosive power. It is a major skill and lesson in martial arts and was the strategy behind Bruce Lee's famous one-inch punch. Indeed, he entertained many audiences around the world with demonstrations of this force that could collapse a hulk of an opponent from only one inch away. You achieve *Kimi* by channeling high-quality, concentrated energy to a very specific area of your body—the fist, foot, palm, or some other area. The martial artist trains by putting this kind of energy behind her strike and then taking her shot. This same technique can be applied to any daily situation to give you explosive power *at the precise moment you need it* in order to accomplish not only physical goals, but emotional or spiritual goals as well.

EXERCISE

APPLY THE PRINCIPLE of focused concentration when you need extra power to complete a job. Relax and center, calmly gather all of your strength, from every muscle in your body, until the very moment you need it. Then follow through with your task.

15.

Empty Your Cup

THE GREATEST ADVANTAGE of an empty cup is that it can be filled. In martial arts you learn to drain your cup, your mind, before you enter the dojo. You empty it of opinions, assumptions, past history, old habits, and old knowledge. When your cup is full, there is no room for new ideas and learning. All arts encourage an open mind-set. For example, the longer-ranged kicking and punching arts usually explore close-range techniques such as those found in judo or jujitsu, and vice versa. The anthem of grapplers is that most altercations wind up on the ground. The anthem of kicking arts is that most altercations are over before they wind up on the ground. The most successful martial artist, of course, is the one who can be proficient in both methods. If you wind up on the ground, you need to know how to get up again. If you are outnumbered, it is good to know how not to wind up on the ground. In life, just as on the mats, it pays to empty your cup and try what is different. You grow. You become more adept. Don't let old methods get in the way.

EXERCISE

PICK A DAY and identify one major task you would like to accomplish. Instead of going at it in the usual way, open yourself to other methods you could use to achieve the same results. Give yourself permission to try something new. See how it works. What advantages does this approach have over the old? Keep an open mind. Think about what skills you need to sharpen in order to improve your new approach.

16.

Use Visualizations

MOST MARTIAL ARTISTS practice *visualization*. This is a process by which you use your mind's eye to see yourself performing a technique successfully. Visualizations help you see how to execute your skills. They help you believe that you can accomplish a task or goal. They are powerful magic that can make you stronger and healthier. I remember when the concept was first introduced to me. My instructor asked me to close my eyes and watch myself performing a martial arts posture. "What are you seeing?" he asked. "Myself," I said, "performing the technique." "But," he added, "are you watching yourself as if you are outside of yourself, say, from the side or from behind or from above? Or are you viewing the action from your own eyes looking out? Or are you watching from your opponent's eyes?" These were vital questions. Moving your perspective as you visualize gives deeper insight into the behavior you are attempting to understand or sharpen. There is also a deeper use of this principle. Positive visualizations create a positive energy within you that will in turn attract like energies into your life. They create muscular, emotional, and spiritual memory that will help you accomplish your goals.

EXERCISE

VISUALIZE THE PAIN of staying in a situation that you do not like. Try to use all of your senses as you develop your image. In addition to what you see, what smells, sounds, and so forth do you envision? Now, using a variety of perspectives, visualize a new way to deal with the situation. From each perspective, imagine the pleasure associated with this new technique. Consider what skills or patterns you need to develop in order to enact this change. Now, do it!

17.

Observe the Natural Balance of All Things

MARTIAL ARTS TEACH you that part of balance is to stay connected with your earthy nature. In the dojo, you are encouraged to observe how balance is achieved in nature and to learn from it. For example, when the wind blows, the tree limb bends, a leaf may sway, or it may let go and flow with it. A hawk can fly with the current, above it, or below it. A cat can remain completely composed until a predator moves close enough to become a threat. When it is out of range, the cat will either just peacefully head out somewhere else or simply put the predator out of its mind and carry on with whatever it was doing. Water may flow, over, around, or through potential obstacles. It may freeze until it is rock hard, or it may vaporize into invisibility. Balance is everywhere in nature and is embedded in everything we do. If you lose touch with that part of yourself that is connected to the earth, your emotional and spiritual powers will diminish. Your job is to stay connected to the powers of both heaven *and* earth.

EXERCISE

MAKE AN ATTEMPT to spend some time in nature. Observe a flower, a family of nesting birds, a boulder, a fruit orchard, or any other aspect of the natural world. Use your senses: touch, smell, sound, sight, and taste. Try to identify acceptance, cooperation, motivation, discipline, commitment, courage, and self-trust in what you observe. Ask yourself what knowledge you can extract to employ in your current life.

18.

Eliminate Susceptibilities to Being Drawn Off Balance

SPARRING EXPOSES YOUR opponent's vulnerabilities to being drawn off balance, but it also opens your own. You pay closer attention to your movement—and in particular to those things in the environment that influence it. For example, if you find that you lose balance whenever your opponents screech or whenever they start throwing high kicks, you train with that circumstance in mind and practice phasing out the behavior that it triggers in you. Doing so is not so difficult. It just requires attentiveness. In the dojo, there is a drill where you freeze in mid-attack, considering what actions you can take to overcome what is skewing your balance so that you can act effectively. You do this until you develop a lot of techniques to deal with susceptibilities. For instance, you might have several training sessions just on what you could do if someone charged you and tried to tackle you. You would train with this situation in mind until you felt confident that you could handle the situation. One by one, you learn to eliminate each of your susceptibilities and strengthen your ability to maintain balance. Here's how you can use this principle.

EXERCISE

ESSENTIAL HERE IS that you are not attempting to escape life. Rather, you are training to strengthen tools that will make your participation more effective. Identify a circumstance that causes you to lose your composure. Visualize yourself in this situation. Bring as many of your senses into play as you can. Then, using your mind's eye to freeze the action at a variety of different points, ask yourself what moves would be effective in turning off what is triggering you, thus maintaining your balance. What responses to the situation would lead to a desirable and peaceful resolution? Make a list of these responses. When the circumstance arises, take your best shot.

19.

Don't Take Things Personally

MARTIAL ARTS TEACH us to move without taking things personally. Just as when the wind blows and the tree bends, when the attack comes, the response follows—quickly, smoothly, naturally. You react in a way that seems like natural law rather than *personal* law. If a boulder were coming at you, you would reflexively move out of the way. You wouldn't start cursing the rock, its entire family, every rock that was of the same age, and so on. You wouldn't be bad-mouthing the rock later that day and for days to come. Martial arts teach that people fight because they feel diminished in some way, because things have become personal. This kind of response to daily life stresses you out and eats up the energy you need to deal with the situation properly. The key is: don't diminish others, and remember that only you can diminish yourself. Don't let anyone or anything rob you of your positive energy. Detect potentially irritating situations and defuse them before they get to you.

EXERCISE

FOR ONE WHOLE day, refuse to take anything personally. Assess your situations, and when you see one that is a potential stressor, deal with it smoothly and naturally, as if you were sidestepping a boulder. Move only as much as you need. Enjoy the proficiency of your movement and your ability to protect yourself. Move on through your daily routines with your spirits and energy high. See how you feel at the end of the day.

20.

What You Do
Matters in the Short Run

IN THE DOJO, you are constantly paying attention to the immediate consequences of your actions—on yourself as well as others. For example, if you are sparring and your opponent starts to spin, and you don't recognize what is coming next, you'll get tagged by either a fist or a kick. If you move just right, you will land yourself in a position of advantage; if you move the wrong way, you will step right into your opponent's attack. The point is this—the more experience you have, the easier you learn to move out of harm's way and into positions of advantage. A more subtle realization is that your movement can also make a situation that is already good even better. You learn to seize the moment. When the target surfaces, you are there, ready, and moving in the right direction to make the absolute best of things.

EXERCISE

WHENEVER SOMETHING ADVANTAGEOUS or disadvantageous occurs throughout your day, map your actions in reverse to see what movement led you to that point. Do this often. Begin to learn the effect(s) of certain actions, especially those that create significant high points in your daily life. Write the following words down on a note card and place it somewhere you will see it regularly: *Everything I do opens or closes windows.* Know what works immediately and what doesn't. Watch as life shows you how you create.

21.
What You Do
Matters in the Long Run

ON THE MATS, just as in daily life, you find that the longer-term goals and effects of your actions are cumulative. For example, if what you want is to develop a lightning-fast back-fist strike, you can focus on training in just that and achieving as much precision as you desire. You can also break the technique down into the various aptitudes needed to make it work—strength, speed, positioning, mind-set, circulation of Chi, and so on—and train each of these individually. Eventually, your cumulative training will get you to where you want to be. In the meantime, learn to enjoy your progress. A positive attitude begets the positive energy you need to reach your goal. Indeed, peace, tranquility, and enlightenment continue for your entire life: It is important to remember that your *accumulated daily actions and training* affect your ability to achieve and enjoy these goals, too. Everything you do from white belt to black and beyond matters. Daily life is no different.

EXERCISE

TAKE SOME QUIET time and identify a long-range goal that you would like to reach. Consider what aptitudes you need to reach this goal. Begin training in each of the aptitudes individually. Try to achieve precision in each of them. Let yourself feel a sense of accomplishment as your proficiency advances. When you are ready, target your goal and take your shot.

Observe Yourself
in Relationships with Others

MARTIAL ARTS ARE all about self-discovery. Partners are vital in this process. Interacting shows whether your chosen techniques are functional and genuinely "you" or extensions of fear and doubt. For example, when sparring, some players keep a distance because they can kick and come in on opponents with lightning speed. Others keep distance because they fear or distrust closer range, even though they may have the aptitude to handle closer sparring. Some players stay close because they compulsively believe they give something up by allowing others more space. Some prefer self-defenses to katas, movements used by many martial arts that look like dances and contain prearranged martial techniques for practice. Is this because their main interest is truly self-defense? Or is it because they don't feel graceful? Honestly knowing why we choose to do things is essential for reaching our full potential. Each opponent or obstacle we face helps us discover who we are—which parts of ourselves we like and which we would like to strengthen or change. Opponents inform us whether our behaviors bring us closer to or farther from the way we want to live.

EXERCISE

AT THE END of your day, take some time to reflect on a few of the day's events. Let yourself feel each event fully. What is the difference between how you saw yourself earlier and how you see yourself now? What do you like? Smile at yourself when you like what you see. Study what you wish to change. Be honest—and a little humor helps.

23.

Be Amused by Your Strengths and by Your Weaknesses

WHENEVER YOU learn a new technique, you feel that sense of clumsiness you felt as a novice. But this feeling keeps life interesting. Mastering clumsiness generates confidence and satisfaction! Martial arts teach you to embrace these moments as opportunity for personal growth. Sometimes beginners are so hard on themselves that what develops is a lack of confidence and lowered self-esteem. This leads to a loss of calm, an increase in stress, and a weakening of spirit. Some people eventually stop trying new things. Resisting life's flow, of course, is in opposition to the martial Way. Indeed, according to ancient practices, there were no black belts—only white. As tradition tells it, with years of training, the white belts would soil, eventually turning black. Then, after many more years of training, the fabric would fray, and in time the belts would turn to white again. The cycle from weakness to strength, from beginner to master, would continue over and over. How beautiful it would be to be brought up this way from infancy. We all move from beginner to master many times in the Earth dojo as well. Our job is to enjoy the process.

EXERCISE

CLUMSINESS APPEARS IN our lives like prompts on our computer screens. Today, whenever you feel a sense of awkwardness, lighten up, don't be critical. Instead, be amused. Tell yourself that life has funny ways of communicating. The situation has occurred because it is something you need in order to better the quality of your life. Learn from it. Trust and have fun on your way.

Don't Worsen Your Opponent's Game—Improve Your Own

IN A REAL SPARRING situation or in everyday life, a cheap shot will most likely land you on your back. It's *skill* that makes martial technique effective, not packaging. Martial arts teach you to focus on what matters. Sometimes lessons are hard. I once watched a novice (who still had to learn lessons of skill as well as respect) intentionally try to make a higher-ranked partner look bad. The novice threw a cartwheel kick like you might have seen in the movies, hoping to score some impressive points. But the mats are a great reality check. Indeed, the novice was totally outclassed. His partner completely dodged the kick and countered with a flurry of punches that led to a takedown and if allowed to continue, would have resulted in a knockout. I remember our instructor saying, *The best way to look good is to get good.* He was right. The next time I saw the aforementioned student, he looked a lot better—not because he was busy trying to belittle his partner, but because he had been busy sharpening his own skills. This principle is true in daily affairs as well.

EXERCISE

IF YOU FEEL the urge to cut someone down, press your pause button. Ask yourself, instead, why you feel smaller in stature. Consider what you need to do to improve your own game. Then do it.

25.

Grow through Your Relationships with Others

A MAJOR ANTHEM of martial arts is that everyone has something to offer. Early in my own training, I entered the dojo to work with a highly skilled Kenpo karate master. He was conducting a workshop on a technique that I had learned years before. I recognized the drill, but it appeared somewhat different from my more traditional version. When I asked him about the difference, he proudly explained that a few days earlier, a new student was training in the technique and just naturally started doing it this way. "It's a great adaptation, don't you think?" he asked. "I'm teaching it both ways now." I was deeply impressed by this senior master's humility, honesty, and ability to keep growing—no arrogance, no elitism. It didn't matter if the technique came from the top down or from bottom up. If it worked, he intended to use it. He simply wanted to do what was best for him, his students, and his art. *Everyone* grew that day. This lesson applies in the Earth dojo as well. Your job is to spot such gifts and use them. Doing so creates a win-win situation for all.

EXERCISE

SPEND SOME TIME today just watching how others get things done. It doesn't matter what kind of work they are doing, whether similar to yours or not. Perhaps it is just a skill of focus, disposition, or relaxation. Ask yourself what you can borrow and incorporate into your own routines. Follow through.

Alternate: Consider a circumstance from your current life. Imagine someone who has been in a similar situation. Ask what he or she would do to enhance or correct things. Try to adapt this method into your planning.

26.

Conquer Anger

MARTIAL ARTS TEACH that it is not bad to feel anger or hostility—what's bad is letting such feelings take over your nature. Acknowledging your emotions keeps you authentic and allows you the opportunity to consciously choose your next move rather than having it dictated to you. Anger tenses the muscles. It strains your mind, frazzles your spirit, and diminishes your fluidity. It will make a pawn of you if you let it. An angry mind is so focused on striking at any cost that it loses sight of real targets that may come around. What's more, a mind that is distracted by anger is oblivious to its vulnerabilities. Senior students love to spar angry beginners, who move slowly and can be easily manipulated. They will predictably chase fake or insignificant attacks and never see the real one coming. In the end, they defeat themselves. Acting in anger only breeds more conflict. It brings out hostility and aggression in others. When you lose your temper, you lose self-control, and you cannot control a situation if you cannot control yourself—on the mats and in daily life.

EXERCISE

FOR ONE DAY, whenever you feel yourself getting angry, press your pause button and refocus. Don't resist your feelings. Instead, acknowledge them. Whatever you do, don't telegraph your feelings. Simply let them flow through you like water through a hose. Don't get ruffled. Watch the myriad more harmonious opportunities arise to help resolve the problem at hand. See what a difference a few moments of calm can bring.

27.

Keep Your Good Energy Flowing

SCIENCE TELLS US that bad energy is real. We can attract it. We can generate it. But we don't have to hold on to it. The dojo teaches that your body is a vessel and can hold only so much energy—good or bad. One way to purge bad energy is to keep your *good* energy flowing. This pushes out negativity and replaces it with positivity. A typical martial arts session immerses you in physical movement that requires your full attention and takes your mind off stressors that are consuming you. Relaxing your mind in such a way begins the process of generating healthy energy. How you breathe is important. Typically you inhale through your nose and exhale through your mouth. You visualize pure, healing energy flowing into your body when you breathe in and negative energies streaming out when you exhale. Sessions end with a moment of quiet meditation, allowing all the positivity you have produced to soothe you from muscle to spirit. You feel yourself feeling good. This is how you are *always* meant to feel. And although the terrific energy you have created will need to be regulated again and again, you can revel in knowing how to do it. Here's how to use this principle in daily life.

EXERCISE

DO SOMETHING PHYSICAL that requires your total attention, such as painting, gardening, sport, or housework. When you are finished, sit quietly. Relax. Regulate and deepen your breathing. Cast out any residue of negativity. Imagine any negative feelings flowing from your body straight into the earth. Don't worry. The earth can handle it. Your body cannot. Feel yourself brimming with positivity. Remember, your body can only hold so much energy, good or bad. Choose good.

28.

Monitor Your
Energy Environment

HAVE YOU EVER walked into a circumstance feeling great and felt an onslaught of negativity coming at you like pollution? Your body is capable of exchanging energy with everyone and everything around it, particularly those in close contact. When a dojo is a place of clean, spirited energy, you attain a similar energy. When a partner is brimming with positivity, you receive that energy as well. If the opposite occurs, however, you walk away from people, places, and events, feeling like someone unplugged you. What does this ultimately mean? It means that the people, places, and events you team up with will affect your overall physical, emotional, and spiritual health. They will contribute to your perspective on life and the quality of energy you require, thus creating the successes you desire. A good environment is one that fills you with strength and happiness. In daily life, just as in the dojo, you can choose to partner with those who will drain you, do nothing for you, or revitalize you. Choose carefully and well.

EXERCISE

KNOW WHAT MAKES you glow. At the end of your day, make a list of the people, places, and situations you encountered. Allow yourself to feel each of them through your senses as much as possible. Highlight those people, places, and situations that charge your spirit. Make them a part of your environment often. Keep your list on an index card, or put it in a nightstand or wallet. Review and use it whenever you need an energy boost. It will help make good times better and rough times smoother. Consider this list a prescription for good energy medicine.

Don't Assume a Woman Is Less of a Warrior than a Man

LEGEND HAS IT that after escaping the initial destruction of the Shaolin Temple, a nun named Ng Mui taught her adopted daughter, Wing Chun (whose name translates to *Beautiful Spring*) her style of martial arts. As the story goes, Wing Chun, after whom this form of kung fu was named, was being harassed into marriage by the town warlord, whom she eventually challenged to hand–to-hand combat before the entire community. The stakes were high. If she lost, she would be his. If she prevailed, he would disappear from sight. After learning her mother's techniques of self–defense, she was easily able to defeat the harasser in front of everyone and then marry the man of her choice. The point to the story is clear: you cannot assume that a woman is less of a warrior than a man or that a woman's skills are less proficient. A man can outperform a woman, but not simply because she is a woman, just like a woman can outperform a man, but not simply because he is a man. Performance is based on skill, both on the mats and in daily routines.

EXERCISE

WHEN YOU ENCOUNTER a woman with a warrior spirit, do not lessen your expectations of her because she is a woman. Treat her with admiration and respect. If a job needs to be done, entrust her based on skill. Show your confidence in her. Notice how this makes you feel. Pay attention to how this attitude results in a winning situation for all.

Don't Assume a Man Is Less Sensitive than a Woman

YEARS AGO I had the pleasure of working with an aikido expert. He was a giant and towered over everyone in the dojo. He was the most massive human being I'd ever seen. He had a technique he liked to demonstrate. It was designed for sensitivity training—that is, becoming attentive enough to an opponent's energy to literally forecast his next move. Blindfolded, he would place one finger anywhere on your body and divert your next move before you finished it. It didn't matter if you were lightning fast, he was right there. Even though he was the size of a wall, you couldn't land a hand on him. Looking at him, you expected him to use his obvious physical force to defeat you. But instead he relied entirely on sensitivity. Martial arts teach that neither size nor gender have anything to do with sensitivity. Indeed, sensitivity comes from the release of all tension in your body and a sense of calm that is so deep you can literally *feel* where your opponent's next move will be before he or she makes it. Sensitivity helps you avoid conflict by never getting tangled up in the first place. Even though many years have passed since this lesson, I still think of the wise and gentle giant who embodied the mind of martial arts.

EXERCISE

OBSERVE THE SENSITIVITY in men. Treat it with admiration and respect. Encourage it. If a job needs to be done that requires sensitivity, do not base your attitude on gender or size. Show confidence. Notice how this makes you feel. Pay attention to how this attitude results in a winning situation for all.

31.

Test the Quality of Your Energy Often

IN THE DOJO, you learn to test your energy often, because optimum awareness and strength are important requirements for success. Failure to monitor the quality of your energy can result in injury to yourself or others. Practitioners can run a quick test by seeing if they can stay focused on an intended activity or if their mind wanders. If you are able to focus, you then test to see whether your movement is strong and fluid. Do you feel invigorated, or do you feel weakened? Do you feel stuck, fatigued, or sidetracked? Do you feel any body or mental tension? You can apply this same strategy in daily life. Test yourself frequently. Learn to adjust as you move through routines. Here is how.

EXERCISE

WHENEVER YOU FEEL depleted, try condensing your energy to give yourself a boost. First, clear your thoughts. Relax. Stay softly focused. Regulate your breathing. Note: Where your mind goes, your Chi will go. With each in-breath picture your Chi moving from your extremities to the center of your body, condensing it tightly into a smaller and smaller sphere, like sunlight tightened into a dot by a magnifying lens. Then channel its concentrated form back into your arms, hands, feet, and legs with your out-breaths. Feel yourself restoring. Channel your energy to where your body needs it most.

32.

Practice Energy Drills with Your Partner

THE DOJO USES partnered energy drills to demonstrate the power of *cooperative energy*. The objective is to create higher-velocity energy than you could on your own. Depending on how long you train, the effects can last days. The first time I ever tried using partnered energy drills, the instructor emphasized that such drills are noncombative and noncompetitive. Movements are short, rhythmic, repetitive, and synchronized, and the drills last from five to thirty minutes. Harmonizing is important in order to keep the drill going and to reap full energetic benefits. Stress dissipates. Egos dissolve. By perfecting your part of the action, you learn to fit into a larger movement, which in turn fuels you and your partner, both individually and collectively. When everyone in the dojo partners up and works such drills, the whole room fills with intense positivity. Cooperative energy is a great natural resource.

EXERCISE

TRY THIS EXERCISE with a partner. Stand about two feet apart and facing each other. Bring your right arms downward and cross them so that the upper side of your forearm is touching that of your partner midway between wrist and elbow, forming an "X" at about six o'clock between you. Gently tap your forearms together, then continue in a clockwise motion, bringing your right arms to twelve o'clock, and tap forearms again. Draw your right arms back to your side, and do the same with your left arms. Repeat this action, alternating right and left arms, for one to two minutes. Feel your energy surge. Carry this positive energy with you, and tap in to it often throughout the day. There are countless times in life when we need to work in cooperation with others. Remind yourself that these can be amazingly high-energy moments. Seek them regularly.

33.

Become an Energy Partner

IS YOUR ENERGY tense, fluid, high, low, alert, distracted, smooth, jumpy, strong, or weak? Sometimes you can't tell. Your partner, on the other hand, can. Once in my own training, I was carrying around a full tank of tension for days. I had gotten so used to it that it felt normal. My instructor, however, noticed. He commented that my energy needed to even out. In contrast, he appeared strong and relaxed. I remember thinking that was what I wanted to be like. His routine was to test everyone's energy at the beginning of class. If someone's energy was off, he would help that person realign it. After a while, everyone started testing one another's energy before he could get around to it. It was kind of funny. In looking out for our own energy, we were also looking out for the energy matters of others. When our instructor realized what we were doing, he was amused and made this a permanent part of our routine. From then on, the whole dojo took pride in how we could make a positive difference in one another. We became energy partners.

EXERCISE

TRY THIS EXERCISE with your partner. Stand, facing your partner. Extend your right arm, straight out and to the side, palm down. Have your partner use his or her right hand to moderately press downward on your extended arm, using steady, even pressure. Use your strength to resist the pressure. If your arm collapses easily, your energy is weak. In this case, gently massage the center of your breastbone or sternum with your fingertips. You can do this yourself or ask your partner to apply the massage. Visualize yourself filling with energy. Then test again. Your energy should be restored.

Practice Mind over Matter

MARTIAL ARTISTS HAVE, out of necessity, developed methods of dealing with pain. In the dojo, this Zen practice is known as *mind over matter*. When I was training in Chinese Kenpo, my instructor demonstrated an explosive close-range strike. In fact, he struck through a slab of concrete at full bore and seemed to feel no pain. When I tried it, I felt like my entire hand had splintered. The pain was enormous. I asked why he hadn't felt anything. "I put my mind somewhere else," he explained. I tried again, but still felt excruciating pain. Months later I was at home working out on a kung fu apparatus when I mistakenly slammed my elbow hard into one of the oak arms on the device. The pain was so excruciating that I fell down. I analyzed what had happened and the extent of damage. No broken bones. Still, the pain was intense. I used visualization and placed my mind somewhere else. The pain didn't entirely go away, but it drastically lessened. Since then, I have relied on this technique often, not only emotionally and spiritually, but physically as well.

EXERCISE

TRY TO CREATE enough of a diversion to stay in the game. Use this meditation the next time something causes you physical, emotional, or spiritual pain. Center. Regulate your breath. Bring your attention inward, away from the source of your pain, and focus on hearing the sounds: *hem* (with in-breaths) and *so-o-o* (with out-breaths).

Alternate: Focus your attention into a space the size of a dime, first on the center of your left hand, then the right, your upper and then lower lip, or on anything in your environment.

Don't Care So Much

HAVE YOU EVER stopped caring so much about what you're doing that you ended up doing your best? You learn this dojo lesson as soon as you attempt your first kata. Paradoxically, those who try the hardest look anything but natural. They may even stop midway, having become so self-conscious that they forget what comes next. Often in sparring, if you concentrate too much on a certain target, others will evade you—or worse, you'll miss and get tagged yourself. When I first began training, I was so concerned about getting hit, that I *always* got hit. My mind, in effect, was frozen. Later I learned that if your mind immobilizes, so does your body. My movement was nimble. I couldn't do what was necessary to avoid getting hit. When you stop caring so much about getting hit, you suddenly discover more options. You're quicker, stronger, and more flexible. You're more likely to find the right action for the moment and nail your target head-on.

EXERCISE

TRY THIS EXERCISE with a partner. Clear your mind of any thoughts and relax. Have your partner hold up a piece of paper or fabric (glove, scarf, etc.) as you try to tag it with a punch—but only when your partner slaps his or her hand against their leg. Ask your partner to vary the slaps. Tell yourself that when you are supposed to hit the target, you will. If you miss, don't even think about it. Just keep going. Try this for two to three minutes. Afterward, consider what skills you needed to draw upon or develop in order to hit your target. How can these skills be applied to your current life actions?

Conquer Fear

MARTIAL ARTS TEACH that for every fear there is a technique to vanquish it. One day at our college dojo, I asked my students to identify their greatest fear in terms of self-defense. Everybody had one. Afterward, we assembled a group of instructors from a variety of disciplines, and for the next six months we participated in workshops to address our concerns. One by one, little by little, we began generating techniques to eliminate everyone's qualms. We practiced visualizations to see how to conquer certain attacks before they actually happen. This generated a pregame plan, so that when the attack finally came on the mats, you were ready, and even if you got tagged, at the very least, you weren't defeated by your own fears. Martial arts teach you to discover what you are afraid of and flip through your inventory of techniques for a way to conquer that fear. No matter what the issue, the martial Way is to rid yourself of fear, boost your confidence, and live free.

EXERCISE

THINK ABOUT ONE source of worry in your life. Identify which martial principles can be employed to troubleshoot this situation. Consider a plan, and then follow through with that plan. Then move on to your next worry. Trust in the process. Stay with it. Take pride in the confidence you gain. Use it to help keep you fueled.

Alternate: Make a list of other fears (at work, home, and the like). Then identify a list of people, places, and literature that may serve as resources for troubleshooting the issue. Focus on one or two, for starters, and then follow up.

Train, Train, Train

TRAINING—IN MARTIAL arts and in any form of exercise—changes the quality of your energy. This changes your chemistry, and thus changes you. You develop an overall feeling of well-being. You feel stronger and healthier. You think sharper and more authentically. You become more aware of your connection to the world around you. You draw its energy and enjoy the energy you are returning. You develop an overall feeling of calm. Your relationships improve. Family life is richer and happier. You are more confident. You are content more often. You say to yourself that you never realized it was possible to feel this way. These were the thoughts I had when I told my instructor years ago that martial arts had literally changed my life. "Mine, too," he admitted. Once you realize the many benefits of training, how could you ever want your life to be any other way?

EXERCISE

TAKE A DAY to enjoy honing the skills—martial and otherwise—that you draw upon in your daily routines. If you are making a phone call to a business partner, try to polish your communication skills. Whatever you do, consider what skills are involved and use the experience to refine them. Don't bother thinking about results. Just revel in the pleasure of sharpening the techniques that have strengthened your life so far. Do this often. Take pride in your proficiencies.

38.

Use Your Power of Reflection

ANY GOOD MARTIAL artist will reflect on his or her previous performance before heading to the mats again. If an opponent keeps nailing you with a certain kick, you need to figure out why. You replay the shot in your mind until you see it. You scan the strike over and over, scouring detail to help you deactivate the kick and counter—should you need to. In sparring, you might replay the whole match in your mind until you see the fix: a leg sweep. Then you use visualization to sharpen the technique. You go over several scenarios, eventually realizing that for a split-second near the end of his technique, your opponent stands on one foot, leaving him vulnerable to the sweep you have in mind. The target is there, as big as a billboard, every time. The next time that you pair up, you successfully launch your technique. Indeed, you have used his best shot *against* you to your own advantage. On the mats, as in everyday experiences, you learn that with a modification of personal actions, you can transform whole outcomes. Use your power of reflection.

EXERCISE

CONSIDER A RECENT incident that didn't work out to your advantage. Play the incident in your mind. Think about what led you to disadvantage. Look to where your skills broke down and why. Identify the other person's best shot. Evaluate why it worked. What could you have done differently to avoid the incident or to turn the situation your way. List any counteractions you could use to gain advantage. Play it over in your mind. Set up a strategy you can use as a base the next time the situation or a similar one arises.

39.

Turn Down the Intensity

WHEN I FIRST entered the dojo, my teacher pulled me aside and told me I was my own biggest opponent. He told me I needed to turn down the intensity. He asked me to watch him as he performed a kata. His eyes were as wide as a tiger's and didn't appear to be looking at anything in particular, yet they seemed to be taking everything in. His energy was so powerful, it seemed he could collapse someone with just one look. Yet, he appeared totally relaxed. His movement was graceful and flowing, yet it seemed as though he could punch through stone if he wanted. When he was finished, he said, "That's the kind of concentration you want. That's the way you want to move." Your mind should be loose and steady, able to trigger any technique from anywhere—immediately, effortlessly. If you move this way, you may not send a heavy bag sailing off its hinges overnight, but you'll realize a sizable increase in power. I've reminded myself of this lesson frequently in daily life, especially when situations look like they could become extreme or whenever I catch myself about to become loud.

EXERCISE

THE NEXT TIME you are in a sticky situation and about to intensify, press your pause button, refocus, and consider what martial techniques you can employ to successfully maneuver through the incident. Choose attention and precision of technique over a lot of grunt-and-grind behavior. Move toward success with grace. Focus more on what you're doing than on any expectations you may have.

40.

Use Tension Functionally

THERE ARE WAYS to get tension to work *for* you rather than *against* you. In fact, you can perform many katas at full tension. This means tensing every muscle in your body, not just those involved in the strike or stance. The idea is to go through your movements as *hard* (tensely) as you can so that when you eventually loosen your muscles, you let go of all the stress they carry. In the dojo it is common to repeat shorter katas several times or perform longer forms this way. Any movement you perform in this manner releases tension. But energetically, circular movements work best. They heighten as well as smooth the circulation of energy throughout the body—de-stressing muscles, decompressing your mind, and lightening your spirit. This practice leaves you feeling fluid and healthy.

EXERCISE

RELAX. REGULATE YOUR breathing. Form a prayer hand (using either hand) by positioning it vertical to your breast and about twelve inches away. Using your fingertips, trace an infinity sign—a sideways 8—about eighteen inches in width. Don't worry about keeping your hand vertical. Let it relax and change positioning naturally. Make your infinity sign bigger and bigger. Start softly. Then start adding tension. Focus on your breathing, as well as the motion you are making. Picture yourself moving through mud. Start tensing every muscle in your body, head to toe. Now visualize moving through concrete. Then iron. Do this three times for each substance. Finish with your hand in the same position in which it began. Turn your hand palm out and slowly extend it (not fully) forward and slowly exhale through your mouth, releasing your tension with your out-breath. Now do the exercise with the other hand. Concentrate on how you feel. To avoid injury or discomfort, don't do this after eating or drinking anything but water.

41.

Have Fun

MANY MARTIAL MOVEMENTS were historically performed in pure, lighthearted, sometimes even silly delight. Ironically, out of such play came some of the most significant martial concepts and applications. One only needs to look at the beautiful and colorful martial dances—for example, the Lion Dance, Dragon Dance, Fan Dance, and Scarf Dance—to recognize the source of a wide variety of martial arts moves. Even the Shaolin monks played, slicing their brooms through the air in martial patterns, which, remember, they had learned to help them meditate. They became so skilled with the technique that they used their brooms to defeat thieves and other adversaries that would break into the temple. As Japanese dockworkers waited for ships to come in, they used to relieve their boredom by playing with nautical rope, whipping it back and forth in martial patterns. These types of play led to the development of assorted martial weapons and new katas. I personally enjoy doing katas on the beach at sunrise or in the dojo with different kinds of music. Play refreshes you and revitalizes dedication. It inspires new and exciting training. Have fun. Play with your art.

EXERCISE

USE MARTIAL CONCEPTS for fun. Here are a few suggestions. Try a tension releaser in water. Or try a meditation in candlelight. Use music, fragrances, and varied lighting in combination with meditations. Combine movements and meditations. Whatever you choose, be creative, play, and have fun!

Alternate: Have fun at work. If you have a private office, try dimming the lights for a while as you work at your computer. Make a calendar using workplace quotes. Use your figure-eight pattern to open a door. See what you discover.

Be Willing to Detach

IN THE DOJO, detachment becomes an art in and of itself. You keep going with the flow, no matter what. Indeed, the martial Way teaches that whatever sticks becomes lifeless. By embracing rather than resisting, the martial mind flows—staying alive, free, and unlimited. You remain supple and spontaneous. You can modify actions in harmony even when there is no permanent resolution in sight. You see things closer to the way they are, with innocence and clarity. You can change *with* change. Lessons you have learned kick in more naturally, giving you internal strength and external dexterity. In the dojo, you learn to watch your opponent without watching so much. When an opponent comes at you, you know techniques to disarm him, but you don't necessarily feel bound by them. By detaching, you allow whatever ensues, modifying as you go, with confidence and grace. You let life flow and find bliss in the adventure.

EXERCISE

CONSIDER A CURRENT life goal. Visualize yourself having already achieved it. Then detach yourself from actively attempting to achieve the goal. Don't attempt to control every step in the process. Wait for specific opportunities to come to you. Don't try to manipulate the outcome. Just let it all happen naturally.

43.

Conquer the Desire to Win

THE DOJO TEACHES that winning and losing are next-door neighbors. You stop thinking about winning and start thinking of making the best of each movement. And you allow whatever emerges to emerge and then go on to the next movement. Even if you lose a match, reflection will help you refine your actions and grow. Any seemingly botched technique is an opportunity for growth and strength. In the dojo, you don't allow yourself to get flustered by disappointment. Instead, you make adjustments even in mid-motion. A missed block can easily be turned into a devastating counterpunch just by letting your arm roll over the top of your opponent's still-oncoming strike. You can find all kinds of locks, takedowns, and even big throws in this same way. The same is true in daily events. Street fighters always want to win. But life doesn't work that way. It keeps flowing. Every moment offers the opportunity to create the next. Winning and losing are only words based on faulty perception.

EXERCISE

WHEN YOU SEE people doing something in a manner you perceive as better than your own, ask how they did it. You'll be surprised by how cooperative people can be and how much easier your life becomes when you aim to do your best, regardless of whether you win or not.

44.

Stay in Harmony

ONCE YOU HAVE learned how to use the principle of yin-yang to create harmony, the martial anthem is: *Don't break the harmony.* If you do, you make yourself vulnerable to attack and sometimes even defeat. In the dojo, you learn to follow your partner's energy and stay with it. In sparring, as soon as you feel your partner break harmony, you strike. The more disharmonious your partner becomes, the bigger the target he opens. Internal discord works the same way. What's more, such disharmony leads to stress, ill health, and vulnerability on all levels. Likewise, stressed partnerships usually become unhealthy. The same is true of families, workplace, organizations, communities, and nations. Staying in harmony with the people and situation around you is one of the best things you can do for yourself and others.

EXERCISE

KEEP HARMONY WITH others by complementing whatever movement they make. Avoid conflict wherever possible. Pick a day and tell yourself you will not break harmony, no matter what. If others are aggressive, stay soft. When others are soft, make your advance. If they persist in their behavior, remember that if you simply stay with the movement it will eventually go the other way and you can make your move then.

45.

Use Your Internal
Pause Button Often

MARTIAL ARTS TEACH you to see consequences. This helps
you choose your next move. Accordingly, you learn to use your
internal pause button often. When you see a master executing a technique with lightning accuracy, you may forget that she wasn't born
with the ability to move that way. Everything wasn't always so simple
and reflexive. In fact, the dojo utilizes many slow-motion and stop-
motion drills. These help you recognize multiple solutions to every
situation. Your job is to learn the advantages and disadvantages of each,
choosing the best option *for that moment*. Partners frequently take
turns playing offense while the other defends. It is common to freeze
postures so that everyone can examine techniques in terms of usefulness and consequences. Your pause button widens your vision. It soon
becomes one of your best friends, whether on or off the mats. After a
while, you start thinking and acting with pause naturally and more
reflexively. You get from A to Z, as they say, so quickly that there seems
to be no delay in your actions. Use your internal pause button a lot.
Precision speed and inspiration will follow.

EXERCISE

START USING YOUR internal pause button today. Consider the usefulness
of actions before performing them. Choose your best shot and take it.

46.

Extend Your Chi

SOMETIMES ALL YOU have to do is walk into a room and someone's negative energy winds up affecting you. Other times their energy elevates you. Sometimes you think someone is staring at you, and you turn around and find that she is. Accordingly, certain situations can automatically coordinate the strength and will of the mind and body. Stories heralding superhuman strength and power abound, such as the young child who carries two elderly people out of a burning house, the mother who can't swim rescuing her drowning child, or the healer dissolving pain with a mere touch. These are all examples of the great power we can invoke from within, demonstrating strength beyond a pure adrenaline rush. They are all examples of our capacity to extend Chi. Everyone, including those who are not martial artists, can do this. Science maintains that such energy moves at the speed of light and cannot be destroyed. World religions tell us it is the basis for spiritual experiences beyond our wildest imagination. Your Chi influences everything around you, and vice versa. The idea is to consciously make use of this principle. Learning how to extend your Chi is one of the most powerful martial lessons.

EXERCISE

THE NEXT TIME you meet with someone, put yourself in a calm, positive mind-set before entering his or her space. Deliberately take a deep relaxing breath as you speak. Watch the other person do the same in just moments. Study how the energy you release affects that person. See how you can get him or her to follow your positive energy output. Experiment. Incorporate what you learn into your actions.

47.

Connect with the Stillness in Movement

MARTIAL ARTS TEACH that there is concentrated core energy within us. It is at the center of every movement. It is still and unmovable, like the axle of a wheel, like a full moon reflected in water. It balances and powers you, on or off the mats, and is who and what you are at your deepest level. Off the mats, tapping your core is vital to the understanding and experience of your deepest, true nature. Psychologist Ram Dass explains: "We are not human beings having a spiritual experience; we are spiritual beings having a human experience." Every once in a while, as the philosopher Meister Eckhart points out, "you can experience your soul flashing out its uncreated prototype." This core energy is your purest self. It is who you were before you were born and what you will return to when your life on this earth is over. Connecting with this energy gives you stability, power, and purpose. Your job is to get connected.

EXERCISE

RELAX. IMAGINE OPENING a valve on your lower *Dan Tien*, streaming energy anywhere in your body. Feel energy radiating from everything in your environment. If you use music, candles, incense, a fireplace, campfire, or something else to enhance this activity, luxuriate in the energy such enhancements emanate. Stay centered. Extend your awareness into the environment's energy. Draw this inside, slowly inhaling through your nose and exhaling through your mouth. Now visualize your inside and outside environments as one. Focus on the nonphysical part of you observing what is going on. Hold this consciousness as long as you can. This is you at your deepest. You have entered what writer Gary Zukav refers to as the "mind of your soul." It is the part of you that was here before you were born and will continue after you die. Once connected, you will experience a deep feeling of well-being.

Look for the Metaphor

RECENTLY, I WAS working out with my wife, who is a talented martial artist. We began training a close range throw. We worked it several times until we felt we could implement the technique. Then we moved on to long-range kicks, one of my wife's favorite drills. Just for fun, she suggested using some long-range kicking to segue into the throw. We needed to create a bridge, so we combined the kicks with boxing, then trapping (closer-range) techniques. A little practice helped us to achieve our goal. After the session, it hit us that the course of action we had created in the dojo was a metaphor for dealing with a person whose distant behavior had been affecting us both in our daily lives. We worked to create a bridging situation that would bring out his *natural* tendency to come in closer. Metaphor is the lifeblood of martial philosophy. Daily experiences offer many such solutions as well. You just have to look for the metaphor. Here's how.

EXERCISE

LET LIFE SPEAK to you. Look for the metaphor in your actions and in the environment. For example, if you don't usually see hawks on your daily drives and you notice that lately you have seen several of them, try researching the nature of hawks. Consider what connections such details have to your current daily activities. For example, do you need to be more watchful? Do you need distance, speed, and tenacity before or in your next endeavor? Perhaps you need to be still yet able to move swiftly upon demand. If you don't see a connection, open your focus more; consider time of day, state of mind, what else is happening in the picture. Try acting on the message. Start with something small until you get more comfortable with the process. Take note of what happens.

49.

Let Other Voices In

AFTER PHYSICAL ACTIVITY or meditation, it is important to revisit some of the ideas that bubbled up into your consciousness. These may contain useful information regarding current life situations. For example, the phrase "This is a time to celebrate" might be coming to you often, but you don't see the connection between the phrase and what's happening in your life. Then several unexpected incidents occur. Perhaps you have been stressed about finding a way to finance another college degree. Suddenly you are offered a new position at work, for more pay, as well as tuition reimbursement at a local university. This opens the additional possibility of moving to a new apartment or home you have been considering. In the depths of your heart, you know these events are at least part of the celebration for which your mind has been preparing. Martial arts teach that Universal Energy flows through your activities and meditations like breath through a flute. This energy contains information as well as power (or spirit). Listening prepares you for upcoming life changes, whether on the mats or in daily affairs.

EXERCISE

FOCUS YOUR ATTENTION on the images and voices that float through your consciousness during the day. Don't let any of these images or voices stay in your mind, but revisit them later. Ask yourself what life is attempting to say. Don't confuse this spiritual energy with the noise of your ego, which is driven by fear and negativity and can only lead you into harm's way and away from your true self. Train yourself to reject that voice. The message of spirit is *always* one of peace and love, kindness and gentility. Look for connections to your current life. Consider how you can use such information to help bring you more contentment and happiness. Start small. Don't do something drastic like quitting your job while you are learning to become proficient with this skill.

50.

Learn to Use the
Two Faces of Vulnerability

SOMETIMES YOU TRY to tag your opponent and wind up on your own butt wondering what just happened. Or you get hit repeatedly by the same kick or thrown from the same angle a dozen times. You think your partner must be so much more skilled than you are. However, you are just leaving yourself wide open to certain attacks. This kind of vulnerability is often easy to see. Once you recognize it, you think more defensively, get your guard up, and draw your kick back more quickly. But sometimes being defensive is not enough and you can still get tagged. There is another subtler type of vulnerability and your partner may be using it against you. For example, one day you realize that certain of your actions are countered so proficiently you'd think your partner knew you were going to launch them beforehand. What you discover is that your partner is making himself appear vulnerable in order to manipulate you. He is creating an irresistible invitation or target and nailing you whenever you take it. Both forms of vulnerability manifest in daily life as well. Make sure you are not leaving yourself open to harm. Do, however, invite actions that will heighten your joys or extinguish problems before they become harmful.

EXERCISE

THINK ABOUT AN incident that didn't go so well for you. Analyze the movements you made. Identify how you may have been vulnerable in the situation. Consider what martial principles came into play or should have, then think about where and why they may have broken down. Ask yourself what could be done to make them more effective next time.

Alternate: Consider ways to make vulnerability part of your strategy in a current activity.

Conquer Negative Energy

IN ORDER TO excel on the mats as well as in life, you have to eliminate negative energy. It causes illness, slows down functions, fogs the mind, contaminates judgment, impedes the ability to issue and receive positive energy, and in short, poisons you on every level. Martial training tells you to rid yourself of *all* negative emotions. The concept is referred to as *wu-shin,* or empty-mindedness. Remember, fear is the foundation of all negative behavior. Indeed, fear is within the energetic chemistry of anger, guilt, doubt, hatred, superiority, inferiority, jealousy, revenge, prejudice, or what have you. *Wu-shin* doesn't mean that you don't feel anything. Emotions can be used to identify the quality and level (high or low) of your energy. You acknowledge the emotion, the part of your body affected by it (usually by pain), and then let it go. Here's how.

EXERCISE

WHENEVER YOU EXPERIENCE negativity, acknowledge it. Identify the precise emotions associated with it. Let yourself feel these emotions. Then release them, letting them flow out of you like water. Visualize the water getting cleaner and cleaner until it is crystal clear. Then visualize only clean, positive energy entering to take its place.

Boost Your Sensitivity

IF SOMETHING IS moving too fast or slow, the eye will capture it, but the brain cannot interpret the data and provide us with a virtual picture. As a result, we remain "mind-blind." Martial arts train you to balance these shortcomings of sight by utilizing the body's natural sensitivity. Sensitivity is a more organic capacity for discovering truth. Some call it your inner knowingness. What's more, this inner voice will tell you step-by-step what to do in any situation. Following this voice, however, is not easy at first. To this end, many martial drills are practiced blindfolded, forcing you to focus more on what you *feel* rather than what you think or see. In the dojo, this is called "seeing with your skin" and is aimed at boosting sensitivity. You learn to associate bodily sensations (immediate calm, effortless movement, increased energy, more aliveness) with correct responses. You recognize the difference in feeling alive and full of energy as opposed to feeling numb, which is how you feel when actions stem from disingenuous inner guidance. Trust your body. It is a powerful and accurate compass for truth, both on and off the mats.

EXERCISE

EXPERIMENT WITH YOUR sensitivity. Start with something small. For example, before preparing your next meal, close your eyes and center. Try to focus as much attention on your internal body as possible. Ask your body what nutrients it needs. Which will best energize it? Vegetables? Green? Yellow? Leafy? Meats? Liquids? If it helps you focus, hold the product in your hands. The point is to make yourself sensitive to your body's reaction. If you feel positive energy surging, it is telling you the substance is what your body needs. If your body weakens or loses balance, your choice is not right at the moment. You can do this with other kinds of daily decisions as well.

53.

Don't Stop to Analyze

EVERY MARTIAL ARTIST has a story about a shot that almost tagged her, the proverbial "strike to end all strikes." And it may have done so if she had stopped for even one second to complain over what was or could have been happening, or what was likely to happen. Instead, she remained very much present and avoided the oncoming blow completely. This principle holds true off the mats as well. When you begin a new relationship, for instance, you don't start thinking about how much more fun life was with your former partner. If you get a promotion, you don't dwell on how much more responsibility you have. Similarly, if you have just adopted a new puppy, you don't stop to analyze how much less stressful your life was before you got the pet. Such thoughts are regressive, and they can actually be harmful. They sabotage your focus and leave you vulnerable. The martial Way is to be completely wherever you are, see your choices, and take your best shots.

EXERCISE

WHENEVER YOU FIND yourself diluting the present by comparing it to the way things used to be, refocus yourself on the moment. Ask yourself what you want from the situation. Harmonize your actions until you see windows of opportunity begin to appear and when they do, take them.

Conquer Self-Consciousness

MOMENTS OF SELF-CONSCIOUSNESS rise like bubbles surfacing across your mind. They contaminate inspired action and spontaneity. They are driven by the ego, which Joseph Campbell, in *The Power of Myth,* defines as "what you think you want, what you will to believe, what you think you can afford, what you decide to love, what you regard yourself bound to." He goes on to say, "It may all be too small, in which case it will nail you down." Martial arts teach that our real battle is in defeating our ego. A favorite dojo exercise is kicking at the speed bag, which, of course, has a mind of its own, swaying in infinitely unpredictable directions. To be successful, you have to kick with intention, yet without thinking about what your next kick will be, who's watching, or who you are trying to impress, or you'll miss the bag entirely. You learn that when you miss, you have to stay focused, disregard what you just looked like, and keep firing. Whether on the mats or in daily life, there are bound to be many setbacks, but the martial Way is to hold tight, forget about outside judgment, trust your skill, and keep flowing.

EXERCISE

AS YOU ARE about to enter into an action, consider what skills might assist you in seeing the situation through. Let go of thoughts about looking good, impressing anyone, self-worth based on winning or losing, or even perfection. Instead, focus on clearing your mind, staying centered, and moving as though the movement itself is a thing of beauty. Take note of how you feel and where you are led.

55.

Love Your Opponent

IN MARTIAL ARTS, the axiom *love your opponent* teaches how to accept or move another person's flow of energy. Aikido is a perfect example. The word itself—sometimes translated as "harmony way"—literally means "the Way (*Do*) of Spirit (*Ki*) Love (*Ai*)." You learn to love your partner, spirit to spirit. Energetically, love cannot be lost. What you send is what you receive. When your partner's energy is driven by resistance, harmonizing and flowing with him will assure a return of gentle, soft energy. In the dojo, this is called *redirecting*. If your partner executes a hard straight punch, you learn to gently and smoothly direct it away. Your art is egoless. By flowing with your partner's energy, you lead. Although you are in control, you appear ordinary. You are calm and confident. You get the job done. Remember that by not responding to an attack with an equal attack, you resolve conflict with as little damage as possible. The energy you expend comes back to power you with even greater force. When partners flow with each other's energy—redirecting, as well as being redirected—life's joys become more joyous.

EXERCISE

AIKIDO SAYS THAT the only reasonable energy one should send into the world is love. The next time you encounter resistance, meet it with softness. Your energy may not return immediately, but it *will* return.

56.

Use the Whole Blade

MARTIAL ARTS TEACH you to finish a technique—that is, not to get tired or sloppy halfway through and abandon your last few moves. Once a movement is "in the groove," your job is to energetically see it to successful completion. When you launch a kick, you don't just halfheartedly draw it back. This can destabilize you and leave you vulnerable. You learn, instead, to promptly snap the kick. If you are going for an armlock, you don't stop once you have your hands on an opponent's arm. You learn to gather your energy, turn the arm, lock the joint, and go for the takedown. The martial axiom is "Use the whole blade." Whether I am painting the house, writing, teaching a class, or some other activity, I have often reminded myself that life is subject to the same principle. Once you bring out your tools and move into action, finish the job.

EXERCISE

WHETHER MEDITATING, DIETING, having a conversation, or whatever else you engage in, make a point of finishing what you start. Pool your energy and use it to bring yourself to a clean and desirable conclusion.

57.

Bend with Adversity

A FORCE THE size of a tornado can snap telephone poles and collapse buildings, yet a blade of grass or a leaf can make surviving such power appear graceful. Indeed, what is soft and flexible can withstand great force, and what is brittle breaks. In the dojo, you train to bend with circumstances, no matter what. Everyone knows it's easy to say, "Lighten up," but sometimes that's difficult to do. Thus, martial arts teach you to constantly remind yourself to stay loose, even in the face of adversity. A judo player I used to work out with always said, "Practice not being afraid to 'take' the throw—the *fall* is part of the movement." She would say, "You and the movement are one." If you can let go of inhibitions about hitting the ground and learn to roll with the movement, you will land in a place of advantage. You will gain confidence in falling and stop feeling like you have lost control.

EXERCISE

DON'T LET ANYONE or anything stop or spoil your calm. Don't get sucked into any disputes. Visualize yourself like a cork floating atop water; no matter if the current is smooth or turbulent, tell yourself you can remain peaceful and content. Just relax. Luxuriate in life's Chi flowing freely through you and everywhere around you. Watch as anyone trying to bully you becomes frustrated and self-extinguishes.

Learn from Adversity

LIFE HAS A way of self-cleansing or pruning itself. This is how all of nature grows: A tree that has stood for years collapses in a storm and dams a brook until the water flows around it, giving growth to new wildflowers that in turn create a meadow of flashing color where there once was nothing. Sometimes growth is difficult to see. Response is everything. For example, a car is pulled over on the expressway and the driver is issued a ticket. Afterward, he begins to drive more cautiously, avoiding, if you will, a more serious adversity down the line. Then again, some drivers ignore such warnings and eventually drive themselves into more serious circumstances. Beginning martial artists often get jumpy when their partner mops the mats with them. Nevertheless, after a few such episodes, you learn to calm down, stop keeping score, and instead focus on staying alert. Whether you are inside or outside the dojo, working through adversity vaults your art to higher levels and goals that are closer at hand.

EXERCISE

THE NEXT TIME adversity strikes, don't flare up. Try to remain as objective as possible. Ask yourself what got you into the situation. Was it something you did? Something you didn't do? Sit back and gather information. Ask yourself what needs to be done to correct the situation. Don't get personal or defensive. Ask yourself what you can learn from the circumstance. What tools can you create from this knowledge that will benefit you in the future? Put them in your toolbox for future use.

59.

Do without Trying

MARTIAL ARTS TEACH that the best technique is the one that requires the least effort. The more you have to try to get something done, the clearer it is that you are on the wrong trail. You can't muscle harmony. My wife and I like using target drills in the dojo. They're fun. You take turns randomly holding a mitt out for your partner to kick at. Here's the lesson: Whenever you think, "The next time she puts the mitt out, I am going to throw some impressive-looking kick," you almost always flub it up. The more you try, the worse it gets. Unless you like tripping up a lot, the exercise has a way of making you stop going for anything in particular and learn to just get the job done—that is, hitting the targets as hard and proficiently as you can without caring what kind of kick you're throwing. Daily life isn't any different. The idea is to stop trying to hit the targets. Just practice your technique, and when the targets expose themselves—strike!

EXERCISE

NEXT TIME YOU find yourself trying to get something done, take a break. Clear your mind. Come back to the job later with a "just get the job done" approach, one you believe requires less effort. Take note of what happens.

60.

Follow Your Bliss

OPPORTUNITIES CHANGE MOMENT by moment. Your job is to recognize these changes and make your best selections. These opportunities and choices, of course, are what make life so interesting and so much fun. When you follow your bliss, you act from deep genuine need. You are awake to who you are and maintain a profound respect for others. Life opens and you learn to energetically trail what sustains you. You learn to feel the difference between what nurtures you and what doesn't, what makes you feel robust as opposed to weak—physically, mentally, and spiritually. You are at peace and express yourself naturally. You initiate change in your life and in others around you. You seek to be part of all things and to see the Infinite in them. When you follow your bliss, every moment of life becomes endlessly exciting and anything is possible.

EXERCISE

NEXT TIME YOU find yourself overthinking something, center and clear your mind. Ask yourself what you need. Stop trying to think of a solution. Just wait for your window of opportunity to open, and when it does, take it. This may not occur right away, so you will need to keep monitoring your need. Remember, your need is subject to change moment by moment. Don't get stuck to dead desires. Bliss, like all other energy, flows. Get excited about life. Let your bliss evolve.

61.

Use Your Imagination

HAVE YOU EVER visualized a sequence of actions and discovered later that they worked out just as you imagined. You think, "Wow, did I do that?" This happens in the dojo all the time. Indeed, your body mechanics perform as though they have already executed your imagined technique a hundred times before. Martial philosophy stresses that visualization works because the imagination is able to tap in to the body's biochemistry. It can flex muscles and even give them memory. What you imagine energetically prewires you for results—just try doing something you absolutely cannot imagine yourself doing. "It's all right here," a colleague of mine likes to say before he demonstrates board-breaking techniques. "You have to see it here first," he adds, pointing to his head. Then, with boards positioned in a large rectangle around the room, he rapidly moves from one to the other, breaking them with fists, elbows, knees, and even his forehead. Whether you are on or off the mats, use your imagination to power everything from your martial postures to your physical, emotional, and spiritual health.

EXERCISE

CHOOSE A GOAL. THINK small at first. Identify what skills and aptitudes are necessary to reach that goal. Imagine someone who excels in these. Recall how he or she maneuvers. Imagine yourself as that person. See yourself reaching the goal. Put your mind "in" your body. Feel the imagined scenario with your body, not just your mind. Give your physical self time to absorb the information it needs into muscle memory. Repetition helps create memory, so play it over until you feel it. Incorporate power words like "focus," "strong," "power," and such to heighten your mind's ability to mobilize your body's resources. Use these words later to help access information when you need it. Try your new skills in a real-life situation.

62.

In the Dark,
Strike to the Center

WHENEVER YOU FEEL as though you are in the dark, martial arts emphasize "doing the fifty-yard dash down your opponent's centerline." The centerline is where a person's major energy centers are located. Striking here will take out an opponent's offensive, as well as defensive, power and structure. Likewise, you can engage a partner by imagining the transmission of high-quality energy to this location. In everyday life this means recognizing what fuels people—the heart of an issue, so to speak—and delivering. To achieve the best results with this technique, the dojo teaches to lighten your advance to such an extent that no one can see it coming. Remember, whenever you feel like you're in the shadows, move toward center.

EXERCISE

NEXT TIME YOU are in the dim light of conflict, tell yourself to relax. Center your consciousness. Stay in touch with what you are feeling, but try to keep your emotions in check. Imagine yourself as transparent, like a glass statue. Ask yourself what you want from the situation, but don't telegraph that desire. Then bring matters to the heart of what you need. Note: You can use the same process to heighten life's pleasures as well.

Basics Are Best

EVEN THE MOST senior martial artists admit that in real combat the basics work best. The idea is to never lose sight of core principles—because they work! I recently watched an advanced martial artist spar with a brown belt. The more advanced student tried to show up the brown belt by launching a series of spectacular-looking spinning and cartwheel kicks. The problem was that he completely missed his target. I remember hearing the brown belt comment, "Was that an offensive or defensive move?" At that point, the brown belt whipped into a series of basic straight punches, which he executed with power and precision. The flabbergasted advanced student, who was still recovering from his misdirected kicks, got tagged and wound up flat on his back. He had learned a tough lesson. An old dojo maxim says: "The basics became basics for a reason." This adage is true on or off the mats.

EXERCISE

THE NEXT TIME you have a job to do, start out by considering what skills are necessary to achieve successful results. Chart your most basic path. Follow through. Assess your outcomes. Take note of how you feel.

64.

Respect Your Body

THE MORE YOU train, the more you feel the connection between how well you take care of your body and the quality of your internal energy. Dr. Wayne Dyer tells us "higher energy is better than lower. The higher your energy, the more capable you are of nullifying and converting lower energies, which weaken you, and the more you can impact in a positive way everyone in your immediate and even distant surroundings." This means if your body is out of tune, your spiritual power diminishes, and vice versa. In the dojo, you explore this connection without anyone telling you to. Diet, meditation, and training all affect outcome. At first you may just be looking for a competitive edge. But ultimately you start craving the higher energy generated by a finely tuned body, whether in the dojo or out. You start to see its connection to all of your various successes. When this truth finally sinks in, you begin to take better care of your body. Respect your body. Take good care of it. It's a vessel of Divine energy.

EXERCISE

CONSIDER HOW YOU feel about your body, both the positives and the negatives. Tell yourself that your body is doing the best it can. Send it love.

Alternate: Restrict habits such as excessive use of saturated fats, alcohol, carbohydrates, sugars, and the like. Eliminate smoking and recreational drug use. Replace these habits with healthier dietary practices, and work up to forty-five minutes of physical exercise three to five days a week.

65.

Respect Your Mind

IN THE DOJO, if your mind generates negativity, your body generates negativity. Your muscles tense, you develop pain, and you nosedive. All the good energy that you've grown used to producing seems unavailable. You wonder what just happened, although in your heart you already know, because of course it wasn't anything the dojo did to you, it was what you brought into it. You go home, review, and tell yourself you'll never let *that* happen again. What you realize is that your mind sees things as *you* are—not necessarily as *they* are. You realize that the quality of mind you bring into situations can determine their outcome. Rarely does a polluted mind lead to successes on the mats or in daily life.

EXERCISE

TAKE NOTE OF what you're feeding your mind, and reject negativity. Avoid "either-or" thinking. Look at your whole day. If there are five good things and one that is not so good, don't focus on the one bad thing. Whenever you feel stressful thoughts or memories creeping into your field of awareness, don't fight them. That will only stress you more. Instead, try centering and letting them gently float through your consciousness and gracefully out of your mind.

66.

Respect Your Spirit

WHEN YOUR SPIRIT is high and in synch with daily life, you notice that you perform more naturally, contently, and successfully. You are happier and healthier. Relationships run more smoothly. All aspects of life seem better. You experience an overall feeling of well-being. The opposite is also true. These are all qualitative affects of your internal energy and how you are processing it. Remember, negativity generates low-level energy, and positivity yields high energy. Just like you learn to be sensitive to certain actions that affect your body and mind, you need to become aware of which actions affect your spirit and how. Your job is to keep your energy high. This will enable you to create the most successes in life with the least effort. Keep in mind that the terms "body," "mind," and "spirit" are just words to help us talk about these concepts as separate functions of energy. In essence, they are really the same thing—energy. What you do to one, you do to all. Whether you are in the dojo or outside, all three of these elements are part of self-respect.

EXERCISE

THE POWERS OF suggestion combined with repetition can drastically affect the quality of your life. Take note of what you're putting into your spirit. Put yourself in close proximity to people, places, and things that lift your spirit. As the expression goes, "Don't let anybody rain on your parade!" Think positive. Be good to yourself. Let your spirit soar.

Tap in to Your
Body's Energy Pumps

MARTIAL ARTS TEACH that some of the most wonderful personal transformations evolve around your ability to tap in to the body's internal energy centers. These can be understood as pumps inside your body that are capable of channeling energy throughout the body and beyond it, as well as receiving it from anything in the environment. There are seven internal energy centers in all, and they are located along the spine:

1. *At the rectum:* drives our instinct to survive.
2. *In the pelvic area:* drives our urge to procreate.
3. *Behind the solar plexus:* drives our will and urge to conquer, master, or achieve.
4. *In the center of the chest:* drives emotional healing, compassion, and love.
5. *In the throat:* drives communication.
6. *In the center of the forehead:* drives perception.
7. *At the crown of the head:* drives spirit.

Martial artists learn that using the body's energy pumps is a way to refine their ability to issue and receive the power to break boards, explode techniques, and energize all other martial skills. Outside the dojo, you learn to use these pumps to energize your power for healing, resolution, and spiritual experiences.

EXERCISE

CONSULT THE LIST above. Regulate your breath, following it down along each pump, and then back up again. Feel the sparkle of energy as your breath passes over. Use whenever you need a quick burst of energy throughout the day.

Check Your Internal
Energy System Often

ENERGY NEEDS TO move through you smoothly. Its natural flow is downward, entering the crown of your head and flowing to the bottom of your feet, where it reverses and circulates back up, leaving the body where it entered. You can also consciously use your energy pumps to channel this power inwardly or outwardly. Such transmissions can be beneficial even if they happen unconsciously. For instance, your body may be healing itself, emotions may be strengthening, or your spirit may be creating events to bring you happiness. The opposite, of course, is also true—you may be creating a future of landmines. So the more aware you make yourself of the way you are processing energy and distributing it, the more control you have over your life. You can energetically generate any future you want. Your job is to be sure that energies you are channeling are positive and in synch with your desires. You cannot be spiritually empowered and ignore the way the universe's energy enters and leaves your body. This awareness is the beginning of a higher-level spiritual journey. Your job is to check in with yourself as a daily maintenance, whether on the mats or in daily life.

EXERCISE

RELAX AND REGULATE your breathing. Follow your breath down through each of your internal energy pumps and then back up with your out-breaths. Visualize clean, nutritious, white breath flowing through your energy channels. Use your breath to massage each pump. This should invigorate you and stimulate the flow of energy. Unobstructed energy feels terrific. Obstructed energy translates to pain. Pay attention to how you feel. Note: If you discover tension or blockage in any of these areas, don't worry; you can learn to eliminate these obstructions.

69.

Release Negative Energy

SOMETIMES YOUR ENERGY gets blocked, impeding its flow like a knot suddenly appearing in a garden hose. Blocks can be physical, mental, or spiritual. They are the result of negative energy welling in your system. In the dojo, you learn to use your body's signals to recognize blocks. These appear as tensions and sometimes as pains—the greater the blockage, the greater your discomfort. Perhaps you can't execute a takedown because of an ache in your shoulders or lower back. You may notice similar patterns of pain outside the dojo, as well—headaches or other body ache creeping in as if on schedule. Martial arts teach two ways of addressing these. The first, which is merely temporary, is to treat the symptom—remember, your body can only hold so much energy. Thus, you can release negative energy and replace it with positive. The second way of taking care of aches and pains is to treat the cause, identifying and eliminating the reason(s) for the blockage. Because it is easier and often quicker, most people choose the temporary solution, to empty out the destructive energy and replace it with good. This gives some breathing space, for the short run, until you find a more permanent solution.

EXERCISE

REGULATE YOUR BREATHING. Follow your breath down through each internal energy center and then back up. Imagine each pump as a different color. Dull colors will indicate blockage. Feel the blockage as your breath moves through. Use your breath to massage blocked centers. Pull in clean energy from the center at the crown of your head, and guide it to the blocked area. Imagine it effervescing with energy and bright color. Use your fingertips to massage the area if you like. When unblocked, energy will pass through it smoothly, the color will become vibrant and strong, and any pain associated with the center will disappear.

70.

Use an Emotional Scan

BOTH MARTIAL PHILOSOPHY and Eastern thought and medicine tell you that blocked energy is directly related to the way you process emotions. Thus, to eliminate pain and illness, you need to understand what emotions are triggering you. To this end, martial arts encourage you to scan your energy centers often. You learn to use your body as a way to understand your emotions, and vice versa. This is the first step in clearing energy blocks and eliminating their causes. Here is how you can use this skill.

EXERCISE

THIS EXERCISE TREATS the *source* of blocked energy. First, identify any pains, tensions, and ill health you are coping with. Sink your consciousness into your body. Scan each energy pump. Identify any blocks. Don't be surprised if you discover more than one. What emotions do you associate with each block? Feel each emotion. Do you feel tension or tightness anywhere in your body, for example in your abdomen, chest, arms, or legs. Scan your emotions throughout the day; keep a list of people, places, and things that trigger negative emotions. Stress grows out of nonacceptance, and ill health grows out of stress. These emotional states indicate that you are processing energy through negative emotions and blocked centers. Your emotions will identify your stressors. Ask what you are resisting. Where does fear play into your inability to just accept things? Martial arts emphasize that fear is at the bottom of all energy blockage. To treat the source of the infirmity, you have to verbalize it. Say to yourself out loud: *I am afraid of this* _____ *and so I am resisting* _____. Just putting your feelings into words lowers stress. Tell yourself that no matter what, if you remain calm and open, life will land you in a place of good. Note: For chronic blockage, you may need to combine this exercise with other therapies.

71.

Eliminate
Compulsive Behaviors

AN INSTRUCTOR OF mine once told me that the only way to make yourself feel blissful is to generate good, positive energy. He used to emphasize this point whenever anyone mentioned compulsions such as eating junk food, abusing alcohol, inflicting cruelty, adopting risky behavior, overworking, and other addictions. Generating positive energy and eliminating destructive compulsions became a major theme in our dojo. Addictive behaviors are dysfunctional because they numb pain, thereby silencing its attempt to speak and throwing you off track on your path to wellness. Martial arts teach that merely eliminating these behaviors from your life will not dissolve all blockages; doing so requires a new approach to living. Nonetheless, getting rid of compulsive behavior is a significant step in the process.

EXERCISE

IDENTIFY WHICH OF the following you rely on to override pain: abusing alcohol, tobacco, or caffeine; overworking; overeating; adopting risky behavior; having obsessive thoughts; and inflicting cruelty. Sometimes choices in these matters seem overwhelming, but we have to acknowledge that ultimately they exist. Consider yourself having done the best you can up until now, but acknowledge that you have a choice and can create different options. Visualize yourself as being ten feet tall and indestructible, filled with respect, and clear of all blockages. Enjoy the idea of yourself functioning with such premium quality.

Use an Advanced Scan

ONCE YOU START practicing emotional scans, you will begin to recognize patterns. Using an advanced scan can help you close in on pollutants. For example, you may find your compulsive aggression at work spreading to your family life, the dojo, and so on. An emotional scan might reveal several blocked energy channels, including areas of spirit, communication, or aggression. Associated with these blocked channels are feelings of anger and depression. You may ultimately find that avoiding a conversation you need to have with a colleague is at the root of both recent body pain and negative behaviors. You can work toward a solution by choosing to open a dialogue with your colleague. This skill requires patience. You need to slow down, look for patterns, and react less.

EXERCISE

SPEND A WEEK looking for a pattern of negative emotional reactions. For example, do you find yourself getting angry with a colleague at work, then at a cashier, then at someone in your family? Everywhere you go? Scan your emotions and energy centers. Which of them are affected? Look for the root cause. Consider what action steps you might take to eliminate the pattern. Then follow through.

Use Avoidance—For a While

IF I KNOW that every time I go up against a certain partner I get clocked with a combination of kicks that end at my head; necessity will convince me to avoid tangling up when I see the kicks emerging. In fact, I will begin to look for how my partner forecasts the attack so that I can sharpen my avoidance. This kind of avoidance works for the short run. If, however, I want to grow as a martial artist, I will need to learn to defend and counter against such a scenario. Mentally reviewing the situation works. But sometimes you may have to seek information from others. In the dojo, you are more often than not encouraged to consult your instructor (or partner) for ways to respond to techniques that are getting the best of you. They will either resolve the problem for you or direct you to ways you can solve it yourself. I have used this approach off the mats—at home, work, and other places—from both ends of the stick, so to speak, and found the results quite rewarding.

EXERCISE

IDENTIFY A POINT of unresolved conflict in your current affairs that you have been ineffectively treating. What have you done to remedy the situation that has thus far been unsuccessful? Look for signs that telegraph the conflict. Then allow yourself to avoid it. Continue to look for a solution. If you can't find one, try discussing the matter with the person with whom you are in conflict. Whatever you do, don't stay stuck.

Use Your Chi to Uplift

I DON'T THINK I'll ever forget the day I was tested for my black belt. It was a grueling, humid August afternoon. At times I felt I was going to pass out from all the heat and expenditure of energy. Then, just as I thought I was past the tough stuff, my instructor asked me to perform a smashing four-star—a partnered bone-to-bone karate drill where you crash forearms at full torque. I chuckled to myself. Here I was teamed up with a person who'd literally splintered oak posts with his arms. I thought this would be a good time for me to conduct my own test, so I decided to implement two martial concepts to help me survive. I summoned as much Chi as possible to my energy center for aggression. Then I pumped as much energy as I could to my arms, charging their ability to ward off injury. Rather than leaving me exhausted and in pain, the smashing four-star drill gave me even more power. You can use this method of warding off bodily, emotional, or spiritual injury, whether on or off the mats.

EXERCISE

SCAN YOUR ENERGY pumps. Identify areas of weakness. Relax. Center. Pull Chi from everywhere in your environment: physical movement, your own and that of others; the earth, the sky—from anyone and anything. Send it to the affected energy pump and use your breath to help unblock it. Then begin pumping Chi wherever you need it.

Strengthen Your Positive Energy

DOJO TRAINING OFTEN includes studies in Chi Kung—a martial practice created in China primarily to supercharge Chi. Nearly everyone in the dojo is initially fascinated by how this technique can make self-defense tactics more explosive. However, the more everyday benefits you begin to realize through the cultivation and use of positive energy, the more you seek it for its real purpose: to sustain health and enhance spiritual experiences. A favorite dojo exercise involves using massage to heighten and release energy throughout your energy centers. A fellow martial artist once told me that she used this technique to wake herself up, during very long drives from New York to North Carolina. And indeed you can, too. Once you generate high-level Chi, the energy is yours to do with whatever you like, whether in the dojo or out.

EXERCISE

DO THIS IN the morning or when necessary during your day. From a seated position, relax and center. Regulate your breathing. Rub both hands together until they warm and then gently rub your lower back, in proximity to where your kidneys are located. This is a storage area for unused Chi. Feel the good energy releasing, and use your breath to guide its nourishment wherever you like in your body. Use your fingers to rub the bottom center of each foot. This Chi point is called the *bubbling well*. This area stores a lot of energy, and when released it is quite luxurious. Now place your hand at your breastbone and focus on your heart. Gently rub in a circular motion. Think of something beautiful, like a sun or moonrise or anything in your environment. Pull its energy into you and circulate it through your body. Feel the warm, tingly sensations this produces. Enjoy.

76.

Use Your Power to Cleanse

BECAUSE NEGATIVITY IS so destructive, the dojo teaches several ways to cleanse your body from its toxicity. If you can simply empty your mind of it, then by all means let go. But sometimes you need help. A combination of Chi Kung and visualization skills offer another way to filter negative energies stored in your body, on into the earth. Remember, the earth can withstand that kind of concentrated negativity, but you cannot. When you are being poisoned by a person, place, event, or what have you, you need to purify as soon as possible, as this kind of contamination has a nasty habit of spreading quickly. It starts as a tiny drop of toxin that begins in one room of your life, so to speak, and then rapidly infects your whole domain.

EXERCISE

USE A SEATED position. Relax and center. Begin with an emotional scan, locating any blocked areas and identifying causes. Then use your Chi to unblock those areas. Visualize all of your negative energy. Assign a color to it. Feel the ground below you. Then stream all of your negative energy out of your body. Image it pouring down into the earth. Feel yourself clearing. Feel your balance restoring. regulate your breathing. Stay silent. If time and place allow, gently place your hand over your heart. Listen to the beat of your heart for three minutes. Feel yourself filling with good energy. Use Pump 4 (center of chest) to send this energy to your entire body. Acknowledge the earth for protecting you. Send it your love.

77.

Strengthen Your Virility

ANOTHER AMAZING USE of martial principle is toward the enhancement of virility—for both men and women. When I first began studies in Chi Kung, my instructor had mentioned that enhanced virility was a terrific side benefit of the art. You hear a lot of things in martial arts, many of which remain in the zone of "Well, okay, but until I experience this myself, I'll have to maintain a bit of scrutiny." Suffice to say that ever since I put the principle of enhanced virility to the test, I have been richly rewarded in terms of energy and pleasure, and with the birth of my first child. I am aware that there could be many other variables in effect here. As far as my personal experiences are concerned, however, I can no longer write off this aspect of martial training as a myth.

EXERCISE

INCORPORATE SOME KIND of exercise into your daily routine. It can be anything from using exercise machines to running, Pilates, stretching, or anything else that gets you moving. You can vary the activities; however, it is important to perform them three times a day—in the morning, at midday, and in the later evening. If time is a factor, midday exercise is best for this particular effect. At various points throughout the activity, use your in-breath to stimulate energy Pump 2, in the pelvic area. This increases both virility as well as fertility. Note: Follow a sensible diet with plenty of nutritious foods. Avoid an excess of meats and carbohydrates. Use fruits, vegetables, and healthy oils.

Use Your Power of Aggression

YOUR POWER OF aggression is associated with energy Pump 3, located behind the solar plexus. When this energy center is left unmanaged, you can lose stability as well as engage in destructive behavior. This energy station has many positive applications as well. Martial arts teach that aggressive energy can be purified and used to supercharge whatever you do. This type of energy has subtle, perhaps more significant uses as well. For example, it is the power behind razor-sharp focus and assertion. It is also the energy that fuels the ability to create. And it is what powers generosity of spirit, ethical conviction, and ultimately the high-quality energy necessary for advanced spiritual sensitivity and experiences. Unblocked, this energy center will fill you with a feeling of contentment; blocked, your stomach will feel like it is doing cartwheels. Sometimes in order to get a job done, you need heart, soul, and guts. Monitor this energy center often as you cruise through your daily routines.

EXERCISE

ACCESS YOUR POWER of aggression. Relax and center. Use breathing and visualizations to stimulate the energy center. Channel its energy to wherever needed. Note: Negative emotions associated with energy Pump 3 indicate blockage. Check and clear this center frequently.

79.

Release Type "A" Energy

IN THE DOJO, Type "A" energy is associated with *jing,* Chinese for "concentrated life force energy." Concentrating energy is natural. You do it, in fact, whenever you closely focus on anything. The problem is that focused energy creates recoil. This is why Type "A" energy is injurious to the heart. It often reveals itself as tension, especially in your chest. Such energy is harmful and should be taken seriously. Indeed, acute or chronic symptoms may require a physician and combined therapies. The dojo teaches to immediately retract (relax) your actions smoothly and softly to avoid injury, particularly if you are employing an action multiple times or, off the mats, any involved in any intensified single effort for a long period of time. Pullback is as important as the action itself. This is because *jing* recoils, potentially damaging the body, internally and externally. Controlling *jing* is tricky because you can generate it unconsciously as well as intentionally. Allowed to run its course, it will surface in what many people refer to as a Type A personality. Daily maintenance is your best plan for keeping this energy in check.

EXERCISE

MINIMIZE BACKLASH BY calming yourself after issuing energy. When applying steady action, incorporate relaxed and still points as part of those movements.

Alternate: Lightly rub your breastbone for a moment. Focus your attention on your heartbeat. Relax and take a slow, deep regulated breath. Use your breath to direct any *jing* in the area of your heart down into the earth. Visualize this energy leaving your body. Don't allow it to well up.

80.

Tap in to Your
Heart's Power Pump

ONE OF THE greatest gifts of the martial journey is learning to feel good in the world and with the world. You discover that the more you open yourself to life, the more it opens to you. You realize that neither your spirituality nor the power you derive from it depends on anybody else other than yourself. You feel "connected." Your body's energetic center for this awareness is Pump 4, in the center of your chest. Martial arts teach that this center integrates you with heaven and earth. Recently my wife and I spent some time on an island off the Massachusetts coast. On several occasions I awoke before sunrise to jog along the beach. One day, as the sun was rising like a concentrated ray of fire, I decided to perform a kata on the sand. I remember centering and drawing Chi from all of my limbs, from the earth and from the sun, extending it through my heart energy channel and to everything around me. Of course, such experiences are beyond words. But they are not beyond feeling. They are elite heartfelt experiences that everyone can have. Our job is to have as many as of these experiences as possible. Experience life through the heart. Feel alive. Be at the center of everything that matters.

EXERCISE

WHEN YOU EXPERIENCE heartache, you feel your heart is closed, in grief or resentment. When this happens, remember a time when you felt the contentment of love and compassion. Let yourself feel all the particulars. Draw that energy into your heart's energy center. Extend it throughout yourself and into your environment. Feel a soothing energy return. Let this energy restore you, even if it's only momentarily.

De-Stress Your Communication Pump

MARTIAL ARTS ASK you to pay close attention to the quality of energy you send into the world, because that same quality is what you will attract. When Pump 5, your communication center (located in your throat), is open and functioning smoothly, your voice is relaxed and smooth. This is the bridge between inner consciousness and the consciousness of everything around you. When it is unobstructed, you feel like you can speak authentically, freely, playfully, and seriously. Your throat is not dry or tense. You get your point across. Of course, when you are having problems communicating, your energy pump is stressed. Unblocking this center makes you feel better about those you are in relationship with, at home, at work, and the like. Indeed, when this channel is open, you can transmit and receive insight even beyond the limitations of words. You create more amiable social and spiritual experiences. You feel better about yourself, because you are not isolated.

EXERCISE

MAKE YOURSELF ATTENTIVE to bodily sensations in your throat and neck at various points throughout the day. Pay attention to when and in what situations you experience any kind of obstruction. Try to identify the cause. Use your martial skills to remove blocks. Follow up with anyone involved when the time is appropriate.

82.

Develop Your Power
of Intuition

HAVE YOU EVER thought something was going to happen and told a friend, who responds that there is no basis for your thinking, and then it happens? Martial arts tells you that there is a foundation for intuitions and encourages you to rely on them. On the mats, intuition protects you. For example, it prevents you from chasing "fake" strikes intended to set you up for the real shot. It helps you to see consequences before experiencing them. Intuition tells you not to play tennis on your day off, and as a result, you stay home and are there when your child calls from school because he or she missed the bus. The body's center for intuitive energy is Pump 6, located in the center of the forehead. Various traditions refer to this as the "third eye" because of its connection to a higher plane of consciousness some call "superconsciousness." Energetically, your body can only speak the truth, and it is 100 percent accurate. Keeping this energy channel clear helps you know behavioral consequences in advance. Use your power of intuition as a litmus test for life decisions.

EXERCISE

EXPERIMENT. TAKE SOME time for yourself and follow a small impulse. Note what happens. Or think about an incident in your current life, something small and relatively unimportant—maybe a conversation or the like. As you enter the situation, relax and tune in to yourself. Ask yourself, *How do I feel at this moment? What do I want from this situation? What should I do?* Listen to your instincts. Remember, intuition will not lead you into harm's way. Which possibilities leave you with a sense of deadness. Which of them seem to boost your energy and make you feel more alive? Choose the latter. Then act from there.

83.

Fire Up Your Spirit

DR. JONAS SALK believed, as do many martial and holistic practitioners, that humankind's next evolutionary step is spiritual in
nature. He refers to this as the "meta-biological evolution." Martial
arts teach that the energy center at the crown of the head, Pump 7, is
your gateway to pure spirit. Through it, you can draw life force energy
from above you, convert and channel it through each of your energy
pumps. This is your invisible power cord to the universe. A person's
level of development is dependent upon the strength of this spirit
energy. It is important to keep this center clear. When it is unblocked,
you feel an optimistic reverence for life. And when it is fully developed, your energetic capacity in this center will yield the highest level
of consciousness, self-awareness, and peace. When this energy center is
blocked, however, you experience feelings of disassociation, depend-
ency, confusion, and disillusionment. The martial Way is to fire up this
center wherever you are, even sitting on a park bench or standing in
a grocery store. This will give you the power needed to recognize dys-
functions and liberate yourself.

EXERCISE

YOU CAN PRACTICE this exercise anywhere. Relax your breathing, and
bring your attention to the crown of your head. Straighten your posture.
Imagine an invisible cord connecting you to the universe. Then, with your
in-breaths, draw an abundance of energy from above, and use Pump 7 to
filter it down through each of the energy centers to Pump 1. Then filter the
energy back up through each pump, and release it from its point of entry,
the crown of your head. Try this whenever you are feeling depleted. One to
three cycles should do the trick.

84.

Map Your Energy Flow

ONE OF THE best activities I underwent in martial studies was mapping my energy flow to see how each individual energy center affected my life. This process provides a much broader and more personalized picture of energy and the specific ways to process and release it on a daily basis. You discover how the people, places, things, events, and even the language of your life affect the quality of your internal energy. You also discover how the way you process energy influences you. The relationship between these and your successes, contentment, and overall well-being reveals itself.

EXERCISE

TAKE A WEEK and focus on one energy pump per day. For example, if you're feeling a potential conflict with a family member, identify the affected energy pumps, unblock them, and revitalize by drawing energy in from above you. Pay attention to what happens—to you and to your partner(s). Keep a notebook. Record immediate and long-range effects (dreams, emotions, situations occurring that day or week). Map the specifics of your life and your response to them in order to see daily patterns. At week's end, review what you've recorded in your notebook. Ideally, you'll see a pattern where before you saw only isolated incidents. Pay special attention to how events were shaped when the energy you released was in fear or anger, and how they were formed when you released softer energies of compassion and love.

85.

You Create the Next Moment

ENERGY FLOWS THROUGH your body and can exit through any of its energy pumps. It can leave negatively or positively, depending on how you process it. Your job is to consciously keep it flowing smoothly and positively. In the dojo, you learn that no matter what, the way you process and receive energy will create your very next moment. If, for example, your opponent knocks you to the mats and you become depressed, perceiving yourself as unable to recover, you probably won't. If you resent him for the good move, you will elicit one type of response. Then again, offering praise will create a completely different reaction. If you smile, commend your partner, recharge, and use your new position to sweep his legs, you could create yet another possibility. Martial art is about not giving up power to the wishes of others or to the haunts of your past. *You* are responsible for the creation of your next moment of life. Choice by choice, move by move, you sculpt the future. Choose well.

EXERCISE

MAKE A LIST of how many times in one day you do things you don't want to do. Visualize each of them. How does each of these activities affect you emotionally and physically? The next day, if someone says, "Let's do this or that," consider your own needs. What are your options? Choose those that bring you closest to your desires.

86.

Weigh Your Options

ONE OF THE most difficult lessons to learn in the dojo is that sometimes a warrior can win a battle and still lose the war. Indeed, there are many situations in which the person who takes the majority of shots loses the match. Martial arts teach you not to go for pawns when there are bigger targets available. In considering the type of future you want to create, you have to weigh your options. I have had to fight my urges and recall this martial lesson pretty much on a daily basis. For instance, sometimes it can be a lot easier and better to fulfill the boss's request and stay an extra twenty minutes at work than to get into an argument that will dramatically change a relationship and permanently damage your job. Weigh your options. Win the war.

EXERCISE

THE NEXT TIME you get the urge to take an action step, ask yourself if it will preclude other options that may surface further down the line. Decide which step would be more advantageous. Go with that one. Take your *best* shot.

87.

Value Your Teachers

I REMEMBER GIVING a presentation at a conference many years ago. I was the last presenter before lunch. I had notes on the blackboard. One of the headliners came on right after the break. He hadn't been there for my pitch and didn't know me at all. He was my senior, and I had admired him for years. He glanced at what I'd left on the board and erased it. Then he proceeded to write down nearly the same points. Several participants thought we had planned things that way. But we hadn't. Later on, I asked him if he had known my teacher. He said that he had not. As things turned out, however, he had been a student of my teacher's teacher—in Chicago, before I was even born. Since then, I have passed this core information on to many of my students, some of whom continue to pass it on. My teacher died a few months before I began this book, but his flame continues to light my life. For this, I remain grateful and send some of his energy on to you.

EXERCISE

MAP YOUR HISTORY. Think about a favorite teacher. Try to determine who taught him or her. Trace the teacher-student relationship back as far as you can. Honor your connection. One of my colleague's students made such a chart and delightedly mapped his history back to the seventeenth century.

Alternate: Think of your teachers often. Choose one today and find a way to express your gratitude to that person. If the person has passed on, consider writing a letter to his or her family. See how this makes you feel.

88.

Dance with Life—
Perform Your Kata

KATA IS A way for martial artists to practice movements vital to their art. There are all types of katas—from those involving blocking and striking techniques, to those executed with weapons (swords, staffs, and the like), to katas performed with fans and scarves. Katas can be done anywhere—in the dojo, on a mountaintop, in the ocean, anywhere. Most players enjoy doing them in a wide variety of environments. Each kata sparks different energies and new knowledge. However, katas are more than just a way to memorize technique. They are dances with and in Universal Energy—remember the Universal Energy Field? You don't have to be a martial artist to perform such dances. You can employ this concept while performing even your most routine tasks. It is a way for you to play with the Infinite, to literally hold its energy in your hands. A kata's ultimate purpose is to harmonize with Divine power, draw it into your energy centers, and circulate it with intention. A kata helps you achieve levels of consciousness that were previously unavailable—on or off the mats. It is a ceremonial way of invoking Divine presence. It is your dance with the Infinite.

EXERCISE

DO SOMETHING PHYSICAL: walk, jog, or hike—anything. Straighten your posture. Center and regulate your breathing. Open and charge each of your energy centers. Be attentive to how the energy flowing through you enters each action and keeps flowing into the next. Feel its power. Feel its ecstasy. Absorb it. Don't be bogged down by self-consciousness. Have fun. Let yourself flow as freely as the energy moves you. Make this life force energy the center of your movement. Take note of how you feel.

89.

Remember That Your Kata
Has No Beginning or End

THE MORE SKILLED you become with your kata (your dance with life), the more you see that there is no beginning or end to any of life's movements. What looks like the conclusion to one action is really the beginning of another. The day you realize this in the dojo is a big day, because your movement accelerates in terms of grace and continuity. And rather than seeing life as a series of circles and straight lines—or, as they say, in terms of black and white—you start to see interconnectiveness everywhere. You are no longer afraid of life's gray areas, because you realize that no action is isolated. Indeed, these gray areas energetically carry the most in terms of strength, self-discovery, and achievement. Martial arts remind us that therein choices flourish. Out of life's shadows all possibility awaits, excitement abounds, and dreams emerge. Play there. Let this concept bring you peace, both inside and outside the dojo.

EXERCISE

DO SOMETHING PHYSICAL: walk, jog, or hike—anything. Be attentive to how the energy flowing through you enters each action and flows into the next. Move your attention beyond yourself, and notice how you are part of another larger action, and how that is part of another action, and so on until you reach a point of just pure attention. Think about how all movement is really one movement. Hold this mind-set for a while. Feel its ecstasy. Try to return to this state of mind a few times each day.

90.

Tap in to the
Dance of Five Elements

TRADITIONALLY, MARTIAL ARTS (as well as Chinese medicine) offer the interplay between the five elements—metal, water, wood, fire, and earth—as a way of living. Each element represents a particular expression of Chi. Most dojos zero in on the constructive/creative and the destructive potential of each. This helps you to understand many subtler aspects of Universal Energy and to integrate them into your daily life. For example, metal liquefies into water, which produces wood, which produces fire, which produces earth, which sustains all life, and so on. Furthermore, for thousands of years, martial arts have taught that ultimately within any particular element each of the others can be found, and that such is the dance of life— *everything is part of everything else,* a banner that the most current of scientific research enjoys waving. Let such awareness enhance you by bringing you more contentment and clarity.

EXERCISE

VISUALIZE THE FOLLOWING colors for each element: white (metal), black or navy blue (water), green (wood), red (fire), and yellow (earth). Focus on one element at a time. See each element with your mind's eye. Then put them in motion—transforming each into the next in a cycle. Focus your attention on your energy pumps. Notice how each pump is affected as you pass from one color to the next. Try visualizing these colors to energize yourself during your daily routines. Note which elements facilitate which actions. Use this information in future endeavors.

91.

Be Like Metal

A BASIC GOAL of martial training is acquiring enough strength to "cut through" things. Thus, the dojo teaches that at times you must be like metal: solid, hard, and able to strike or withstand attack with the power of iron. Early in martial training most practitioners try to avoid punches and kicks as much as possible. Later, however, with proper conditioning, you learn there are times when your ability to take a shot yields considerable advantages. This isn't to say that you stand there like an iron statue. It's more fluid than that. It's more like split-second transformations from: navy blue (water), into and out of yellow (earth), and white (metal), then back through yellow, to navy blue again. You are taught to remember that iron melts. Nothing stays rigid, because what is rigid breaks. One of the most common dojo anthems is "just keep moving; don't stop!" When your opponent is burning with speed, you turn liquid. If you are liquid, you need to ground before turning solid. If your opponent is liquid, you won't get anywhere; it's better to become absorbent.

EXERCISE

MAKE A LIST of all the properties of metal you can find. Consider how each of these properties may parallel a way of problem solving a particular incident in your life. Visualize how to move in and out of the most useful properties from other behaviors involved in the incident. Remember to keep moving. Choreograph a troubleshooting strategy. Try it out.

92.

Be Like Water

NO MATTER WHERE you go on the planet, water is a symbol of purity, birth, and rebirth. *Be like water.* This is the climactic chapter of the *Tao Te Ching,* an ancient text providing the philosophical basis for a way of living known as *Taoism* (which became a state religion in China roughly twenty-five hundred years ago). The Way (or *Tao*) of both Taoism and all martial arts is acceptance or noninterference. Lau-Tsu, founder of Taoism and author of the *Tao Te Ching,* suggested to *always go with the flow.* Indeed, this has become a foremost anthem of our times. It is simple and perfect. Whatever you do, consider the properties of water, and they will get you through. Sometimes you have to be soft, and other times you must be hard. You can be heated, cold, go over things, under, around, and even through them. You can explode or be still. Sometimes you have to vaporize and become invisible. Be like water, and you will glide through life effortlessly. Your troubles will seem lighter, and your joys will soar higher.

EXERCISE

CONSIDER A POINT of conflict or stress in your current life. What properties of water can be employed to help bring you to a state of resolution and peace? Now just follow through by trying to use some of those properties. See how you feel. Consider how using the same properties may heighten a current source of joy.

93.

Be Like Wood

SOME OF THE most elegant movements in martial arts are associated with the element of wood. These movements grow naturally out of the fluidity of water actions, reaching in all directions. When it is balanced, this energy is direct, even piercing, yet graceful and flexible. Most martial artists learn to make movement associated with this element appear quite simple. For example, one of my favorite postures begins from a very low, almost crouched stance. You rise upward into a standing position and, ever so slowly, raise one leg above your head like a slow-motion kick, until it is fully straightened, extending your arms outward like a figure skater. Much like watching a ballet or ice dance, this is one of those postures that looks so graceful that it's easy to miss the trained strength behind it. It's a great example of what martial arts calls soft, peaceful energy being guided by iron will. Anger and tension indicate that this element is blocked. When such energy is imbalanced, you feel as though you have lost center and have become rigid. You run the risk of snapping. To utilize this element, on the mats or in daily life, you must move from an orientation of water and remain supple—able to bend in any direction.

EXERCISE

CONSIDER A POINT of conflict or stress in your current life. What properties of wood can be employed to help bring you to a state of resolution and peace? Now just follow through and try to use those properties. See how you feel. Consider how using the same properties may heighten a current source of joy.

94.

Be Like Fire

MARTIAL ARTS TELL us to balance the element of fire in our lives. When it is stabilized, it will sparkle your eyes; give you healthy, radiant skin; ward off disease; increase potency and sex drive; as well as keep you trim. Fire is vitality. It is the energy behind good health. It gives you penetrating speed and the capability to be productive. On the mats, when you summon the power of fire, your lines can lengthen in an instant. You can blaze shots high or low in seconds. Strikes mold into fiery grabs and rapid takedowns. You swiftly adhere, penetrate, and get the job done. But fire can be destructive, so summon it with care. If left uncontrolled, fire can dehydrate you. This increases physical, emotional, and spiritual toxins, leaving you vulnerable on many levels. Symptoms of imbalance surface as headaches, body pain, or stomach disorders. In the dojo, you are wary of staying in this energy field too long. Simply put, it will stress you out. When it is prolonged, this element will turn on itself, as is the case with Type A personality. But when it is balanced, it greatly increases your ability to succeed at whatever you do.

EXERCISE

CONSIDER AN ENDEAVOR in your current life. List all the properties of fire that you can identify. Which could be employed to create advantages and ultimately lead you to success? Follow through and try to use those properties. See how you feel. Remember that these elements can be invoked to enhance life's pleasures as well as solve problems.

95.

Be Like Earth

EARTH ENERGY ROOTS and centers you. Martial training says that to be like earth is to feel sure-footed and powerful. Earth energy is downward. So, when it comes to technique, this energy makes it difficult for anyone to push you over. This is why the dojo teaches you to place your consciousness in the lower *Dan Tien* and move from there. It opens a steady flow of Chi throughout your body. It is transformative. Earth is the energy in between postures that allows each to "blossom." It absorbs and channels energy from the universe to nurture, strengthen, and promote growth. It absorbs, cleanses, and protects. On the mats, you learn to let some shots run straight through you like lightning into the ground, and you keep on going, undaunted. You learn that you have the same capacity at work, home, wherever. Blocked of this energy, you become prey to the smallest conflicts. You move in fear and weakness rather than in confidence and strength. Earth energy flows in and out of all transformation, providing a solid foundation for each of the other elements. Settle into your self. Move from the ground.

EXERCISE

CONSIDER AN ENDEAVOR in your current life. List all the properties of earth that you can identify. How can these properties be utilized to provide balance between problem-solving actions and lead you to success? Follow through and try to use those properties. See how you feel. Remember that these elements can be invoked to enhance life's pleasures as well as solve problems.

96.

Use Elemental Energy to Make Peace with Anyone

INTEGRAL TO ALL martial training is the ability to invoke the energy of elements and let the universe's life energy flow through you. Your job is to harness this energy in order to enhance and nurture all aspects of the self and to avoid being controlled. Whether inside or outside the dojo, you will discover that water energy nurtures wood and that wood energy in turn nurtures fire; that fire nurtures earth; earth nurtures metal; and metal nurtures water, and such is the Wheel of Life. On the other hand, you will also find that earth controls water, which controls fire, which controls metal, which controls wood, and so on. Flowing from one element to another is not only the way to move on the mats, but it is characteristic of all balanced living. It is another method for creating harmony with everyone you encounter and everything you do.

EXERCISE

CONSIDER AN ENDEAVOR in your current life. What elemental energy is most likely to get you through? Consider how it can be utilized to lead you to success. Then determine from which element the energy you have identified must flow. Visualize yourself beginning there and maintaining a balanced flow from one element to the next as the cycle continues. Try to visualize what advantages will arise as you work toward success, as well as which energies will need to be controlled and which nurtured.

Practice Discipline

MARTIAL ARTISTS SET goals and get the job done. To do so, they practice discipline. In the dojo, weekly training helps students reach larger goals. For example, months of flexibility exercises help you achieve a full split. Goals and discipline are important in daily life as well. It's the small stuff that prepares us for the big. The martial Way is to find out what makes us discontent and to do something about it. Maybe as a martial artist you flinch whenever your partner starts an approach, and you wind up getting tagged. Set up a drill to help alleviate the behavior, and discipline yourself to practice until you improve your game. Outside the dojo, you may want to start a jogging routine, lose a few pounds, or just have more free time on the weekend. Discipline helps you set a plan and stick to it. It helps you focus on what's important, ward off problems, reduce anxiety, build confidence, and live better. Remember, discipline is just a means to an end. Once you achieve your goal, use its power to go on to something else.

EXERCISE

IDENTIFY SOMETHING YOU want to achieve. Devise a plan and use your power of discipline to see it through. If you don't get there right away, or if you experience setbacks, don't be hard on yourself. Instead, try to find out where and why your difficulties began and adjust accordingly. Discipline requires training, just like all of your other skills.

98.

Let Your Vision
of Success Evolve

THE MARTIAL JOURNEY is one of self-discovery and living to your fullest potential. Of course, all holistic arts tell us this is a never-ending road. In fact, because martial principles work both individually as well as sequentially, you can expect to flow through many stages and levels of self-awareness and potential. In daily life, you may start out wanting to just finish your academic education, get a job, and then become the best you can at what you do. This desire shifts to making more money, having a family, and so on. As you evolve in and through your life, you seek greater peace and a more practical spirituality. Your attention shifts again, this time to the idea that such spirituality can energetically be summoned to affect physical life—even to help create day-to-day events. The point is that as you grow, so does your notion of success. Your job is to create: to bring into your reality the best of what you are able to imagine, live it, love it, learn from it, and then go back into yourself to create again and again. Such is the Wheel of Life.

EXERCISE

DEFINE SUCCESS AS you would have at various stages of your life. Then imagine yourself ten years from now, then twenty. Compose a mental letter to yourself from the future. What would you say about success to the person you are today? Ask yourself how this information can affect what you do today. Do this exercise often.

Practice Meditation

ONE OF THE most important aspects of martial training is achieving and sustaining a meditative mind-set. Remember that martial arts were founded as a means of enhancing meditation. The meditative mind can be described as profoundly calm, yet vibrantly alert. Meditation is obviously a great de-stressor, but its function in martial arts has deeper significance: to reach higher levels of performance both on and off the mats. Most practitioners eventually discover that meditation is key for sustaining good health, healing, better living, and enlightenment. Meditation connects you to the ultimate energy source—call it the universe, infinite, God, whatever you like. Staying connected to this ultimate energy source is necessary for all growth. Clearing the mind, regulated breathing, centering, and learning to channel Chi with intention, whether still or in movement, are all ways to enter this mind-set. Explore and even create various methods that work for you; make time, and practice on a daily basis. Your goal is to operate from this mind-set during everyday endeavors. Doing so powers your highest physical, emotional, and spiritual potential. Meditation isn't easy. In fact, it is a lifelong exploration. On the bright side, though, the benefits are immediate.

EXERCISE

MEDITATE EARLY ON in your day and again at the day's end. Try to meditate for a period of at least twenty minutes. When you're totally relaxed and your mind is clear, anchor it to a special image, sound, aroma, or the like—something you can use to pull you in more quickly during times of need. Try to maintain a meditative mind-set of alert-calm for as long as you can through your day. When you feel yourself slipping, practice using your anchor to put you back in the gap. Remember, this skill takes practice. The more you put in, the more you'll get out.

100.

Get in Touch with
Your Physical Self

EASTERN ARTS AND medicines say that at the cellular level your body is made up of the same living, conscious energy as stars and galaxies—the same as the earth and everything on it. Once in balance, your body is capable of opening and translating this wisdom (some of it ancient) and teaching you whatever you need to know. In the dojo, you learn to listen more closely to your physical self; i.e., your body asks for water, you water it; your body asks for rest, you rest it. You learn never to punish it, because it is always doing its best. Your body will create cycles to facilitate you. For example, say you work out at 7:00 PM. Your body is busy preparing in advance: revving energy, regulating its temperature to provide better flexibility and flush toxins, making itself less receptive to bacteria and allergens, and releasing tensions to provide better cardiopulmonary capacity. In short, your body figures out your goal and creates a biological guide to assist—physically, emotionally, and spiritually. This is why it is difficult (but not impossible) to change habits, even good ones. This is a fact worth remembering, especially when the going gets a little rough—you have to stick to it. Send your physical self the right messages.

EXERCISE

DO SOMETHING PHYSICAL to raise your energy level. Brisk walking works well, although anything you like will do. Set up a daily routine and try to stick to it. Start listening to your body more. Use your instincts. As usual, begin with something small like diet: What food should you have for dinner—vegetables, fish, meat, carbohydrates? Should you eat more today or less, or should you fast? Let your body facilitate. Tell it what you want and watch it create patterns to help get you what you need. See how it works.

101.

Never Stop Studying Philosophy

AT THE HEART of martial arts is a very basic paradigm for living to your fullest potential. The formula includes three elements:

- Do something physical to get your energy going
- Use meditation to get in touch with your energy as it moves through you
- Study martial philosophy to see what can be done with this energy

It's really that simple. This last step, however, is what brings everything all together and gives you inspiration for the creative personal exploration of techniques you have learned. Ultimately you want to incorporate all three into your every action.

EXERCISE

FIND A BOOK of philosophy that relates to the martial arts. I recommend any translation of the *Tao Te Ching*. Read a section of this book, or the whole book (it's short), regularly. You may choose to discuss what you've learned with a partner. Think about how such philosophy relates to martial principles and how you can use this knowledge to inspire new directions for the techniques you have learned.

102.

Scan the Quality of
Energy in Others

HAVE YOU EVER "sensed" the last time you would see someone;
a family member's on-coming illness, even though he or she appears
to be in good health; a friend's depression (and the reason), no matter
how happy a face he or she wears; or a colleague's distant past without
anyone ever saying a word? Steven Johnson, in his book *Emergence: The
Connected Lives of Ants, Brains, Cities, and Software,* explains that
everyone is born with an ability to read other people's energy—
which, remember, is a carrier of consciousness and information.
Martial artists combine skills of sensitivity, intuition, and emotional
scans to increase this natural capacity to envision actions before they
happen, as well as to read the energy that is creating them. This helps
you encourage certain actions and discourage others. In the dojo, you
can stop an attack while it is still in your opponent's head. In workouts, you can give your partner energy he needs for healing and
strengthening without his asking. Depending on your sensitivity, you
may be more in touch with your partner's needs than he is, and vice
versa. Learning to scan the energy of others will help keep goodness
flowing, whether on or off the mats.

EXERCISE

RELAX AND CENTER, focusing your attention on your partner's energy
centers, just as you would your own. Let yourself feel what he is feeling as
you scan. Circulate your awareness within your partner's movement, feeling
where he is weak and where he is strong, where his energy is flowing
smoothly, and where it is blocked. Identify what energy he needs to balance
and, targeting the appropriate energy center, send it his way.

You Can Work with
People of Low Energy

IN SPARRING, ALL other things being equal, the person with higher energy will supersede the person with lower energy. If you are that person of low energy, becoming more proficient in skill can tip the advantage in your favor, giving you time to rebuild your energy output. Everything, however, is not a competition. So your prime objective both on and off the mats is teamwork. You can either adjust your energy to match your partner's or use your higher energy to raise the quality of hers. Be careful. I am not saying "lower" your energy. Rather, I'm suggesting evening its output. Having a full tank of gas is good, but you don't always push the pedal to the metal. Harmonized forward motion will build reserves for both you and your partner, whether on the mats or in daily life. Conversely, some jobs necessitate a lot of pizzazz. Thus, you may work to unblock a partner's blocked energy centers and evenly feed her the energy that she needs. If time is of the essence, you may have to ask her to help by identifying blocks. Don't be shy in asking for energy yourself. Sharing and matching energy makes everything in relationships run smoother and more successfully.

EXERCISE

RELAX AND CENTER, focusing your attention on your partner's energy channels. Decide whether it is best to relax your outflow of energy or to use your energy to boost your partner's. Then proceed with whatever course of action you decide upon.

You Can Work with People of Negative Energy

HAVE YOU EVER had to work with someone whose idea of a routine day is "throwing an attitude"? This is a time to remember that your mind is under your control. Even when negativity contaminates an entire group, you can separate from the pack. In the dojo, you learn to spot negativity fast, because it gets you nowhere. Your job is to boost and maintain a positive energy supply. Don't fuel negativity. You use patterns that forecast negative action to help avoid or extinguish it. Pay attention to which of your movements float others into the positive—even if it's only momentarily. Then you create *those* patterns. Partners will usually follow the trail, leaving old contaminated patterns behind. This may not happen instantly, so be patient, especially in long-term relationships. Sometimes, however, you have to work things out quickly. In this case, if your partner's energy is low, first increase its quality by sending out your own positive energy. Then you can link into an activity that requires so much of his or her focus, it will zap your partner into a new direction. These, of course, are temporary fixes, but they may give your partner enough strength so that he or she can find a more permanent solution.

EXERCISE

THE NEXT TIME you have to work with someone who is operating on negative energy, relax and center yourself. Scan your partner's energy centers. Try extending your good, positive energy to any blocked channels. Shift to an activity that naturally draws positive energy from the person, and try to sustain that for a bit. Tell yourself that no matter what, you are not going to allow any negative energy into your mind. Stay positive. *Don't dole out life force for things you don't believe in!* See how you feel having protected your own good energy, even if you don't achieve desired results right away.

105.

Stay Alert

ALERTNESS SEEMS LIKE such a simple thing, but it is a skill many beginning practitioners of martial theory have trouble sustaining. A large part of the problem comes with early attempts to attain a wider focus—that is, to see more—which, of course, all martial arts insist upon. One of the predictable snares of broadening focus is that until you train otherwise, you tend to withdraw energy from your external senses, drifting too much into a passive state, relaxing the body and reaching a state more like sleep than alertness. This leaves you limited in physical, emotional, or spiritual abilities. But don't frustrate. Alertness is just a matter of getting used to channeling enough energy to reach a comfortable balance between internal and external focus. Your goal is to achieve broad energized field of attention that is able to pierce through things calmly and in full consciousness. Try the following exercise.

EXERCISE

START BY LIMITING your use of things that dull consciousness, such as alcohol and other toxins. Avoid energy sappers, such as overeating, and sensitivity-reducing behaviors, such as getting too little sleep. If you can't do this right away (few of us can), try to do so for forty-eight hours before circumstances that require your fullest alertness. Take care of basic needs so they're not on your mind all day. Then use any physical activity to increase positive energy. Sink your consciousness. Breathe in smoothly through your nose and out through your mouth. Focus on building internal energy. When you feel your energy peaking, briskly sound the word s-a-h with your outbreaths. This balances your attention outside. Repeat this last step if necessary. Heighten all of your external sensory awareness. Let everything float across your field of attention in the present. Scan your energy centers regularly.

106.

Move Instinctively

EVERYONE HAS INSTINCTS and reflexes. For example, when you hear a sudden loud noise, you flinch. If an insect flies toward your eyes, you blink or swat. Science tells us that instincts start in the womb. On the mats, however, untrained instincts can get you into trouble and land you on your butt. On the other hand, you *have to* function instinctively; anything else would be too slow. Actions, however, need to be functional. To this end, the dojo emphasizes experiencing your martial techniques repeatedly in as many varied situations as possible, until they reach the level of instinctive behavior. This helps you generate constructive instinct that can be applied to situations with confidence and success. There is an old samurai proverb that says, "A man who has attained mastery of an art reveals it in his every action." Let the energy of martial arts enter your muscles. Feel it maximize the power of your mind and spirit.

EXERCISE

CHOOSE ANY ONE of your martial concepts, and practice activating it in as many situations as you can for one week. Be creative. Explore modifying the technique as you go along. See how many assorted uses you can discover. Feel it becoming more and more natural in your movements. Choose another concept for the next week.

107.

Be Ready to Accept Guidance

RECENTLY A COLLEAGUE and I put on an exhibition of Chinese, Japanese, Korean, and Filipino martial arts. The demonstration was followed by a workshop. Most students were eager to learn. Afterward, I thought about how each of them had acquired a little gem to take back into their private world and eventually manifest in more public ways. I started thinking of all my teachers along the way and considered how much better they had been than I believed I was—how they always gave me something to strive for. I remembered how impressed I was the day I discovered that, even at his level, my teacher had gone off to study with another master and how that master had studied with another and so on. It was as if I couldn't have imagined someone as skilled as my teacher having to accept guidance from anyone. But he taught me that everyone has a master. Part of growing is sharing. Part of sharing is having more room to grow. This is how you improve, both in the dojo and out. Martial arts are founded on the anthem that everything is alive and informative. Your job is to accept guidance as you go with the flow.

EXERCISE

SPEND A QUIET moment reflecting on your current life situations. Excite yourself about the possibility of finding guidance to help you achieve greater heights in each situation. Seek your guides.

108.

Increase Your Awareness to Hidden Truths

TRUTH IS INFINITE, living, and ever changing. Indeed, discovery and mystery are next-door neighbors. Just recently I found myself explaining a basic martial concept to a new student. Ironically, as I demonstrated the concept—and even though I had taught it for decades—I discovered yet another truth hidden in the technique. This sort of thing happens often. You don't have to be, as they say, "looking for gold" all the time, but you do have to be aware whenever it comes up and stares you in the face. What's more interesting is that such discoveries get qualitatively better and better, in direct proportion to practice. Martial arts teach that there is but one movement in the universe, and it is made up of infinite smaller ones. So wherever you look you'll see layers and layers of meaning. You seek, become aware, see with accuracy, understand, experience, master, and start all over again. I cannot tell you what the truth is for you at any given moment, but I can say this: when you hold truth in your hand, your mind will brighten and strain will diminish.

EXERCISE

SPEND A DAY thinking about how you realize truth. Don't want with either your heart or with your mind. Try not to make decisions based on either being for or against things. Rather, put energy into seeing things as they are at the moment. Where a problem exists, see it clearly. Tell yourself the problem *is* the answer. Understand the answer. Then choose your best action. For example, let's say you need more money but are suddenly unemployed. You would never have quit your job in a time of need. But therein is your answer. This is how *Tao*, or the Way, works. Your life is pruning itself—cutting off your weaker employment to steer you into a more gainful employment opportunity. Listen and follow. Be open to hidden truths.

109.

Strengthen Your Weakest Link

THE MARTIAL MAN or woman is engaged in an ever-growing process of self-improvement. Consequently, you appraise your aptitudes on a regular basis. The dojo teaches you to consider goals and identify what aptitudes are necessary to attain them. For example, say you want to launch an effective high kick. Your ability to precisely deliver the shot can be broken down into individual movements that comprise it—opportunity, speed, balance, range, timing, rhythm, and so on. This allows you to check your proficiency in each movement. If you consider using a checklist, showing your levels of strength for each area, you can then proceed to create a training program that will lead you to accomplish your goal. This method of training can help you reach goals inside or outside the dojo. Locate your weakest link. Strengthen it and strengthen your game.

EXERCISE

CONSIDER A CURRENT goal. For example, say you would like to get a promotion at work. Ask what attributes you need to successfully achieve this goal. Evaluate your level of skill in each. Create a training plan focused on strengthening your weakest link. Move on from there.

110.

Know Your Guides

BECAUSE LIFE IS ever changing and so are you, your guides will also change moment by moment. This is not to say that old guides are of no more help, far from it! New situations, however, will be driven by new information, whether from old or new guides—and in some cases you will respond better to a fresh guide. Martial arts and various sciences teach that *the answer to all questions is within all things.* I like this notion a lot because it puts focus on knowing who or what your source is—for you, right now—not yesterday or for anyone else. Your sources may differ from those of other people, but that's okay. Energy is energy, and consciousness is consciousness. Both speak through every particle in the heavens and on the earth. You can look inward or outward. But just look. Discover who or what is speaking to you. And listen.

EXERCISE

SPEND A QUIET moment to reflect on a current conflict or area of happiness in your life. Brainstorm as many resources as you can that will help you troubleshoot it. Is there a book that could enhance your success, a lecture you could attend, a friend you could consult, a class you could take, a degree you could pursue, a trip you could take? Then relist your results, including only those guides that you feel speak to *you.* What if you took a day off from work? How could you use that time to open yourself to the kind of guides that could heighten the quality of your life? Incorporate some of these into your daily routine.

III.

Embrace Your Guides

IN THE DOJO, once you have identified your guides, you embrace them. You seek their wisdom. This sort of thing happens all the time. I once heard one master say of another before trading techniques, "All I have to do is *feel* that energy one time, and I'll be able to do it." The operative word here is "feel." Guides transfer energy—just substitute the word "download" for "feel" in the sentence above. You absorb and invoke energy from all sources in the universe—physical, emotional, and spiritual. For millenniums, martial arts have looked to nature, exploring the elements as well as five traditional animals, for its guides. Energetically, meditation, scans, visualization, and physical movement have been the way to plug in. The process is like a "copy-and-paste" method of absorbing new energies and awareness. Once you do integrate this energy and wisdom, the essence of your guides is yours, not symbolically but literally. Embrace your guides. Invoke their wisdoms and sweeten life.

EXERCISE

USE YOUR POWER of meditation to help you plug in to your chosen guide's energy. In its pure form you will feel only positive energy. Let your guide's energy trigger each of your internal energy centers. Feel how it affects each one differently. Let it float into your mind-set and inspire you. Note: Any physical exercise you undertake prior to this meditation will enhance it.

112.

Crouch with the Tiger

SHAOLIN MARTIAL ARTS are embedded in the study of five traditional animals: the tiger, leopard, snake, crane, and dragon. Each has its own energy, mind-set, and unique movement. The first animal, the tiger, embodies great forward, offensive power. Every movement is made with intent to close in on its target. It is disciplined, comfortable, and capable in close ranges. It can quickly move through the gap between where it stands and where it wants to be. It can stop on a dime if necessary and resume activity at a microscopic crawl. It will wait as long as it must before making a move. It remains centered whether crouching, jetting, leaping, crawling, or rolling. Crouching, its quiet, calm massive power stills to the point of invisibility and then explodes from A to Z in an instant. Once the tiger reaches a target, its power to adhere is unparalleled. It knows what to do instinctively and does everything to gain positioning. This energy is essential both in the dojo and out. Feeling it and committing this energy to memory allows you access to immense forward focus and drive. Such energy provides dramatic balance and resolve, even when life is doing cartwheels.

EXERCISE

RELAX AND CENTER. Close your eyes. Open all energy channels, and feel yourself pumping strong positive energy. Consider all the characteristics of the tiger. Visualize an action scene for each, from as many angles as you can. Observe the tiger's behavior. Using your in-breaths, invoke the tiger's energy into your muscles. Try to feel its mind and power. Imagine your favorite meditative setting (a mountain forest, a river, or some other peaceful setting). Experience the environment through all the tiger's senses. Be the tiger. Feel the energy. Consider how you can tap its iron commitment to get comfortable at close ranges, as well as sustain pure focus and purpose in daily life.

113.

Shadow with the Leopard

THE LEOPARD RELIES on extreme speed, hypersensitivity, and cumulative effect. It is spontaneously aggressive, yet analytical. The leopard has the unique ability to ricochet off targets and bolt back with heightened force, using an opponent's force to project more power. You can experience this burst of rapid energy just by placing your hand on the corner of a table or doorway, applying some forward pressure, and letting your hand skid off. This sudden surge makes good balance essential. Master of these techniques, the leopard redirects attacks and turns blocks into opportunities to launch a flurry of strikes—and with constant ricochet, the steady accumulation works. Not as massive as the tiger, the leopard builds power from speed. It moves left to right rather than taking a head-on approach. The leopard uses sensitivity to "see" emotional and physical shifts as openings. It "feels" an opponent's intent. Such hypersensitivity allows the leopard to sense things before they happen, thus allowing time to analyze and respond in what appears to be one spontaneous act.

EXERCISE

RELAX AND CENTER. Open all of your energy channels and pump strong positive energy through each of them. Consider all the characteristics of the leopard. Script an action scene for each characteristic, from as many angles as you can. Visualize the leopard's behavior. Invoke this energy into your muscles. Feel the power. Imagine your favorite meditative setting. Experience this environment through all the leopard's senses. Be the leopard. Feel the energy. Commit the energy to memory. Think of times you can tap this resource in daily life to help you act swiftly yet with precision accuracy, turn attacks into windows for increased strength and personal growth, and reach your goals by accumulated efforts.

Soar Like the Crane

THE CRANE IS the ultimate defensive artist. Its techniques, however, may be the most difficult of the five animals. It waits, testing and evaluating movement—its own and its opponents'—until the right move exposes itself. Then it relies on graceful, angled attacks, maintaining a keen stability, yet destabilizing attackers. Its lines can be short and snappy or long and graceful. The crane has the unique ability to remain hauntingly calm, even when being attacked. It faces its opponent, utterly relaxed—circling its environment if necessary, thinking things over, and putting itself out of range until just the right moment. No matter what, the crane will remain composed, alert, and ready to soar for as long as it must. Then when absolutely necessary it will make its move, using a lot of decoys to focus opponents' attentions where it wants them and softly redirecting their energies.

EXERCISE

PRACTICE MOVING WITH graceful calm. Light a candle. Imagine a circle around the flame with a diameter of about nine inches. Rotate an open hand around the flame. Watch how the flame harmonizes with your energy flow. Try to harmonize with the flame's energy flow. Move in when the flame retreats, back when it advances. Keep circling and harmonizing with the flame.

Alternate: Imagine your favorite environment. Visualize a crane circling, analyzing—calm and present, perhaps just waiting for the right moment to land. Invoke the crane's energy into your muscles. Feel its mind and its graceful, *relaxed* spirit. Think of times you can tap this resource in daily life to help you move more softly and timely, with graceful fearlessness. Revisit this energy often.

115.

Strike Directly as the Snake

THE SNAKE EMBODIES the most Chi of any animal. Its internal energy is extremely sensitive and powerful. No wonder understanding this often-mysterious creature was one of the Shaolin monks' earliest undertakings. Some of the most coveted martial secrets are rooted in the snake's ability to completely control attackers with absolute minimum effort. Instead of muscling anything, the snake is known for its piercing focus and its ability to strike in between heartbeats. Its style is punctuated with both intent and avoidance. The snake completely controls its opponents' attacks by slipping in and out of them, moving only as much as absolutely necessary and wasting no time. It is able to read its environment with intense clarity; it moves softly, directly, and precisely; and it targets only what is vital. Invoking this energy will sharpen your attention in tight situations and help you glide through them with ease.

EXERCISE

IN A STANDING position, form your hands into the posture for prayer hands. Turn them over so that your left hand is on top, palm down. Start to move this posture into a sideways figure eight, the symbol for infinity. Invoke the snake's energy. Visualize a target about two feet in front of you. Regulate your breathing. Make yourself as sensitive as possible to the pattern of movement. Feel its energy. When you feel the moment is right, and only then, separate your hands smoothly, and *in the same motion* shoot out your right hand and press your right palm to the center of the target. This should feel awkward at first. You will find that as you learn to read the energy patterns with more sensitivity, you will be able to execute your shot with more authority and less effort. Be careful not to overextend your arm. Consider how reading another person's patterns and shooting straight to the heart of the matter can resolve current conflicts or heighten your joys.

Explode from Stillness
Like the Dragon

IN MARTIAL ARTS, the dragon is a mythical animal with great wisdom. It is strong and hard, capable of riding out and withstanding whatever turbulence is keeping it from happiness. The dragon's energy will guide you through the hard times. It can help you bite the bullet, when necessary, and land a place of advantage from where you can launch an effective shot. The dragon employs long, whole-body movement in addition to short snappy shots. Its power comes from its ability to coil energy tightly within and then explode outward gracefully, spiraling through space in a continuous dance that fuels itself as it unravels. The dragon's secret is that it is all of the other animals combined.

EXERCISE

RELAX AND CENTER. Open all of your energy channels, and feel yourself pumping strong positive energy through each channel. Consider all the aforementioned characteristics of the dragon. Visualize a dragon coiling up, condensing energy, and then spinning its tail in long graceful lines. Feel its explosive energy. Invoke it into your muscles, and feel how such strength could withstand anything that comes at it. Experience the dragon's mind and sheer power of its spirit. Be the dragon. What parts of your body are most affected by this energy? Commit the energy to memory. Think of times you can tap this resource in daily life to help you withstand difficult situations until windows of opportunity open and you explode toward your goals with inexhaustible power. Revisit this energy often.

Focus without Concentration

IN EVERYDAY LANGUAGE the word "concentration" means to single out something, an element, detail, or the like, and tighten your attention to it. Focus and concentration go hand in hand. Contrary to this understanding, however, martial arts teach you to focus without concentration. Thus, the martial eye is less restricted by any single detail. It is instead ultrapresent to the whole. Images in the mind are broader, yet awareness is sharp—similar to when you are at a concert and your field of attention, still intense, quietly expands to the length of the stage rather than on any individual musician. In the dojo, this skill enhances your ability to deal with multiple opponents. Whether you are in the martial theater or in everyday situations, this way of "seeing" engenders greater sensitivity and quantity of information. It quickens your mind, sharpens your actions, and heightens your spiritual experience.

EXERCISE

YOU CAN TRY this activity whether you are alone or with others. Relax and center. Let go of your urge to concentrate on any single detail in your environment. Instead, lengthen your field of vision without restricting it. Stay relaxed. It may take you several attempts to get used to interacting with a wider lens. Just hang in and stay present. Experience the difference in your energy. Your wider lens is more relaxed, calming, and connected. It is more intuitive and unfaltering. Use it to help you sharpen actions and reactions. Take note of how you feel.

118.

Know Your Pressure Points

ONE OF THE most intriguing and secretive elements of martial arts is the notion of pressure points. These are vital spots on the body. Striking one of these points will instantly stun, weaken, or disable an opponent. You don't usually target such areas, but in a life-threatening situation, especially if there are multiple opponents, knowledge of the body's pressure points will quickly and efficiently put you out of harm's way. Deepak Chopra once said, "I'm a medical doctor, and I am not opposed to removing a tumor if I have to." Sometimes, it is necessary to stop a crisis immediately. In these situations, you don't want to spend time chasing after pawns. On the mats, most shots to pressure points are illegal. The concept, however, still applies: identify your attacker's weakest links and strike. If he kicks like lightning, train at close range, where such kicks are ineffective. If he's an expert at close range, you should train long. If he has bad balance but is strong as an ox, train in putting him way off balance. Both on the mats and in daily routines, striking pressure points will quickly put the game in your court and advantage on your side.

EXERCISE

CONSIDER AN INTERPERSONAL situation that is causing you conflict. Assess the source of this conflict. Zero in on what you are trying to accomplish. For example, perhaps you are a new parent and want more time off from your job, but can't afford less pay. Your supervisor doesn't see how this can be done. Identify vital areas where your company is weak. Consider what skills you have that will allow you to create a position that could be handled from home. Perhaps you can work online. You may have to be trained, take courses, or enroll in a part-time degree program; however, this is all part of making yourself competent enough to conquer your company's weakness. Figure out what they would agree *they* need and how you fit the bill.

119.

Try Your Technique
One Thousand Times

MANY MARTIAL PROGRAMS have what they refer to as one thousand _____ days. These are days when you pick a certain technique and perform it one thousand times. It can be anything from certain punches and kicks to whole drills. The first time you give this a crack, you may feel overwhelmed merely hearing the number. Indeed, surviving the session gives you a new sense of confidence. You ache a little, but can't help feeling somewhat more indestructible, as well as mysteriously energetic. What's happening is that you are "downloading" patterns of action into your muscle memory and programming yourself to react in a certain way. This is why you must perform these actions flawlessly. Otherwise, you are committing faulty procedures to memory. Repetition develops precision, reflex, and long-term recall. It is common for most dojos to practice techniques thousands and thousands of times, knowing that in real situations they only activate for seconds. That, nevertheless, is what usually makes the difference.

EXERCISE

FOR PRACTICAL PURPOSES, pick a week. Make it a one thousand _____ week. Utilize visualization. See yourself performing any one of the techniques in this book. Try some of them out in your day-to-day routines. Shoot for one thousand. See how you feel.

120.

Believe in Your Techniques

IN EVERY MARTIAL artist's training there comes a point when you wonder if the techniques you are learning actually work. The best way to test your blocking, for example, is to have someone really come at you with punches. The best way to test whether or not you can execute an effective armlock is to ask your partner to resist your move against him. In these occasions, you discover once and for all whether or not you can "walk the talk," as they say, and the experience can be quite an eye-opener. You usually see that what you have learned in the dojo works. Of course, the effect is synergistic. The more you believe, the more you learn, and the more proficient you become. At some point in most martial training, practitioners attempt to break something that appears stronger than their limbs—wood, brick, and other seemingly impenetrable materials. Essential to the process is that you have to believe you can do such a thing—actually see yourself going through an object—*before* you ever attempt it a first time. Most instructors won't let you jump the gun on this one. By this time in your training, you believe not only in what you know you can do, but also in the skills that have gotten you there. Your focus is no longer only on destination, but also on enjoying the Way.

EXERCISE

CONSIDER A POINT of impasse that has become a problem for you. Make a list of all the martial skills you could employ to effectively deal with the situation. Set up a strategy for dealing with it. Visualize yourself dealing with the obstacle. Identify any possible kinks in the endeavor. Create a strategy for addressing these. Believe in yourself. When you are ready, follow up and see what happens.

Don't Telegraph Your Actions

IN THE DOJO, inexperienced players often unintentionally give their next move away before ever making it. This is called *telegraphing* and is something you try to avoid. There are many ways martial artists telegraph their intentions. Some of the most common are drawing back before striking, shifting in stance, moving the eyes, even grimacing or taking a deep breath before going into motion. An experienced martial artist will not only pick up on such cues, but she will also be looking for them. This can reduce the time you need to properly set up and deliver. Once you have established a pattern, opponents will be able to deactivate your techniques with a lot less effort. You lose the power of surprise. You present the appearance of being easy to sidestep and manipulate. If you can avoid telegraphing, you can move more strategically and easily toward resolving problems, heightening joy, and reaching goals.

EXERCISE

CONSIDER A CIRCUMSTANCE that would have worked out more to your advantage had others not been aware of your actions in advance. What advantages could you have gained by keeping your intentions to yourself until the last moment? How could you have avoided giving your plan away? Although you cannot hold back every signal, practice some strategies that will help you keep your intentions less obvious. Consider your facial expressions, eye movements, body language, breathing, and verbal cues (words and tone). You can always use any of these as feints, to buy you time when you need it. Think of ways you can use this information to reinforce your movement. Follow up by applying what you've learned.

Train in Pulling Back

THE WORD IN martial training is that if you launch a thousand punches, you had better train to do the same action in reverse, the same number of times! Strengthening the appropriate muscles to pull back a punch, kick, blade-hand—any kind of strike—is necessary to deliver the technique with precision, power, and speed, and especially to regain balance afterward. For example, if you are throwing a straight punch at a heavy bag, you train to do the same motion in reverse for an equal number of times. If you are training in doing front kicks, you launch the technique as though you are going to throw *two* kicks, thus building the body mechanics necessary for a second shot, particularly in pulling back. This attention quickens delivery, but more importantly, it trains you to restabilize your coordination and balance. For every step forward there is a slight back-flow of energy—as if you were moving water in a glass—and then a centering or settling back into position. Precision pullbacks make change anywhere in your life easier and more fluid.

EXERCISE

PICK AN ACTION during the course of your day and consider what you can do to employ the principle of pulling back. For example, if a discussion works upward in volume, think of how to smoothly return it to a slightly lower level than it began and then back to its original dynamic. If there is a dip in your energy, think of ways to heighten your activities, but allow them to decrease a small step before stabilizing.

123.

Strike through Your Target

THERE IS A type of roundhouse kick that Muay Thai masters will teach you to swing around like a baseball bat. One of the most important elements of the technique is striking through your target—that is, aiming the kick just beyond bulls-eye. Also important is positioning the body to prevent any damaging recoil. You do this by tilting slightly back as you go into the strike, staying balanced, and readying for the rebound. These principles apply in daily situations as well. Yes, it is good to envision goals. But you have to see through them as well—to where you will be standing after taking action. When you do this, you develop strategies and skills to take care of where you will be, as well as where you are.

EXERCISE

CONSIDER A CURRENT goal. See yourself having reached it. Where will you be standing after? Is this someplace you would *like* to be? Is the route you have chosen the only route? What skills will you need to stabilize? What skills will you need to enhance your new position?

124.

Overcome Power with Precision and Speed

MARTIAL ARTS TEACH that precision and speed will defeat mass. It doesn't matter if your opponent is three times your size. Your job then becomes perfecting the execution of your techniques and performing them with the utmost speed. The combination of these two elements will always defeat massive brute strength. I recently watched a young judo expert who probably weighed less than a hundred pounds completely outmaneuver her male opponent, who must have weighed over two hundred pounds. Her skill on the mats was astonishing. At one point I watched as she went for his throat, his most legally vulnerable target, and put him in a perfect figure-four lock—tying her legs like a noose around the small of his neck. When he stood and tried to muscle her into a pin, thinking he would drop her from over six feet up, she confidently tightened the knot as if it were made of steel. Completely undone, he frantically tapped out (ending the match) before she rendered him unconscious. Size really doesn't matter. Quicken your mind. Live with precision. Fear no one.

EXERCISE

CONSIDER A CURRENT goal. List all of the skills necessary to reach your target. Now, identify as many ways as possible to expand your knowledge and improve your execution of these skills. Perhaps you could seek a new class or refresher course, a book, a workshop. Don't dismiss peripheral information—for example, reading a book on meditation when your goal is to diet.

125.

Have Multiple Weapons

WHAT MAKES A martial artist's skill dramatically effective is the ability to launch virtually unlimited strikes from any position. To this end, you learn to utilize and combine the use of multiple weapons. Each of these tools is intended for a specific purpose and range. For example, certain swords are used at a distance, others up close. Your body can also be considered a weapon—your fingers, hands, arms, legs, feet, head, knees, elbows, and so on—each having its own function and range as well. The idea is to have as many tools in your repertoire as possible and know how to use them. Thus, you learn to make modifications, such as learning how to execute a long kick at close range, forcing new uses of old weapons. Indeed, the more choices you have, the more customized and effective solutions can be.

EXERCISE

GIVE YOURSELF A week. Choose a different skill each day, and explore ways of using it in nontypical situations. For example, if you are a teacher, practice using an emotional scan in classroom discussions. If you are in retailing, try using it on customers. Try using the principle "Don't Care So Much" at work or in a relationship. Experiment. Also vary the "when" and "where" in the execution of techniques. Try combining techniques in unlikely ways. See what happens.

126.

Play Your Own Game

IN THE DOJO, you learn that your tools are not necessarily the same as the next person's. Even when they are, your way with tools is yours alone. This means that it's okay to have your own unique style of doing things. When you follow someone else's way on the mats, you learn quickly that it is not designed for your aptitudes. If you are as skilled as your sparring partners, yet you choose to play their game instead of your own, you will more than likely regret it. One of the most effective ploys of veteran players is duping novices out of their strongest aptitudes and straight into their worst, which, of course, the experienced player is ready to meet with her best techniques. It's amazing how many times this can happen before the beginner catches on. Believe me, I was no exception. Only the rarest of people would be immune to this process. Here's the good news, though: people are genuinely surprised at how easily they can move others onto their own playing field. The first time you do this is quite revealing. You realize just how in charge you really are.

EXERCISE

CONSIDER A CURRENT situation you have been playing on someone else's "field." This can be anything from work to recreational activity. Identify your strongest aptitudes as a person as well as a practitioner of martial thought. How many of these aptitudes have you been able to draw upon? Visualize several scenarios in which you are able to use your best skill in the aforementioned circumstance. Think of a few strategies to move any people involved into your playing field. Follow through by using these strategies.

127.

Don't Worry about
Scoring Points

DON'T GO CHECKING up on life. It's going to keep moving with or without your monitoring. When some people hear this, they think, "Well, then, what the heck." Martial thought, however, says your job is to let life happen without interfering. Forget about scoring points. Does this mean you have no choices? Not at all. Instead it means to focus on the choices. Your job is to participate. The possibilities for each movement are unlimited. Making choices is the ultimate creative act. It doesn't matter, in the end, whether or not you score a point here and there. In fact, if you scored every time it wouldn't be as much fun. The possibility of missing is what makes things invigorating. The match continues—don't worry about that. Even when the little ones are over, the big one keeps on without end. *Experience* the points. That's what it's all about. Celebrate the good shots. Know, however, that they are fleeting. Don't get bogged down. Just keep flowing, transforming, and contributing. Follow life's energy into the next moment, choosing all the way.

EXERCISE

TRY NOT KEEPING score for one whole day. Just place your attention, instead, on all the possible choices you have as you move from one circumstance to another. Take pleasure in all that is available. Remember that childhood feeling of being in a candy store? The thrill of the selection process was perhaps greater than your final selection. Bring that enthusiasm into your life.

128.

Test Your Opponent

ONE OF THE greatest fallacies, on the mats and off, is the notion that people will respond alike to the same technique. It's difficult enough when you are trying to account for partners trained in the same art, but then, of course, those who are trained in other arts seem even more unpredictable. If, for example, you have never gone up against a boxer, you don't really know how he or she will strike. You also don't know how that person will react to your techniques. Many schools of martial arts bring in experts from other disciplines so that practitioners can all learn how the other styles express themselves. Whether you are training within your discipline or not, the objective is to test your partners. Differences in response are the rule, not the exception. So throw a wide variety of shots out there and analyze reactions. You will learn to adapt your own techniques from slightly different angles: harmonizing, disarming, and defeating when necessary. Often, you create new skills. This is how you grow as a martial artist and as a person.

EXERCISE

WHENEVER YOU MEET someone whose orientation is different from your own, try testing that person's reactions to techniques. See if you can identify what kind of system or rules they draw from. Play your "game." Notice which of your techniques work with them. Modify where necessary. Add any effective techniques from this exercise to your toolbox.

129.

Your Way *Is* Your Way

HISTORICALLY, THE HEART has been known as the primary organ of consciousness. In martial training this concept is known as *Xin* (heart consciousness). *Xin* is your open line to the Way. Unfortunately (or perhaps fortunately) the language of the Way is not English, German, Russian, French, Italian, Spanish, or the like. Its language is feeling: feeling what is truly in the pit of your heart—*Xin*. Joseph Campbell calls this "living from the heart" or "following your bliss." *Xin*, however, doesn't mean to live whimsically, and Campbell didn't mean that either. *Xin* is a deep exploration of the heart to discover who you really are, the reason you are on this planet to begin with. Then, instead of going *outside* and gathering "things," martial training emphasizes going *inside*. The more keenly you recognize and nurture what's in your heart, the quicker and easier people, situations, events, and the like begin appearing in your life. Be present. Open your heart wherever you are. The secret is to be yourself—because you and the Way are one and the same.

EXERCISE

CHECK IN WITH your heart often throughout the day. In fact, try to live your whole day like this. Think about who you are at your deepest. Consult your feelings from right there. Honestly reflect upon what you want from situations. Spend your energy on knowing who you are and what you really want, and watch for appropriate openings to appear in your routines. Take them. Trust that you are who you are, where you are, and when you are, for a reason. Stay present and watch with interest as everything slips into place.

130.

Don't Expose Your Power

MARTIAL STORIES ABOUND with legends of multiple thugs preying on unsuspecting people of small stature or of old age. The anthem of these tales is similar: that the victim's martial skills are so adept, there is never any question as to how the attack will conclude. The martial artist disabling attackers to within an inch of their lives is surprising only to the thugs themselves, who end up wishing they had never gotten out of bed that day. A subtler theme is that you should refrain from exposing all of your power. As soon as you do, it becomes less powerful. You are most effective when others discover your strengths on their own. In the dojo, this is known as "the element of surprise." Martial arts teach that any power that needs to be "shown" is of lower quality. Supreme power is as invisible as thought. This is true in martial arts and everywhere else in life.

EXERCISE

SPEND A DAY putting the brakes on every time you are about to consciously show your powers to anyone. Let people discover your powers through your actions. See how different you feel at the end of the day. Watch as personal power and relationships grow.

Let New Movements Create New Patterns

TO REMAIN FUNCTIONAL, martial skills morph from one instant to another. Practitioners who talk or act with a this-is-the-only-way mind make themselves vulnerable to a good player coming by and shutting down their skills before they can blink an eye. Life is ever changing. Martial training emphasizes entering the flow and letting new movements emerge naturally. Interference only causes stress, conflict, disharmony, anger, and a swarm of other negative feelings. Many times in the dojo, you learn a specific posture and apply it for years. Then one day your instructor chooses to show you a higher function of that same movement. Sometimes you discover this yourself, out of necessity. Either way, your job is to embrace every opportunity to go beyond the known. Let these create sharper patterns of response in your actions. Routines outside the dojo are no different. Stay open to change. Replace old patterns with new ones. Download these like updates in your mental software.

EXERCISE

NEXT TIME YOU are walking through a crowded area, notice how you are maneuvering around people. Consider speed, distance, straight and circular movements, stepping forward or back. Try moving a little differently to make life easier for yourself and others. If you discover a new pattern, use it the very next time you are in a similar situation. Follow this same routine with interpersonal maneuvers.

Truth Comes in a Flash

BUDDHA SAID, "TRUTH comes in between breaths." When I first began my experience with martial arts, I thought that this statement was literal and had something to do with regulating your breathing between movements. Later I realized that Buddha meant that truth comes "between thoughts." This, of course, is a major Zen tenet—that is, when you least expect it, you will discover what you have been looking for. Truth will come in a flash. This axiom proves itself over and over in the dojo. Your partner nails you with a certain technique for weeks. All of your countermoves are duds. You dizzy yourself trying to figure out a good response. Then, one day while doing something that is so apparently unrelated its funny, the answer flashes across your mind like a godsend. You don't have to dwell on it, because you already know it will work. It is the perfect move—the solution. This happens repeatedly in daily life. Just remind yourself of this principle whenever stressors start sneaking in.

EXERCISE

CONSIDER A CURRENT problem that you keep knocking yourself out trying to resolve. Instead of recycling energy one more time and coming to the same point of nonresolution, treat yourself especially well for a whole day. Do a variety of things you enjoy. Have fun. Wait for the answer to come to you, easily and naturally.

133.

Channel Your Opponent's Energy

CHANNELING ENERGY MEANS to send it elsewhere. For example, if a punch is coming straight for your face, you have choices for getting out of harm's way—one of which is to remain loose and, with the lightest possible touch, direct it away. To do this, you have to keep yourself from tensing up, maintain a wide and present perspective, make contact without trying to stop the motion, and adhere to it, angling it away. You don't have to do any more than that. If you have to return fire, wait till your opponent breaks harmony. Balance is important while executing the maneuver so that you will remain stable when the attack is removed. On the mats there is often an opponent you forget about—your own mind-set. This comes in the form of urges, emotions, past behaviors, and the like. You learn to rechannel these by dissolving such thoughts and taking their energy and releasing it into your focus. This will fuel your presence, as well as your actions. The same principle works in daily affairs. Here's how.

EXERCISE

THE NEXT TIME you feel an offensive action coming at you, try this. Relax and center. Remain balanced and calm. Empty your mind of any urges, emotions, past reactions, and the like. Take a deep breath if you have to. Just stay present. In this mind-set the action will appear in slow motion, rather than as an ambush. Remember the leopard. Let your opponent's shot come. Find something in what the person is saying or doing that you can latch on to. Respond positively to those words or behaviors. Remain positive, no matter what, otherwise you will leave yourself vulnerable. Keep moving the interaction bit by bit, looking for a point where you can harmonize and work the issue together rather than in conflict.

Know Several Finishing Techniques

MOST MARTIAL SYSTEMS rely on a three-move model: contact, stun, finish. The contact phase in karate and kung fu systems usually involves some form of block or parry, followed by a punch or a kick. From this initial point of contact, known as your *reference point,* you learn to fire an unlimited number of techniques intended to stun opponents. The idea is to take their attention away from what they are doing and put it on where they just got hit. Then, if they are still standing (you can never predict), you launch your final or finishing technique. These are intended to end confrontation. Lots of different kinds of movies like to play with this concept, showing what happens when you *don't* finish this three-step process in actual altercations. The result is always the same. The attacker will attack again, often with a more powerful comeback. Everyone has been taken advantage of in this way. The best way to avoid this scenario is to have several back-up strategies and to relentlessly stick to your goals until you reach them or until your strategies are completed.

EXERCISE

PRACTICE IN ULTRASLOW motion. This exercise is based on the famous 1-2 drill. Stand at an agreed distance from your partner. Your partner may take two shots at you (not really hitting). The idea is to find a way to close the distance and make contact. The first shot is free, no blocking. However, with the second shot you may block, parry, or whatever, as long as you keep contact. Your objective is to just get it out of your way. Then you get a free, unblocked shot, followed by a second, which your partner blocks. Keep trading off. Agree on three bull's-eyes, which if struck will end the drill, winning it for whomever hits the target. Your job is to protect your vulnerabilities, learn to divert your partner's attention, and hit targets capable of finishing conflict. Later, consider how you can place skills in this book into this three-step model and apply them in everyday life.

135.

Increase Your Energy
while You Move

HAVE YOU EVER noticed your body charging up and giving you the energy you are going to need to accomplish a task *before* you actually attempt it? You're using this capability all day long, you just aren't aware of it. For example, your body knows you wake up at 6:00 AM and starts kicking up energy for you to go through your morning routine. It knows you take a break at 11:00 AM and starts resting its engines. It knows you fuel it at noon, so it makes itself hungry. It knows when you sleep and unplugs. Your body works from models or patterns. When your schedule changes, you are working against it for a while—that is, until you create a new pattern. All coaches know this. Thus, they tell you to pour it on when you are about to fatigue. Your body, of course, is there to assist. Little by little it will attempt to create new patterns to give you what you require in advance. Thus, it needs to receive the *right* messages. Here's a secret: your mind and your spirit work the same way. Synchronize all three.

EXERCISE

TAKE TIME TO reflect where your skills are "fatiguing." Ask yourself what you need to improve to stay in the game. Be specific. The next time you are in a situation that calls for these skills, put more into using them. Test these skills repeatedly in similar situations. Help yourself develop new patterns. When you do, your skill will sharpen. Your actions will become reflexive.

Put Your Guard Up

PUTTING YOUR GUARD up doesn't mean that you live in a box. It is a way to let others into spaces where you excel. Of course, your guard may change in a split second. Indeed, at certain moments, you will even drop it completely—for an unlimited number of reasons. Dropping your guard completely is an advanced and very functional skill, and if used improperly it can land you on your butt. Martial arts is about keeping you in the game, not knocking yourself out so that your opponents don't need to. For this reason, martial training will have you using your guard until it is as natural as breathing. Your guard protects what is vital. It can deter opponents from taking shots that could cause you serious damage. Additionally, if your guard is effective, it will leave you in a position of advantage. Whether on the mats or in daily life, you need to know two things: the first is what to guard. The second is how to accomplish this effectively. Then, nothing beats experience.

EXERCISE

CONSIDER SOMETHING IN your life that you are trying to change and yet keep messing up. For instance, perhaps you are trying to limit carbohydrates or fats in your diet. What factors are making you vulnerable? Maybe when you get home from work, you are famished and there is nothing to eat but what you are trying to avoid. Perhaps, a friend you meet for lunch compulsively goes to shops that only serve these foods. What guards will keep you from harm's way? Maybe cooking up a week's worth of delicious low-fat, low-carb treats before your week begins will eliminate the temptation. Consider a lunch with higher protein. Perhaps you can think of a great place to take your friend to lunch that also serves foods you can partake in. Make a list of possibilities. Follow through on your ideas.

137.

Open Your Guard
with Purpose

THE WORD IN martial arts is that you can't guard everything at all times. It's simply not possible. If you section the body off, from top to bottom, into three equal meridians, you can successfully guard two at once. The same is true if you consider a horizontal field that opponents can try to enter from the sides. There will, however, always be one meridian open. For example, players can guard their high line with their hands and arms, the middle line with a knee and leg, but that will open the lower line. There are many such variations. So an advanced understanding of putting up a guard is also *consciously selecting* what line you are going to open. This process can be a powerful strategy. What you are doing, in essence, is inviting your partner in. By making the target irresistible, you can position opponents precisely where you want them, which, of course, will be in synch with your best skills as well as strategies. This principle can be utilized in any aspect of daily life as well. It can increase joys and help vanquish conflict.

EXERCISE

TRAIN IN OPENING your guard with purpose for one whole day. See how you can create irresistible targets that people you encounter will trail. Take note of how the process works: who trails what, at what speed and intensity, how they position, how the target affects their balance and emotions (as well as your own), and especially what techniques you can launch from these points. Try to align all of the above considerations with specific goals you are attempting to achieve in a particular situation.

Protect Your Center

IMAGINE A VERTICAL line extending right up the center of your body. All of your major organs are located along this path. In the dojo, you learn to safeguard this line. This is called *holding center*. By holding center, you protect yourself against physical injury that can quickly debilitate you. But there is a hidden meaning to this maxim. Remember your energy channels. This centerline is also the location of your body's energy pumps. You need to protect these as well. Injury to your energy pumps will result in mental and spiritual depletion— or worse, poisoning. This is also true for daily matters.

EXERCISE

SPEND A DAY noticing how close the people you encounter come to landing shots into your centerline. How are they doing this? What actions and words are they using? What are they withholding? Consider each of your energy centers. Which are affected? When you locate one, don't stop there. There is a high likeliness that others are being affected as well. Do you feel any physical pain? What emotions do you feel? What happens to your spirit? How do these feelings play out throughout the rest of the day? Consider ways that you can guard your center the next time you encounter these people or are in similar situations.

139.

Give Center

ONE OF THE many things that I love about martial arts is that they are an antidote to "either-or" thinking. Yes, your job is to protect your centerline. But the reverse of this works, too. You can sometimes best protect your center by giving it up. The irresistible target of your most vital zone—in daily living, in the very sustenance of your life—can draw people where you want them. The question is, why would you want someone in your most vulnerable area? In the dojo, the answer is simple: because you have been training in angled techniques. The same is true in your daily routines; however, you may also want to invite certain energies because they nurture you. For example, everyone has experienced being down in the dumps and needing a little "attitude transplant," as they say. You may have a friend that works magic for you, radiating power into the very energy centers you feel have drained. Just getting near this person makes you feel better already. Know what people, places, and things transmit energy that coincides with your goals. Open yourself up to them.

EXERCISE

PICK A PERSON, place, or thing whose energy plays into your current goals. Try inviting that energy into your centerline. Consider what kind of target is needed. For example, perhaps there is someone at your workplace who has proven trustworthy and who animates you but with whom you are not close. Consider inviting him or her over for dinner or out to a café. Share a few details about your goals. Which of your energy centers are affected? What do you feel physically? Emotionally? What happens to your spirit? How do these feelings play out? Perhaps your overall energy is heightened. Consider other martial principles that might help make the process even more pleasurable in the future.

140.

Protect Yourself from
a Sideline Attack

IT'S EASY TO get so hyperfocused on protecting your most vital zones that you forget about the sideline attack. In fact, as far as the mats are concerned, some opponents have trained in launching the majority of their techniques from these angles. Kali (a Filipino martial art) players, for example, execute a flurry of strikes and traps down your right and left lines. The adage is to maintain a wide-angle lens at all times. You can't give your entire field of vision to center, or you'll wind up on your back. Tae Kwon Do and karate practitioners love setting you up for a center strike and then snapping kicks in from the sidelines. Outside the dojo, such strategies are equally effective. There is always that person whose real agenda surfaces from the sidelines. You don't really know what the heart of the issue is until it's too late. It's just the way they play. Indeed, most of us operate preferring either one line or the other. The idea is to expand your peripheral vision. Practice launching your techniques in those directions as well. Laws of balance suggest that equal proficiency is best.

EXERCISE

MAKE YOURSELF ATTENTIVE to the angles that people in your life use to approach you. Identify the sideline players. Observe the specifics of how their agendas surface. Do they set up smoke screens? Do they telegraph their moves? Do they use body language? Words? Moods? How can you use these to help you select a better response? Spend a day practicing martial principles on people who use this approach so that you build proficiency and confidence in these waters as well as in your own regular comfort zones. Repeat often.

Train to See Multiple Targets

SOMETIMES YOU HIT your target, sometimes you graze it, and sometimes you miss it entirely. Sound familiar? This is true whether you are on the mats, trying out a new recipe, having a discussion with a loved one, or going for a promotion at work. Thus, martial arts train you to see more than one target. For example, you notice your sparring partner is vulnerable to a highline, upper ⅓ of the body, shot. The window, however, may just be a ploy. You look for other openings. You see several possible low-line kicks. If he blocks, he'll open the opportunity for a leg sweep or other techniques. You launch the high strike. It gets blocked. All the other anticipated targets are covered, so you let the shot roll along the arm, see a new target en route, and land a shot to the head. Martial vision is roving and panoramic. It is like radar locating targets as they morph from one action to another. Whether in the dojo or in life routines, opportunity is part of the evolution of actions. Train yourself to see multiple targets. Remember, they may only last a moment. Your job is to be there.

EXERCISE

SPEND A DAY identifying goals as you proceed from one situation to another. Before acting, set your pause button and be prepared to refocus. Identify the most obvious path and target. Then identify several others as backup. Follow through and act on one of these paths. Keep a roving eye for new and perhaps better targets as you go along. Observe what happens. Later remember any new angles from which these targets necessitated employment of skills. Was there anything you could have done differently to improve their execution? If so, train and modify. Add these improved skills to your repertoire.

Decide on a Course of Action and Proceed Calmly

MARTIAL ARTS TEACH to decide on the best course of action and to proceed with a calm and open mind. You also learn to keep room for your plan(s) to evolve. Training strategies are good examples. Your goal may be to develop a quicker snap punch. Before you can generate a plan, you need to isolate the components of the technique and consider what aptitudes are required. You decide that you need work in several areas: body mechanics, strength in all the muscle groups necessary for executing the strike, positioning, and mental focus. Next, you decide on a training plan for each element. This enables you to use your time wisely and get the most from it; some elements may require more attention others. The next step is putting it all together. Then you're ready to test your shot, evaluate its overall effectiveness, and retrain certain components if necessary. Sometimes in everyday life you have to make decisions in split seconds. The process is the same as it is in martial arts. Decide on an action with backup, isolate its components, identify necessary tools (or skills), and act in calmness.

EXERCISE

IDENTIFY AN AREA of your life you would like to improve. Decide on the best plan of action today. Then proceed. Act calmly. Let things evolve naturally.

Allow Yourself to Be Content

MANY ACHIEVEMENTS IN martial arts are sequential. There is, however, no limit to how much you can accomplish. That has to do with willpower and goals; although, the martial Way—if you give yourself to it—naturally ebbs and flows to greater heights. In the dojo, you learn to be content with where you are in training, because just like all other places you have been, your current experience will pilot you to more advanced ranks. You celebrate the thrills of achievement, because these moments, like all others, must pass to make way for new experiences and higher highs. You come to embrace the clumsiness of an "ebbing tide," because this means you have entered another learning phase that will increase your joys even more. You are content with everything that comes your way, although at times you must remind yourself that the Way does not abandon. Remember the cycle of yin-yang. Be content wherever you are. Participate with interest in your own evolution. Trust that life is good.

EXERCISE

FIND A QUIET place to reflect. Take a good look at your current life situation. Trust that it will carry you toward goodness. Don't judge anything. Just tell yourself to open to the idea that everything is the way it is for a reason. Your presence to this purpose and ability to develop it will parallel the depth of richness you gather. Put your energy in understanding the moment—exactly what it is that you are supposed to learn. Forget about the outcome. Let life deal with that and pleasantly surprise you. Be content with your discovery of lessons. They will flow you to higher levels of living. Be wary of *not* seeing life lessons. You need them to grow. Be present and open-minded to them.

144.

Maximize Now

A PRIME ANTHEM of martial thought is to maximize the present, to seize your greatest opportunities and run with them. To do this, however, you need to see opportunity, and when you do, confidently go for it. When you are sparring, for example, if an opponent loses his focus, even just for a second, you take the shot. Then you go all out, launching your best material. Achievement isn't the point. Being in the moment and doing your absolute best is! You don't *have to* hit every target. Believing in your skill, remaining optimistic, accessing attempted techniques, modifying, and trying again not only keep you in the game, but also strengthen your potential. Your job is to stay in the game and take from each round as much as possible. Success may come today or perhaps on a later day. But it will come. Make the most of the moment.

EXERCISE

FORGET ABOUT GETTING what you want. Focus on wanting only to do your best work. Invoke as many skills as appropriate to assist you.

145.

Don't Be a Slave to Technique

MARTIAL ARTS TEACH you to be fluid in thought and action. What is rigid breaks. This maxim holds true with respect to attitude toward technique as well everything else in life. Consider a technique calling for three quick, straight punches, a back-fist, a low kick, and then takedown. Your opponent unpredictably leans out of reach during the triple punches so that you can no longer make the back-fist. You can't think, "I *have* to get the back-fist in." If you do, you'll be serving yourself up to your opponent on a silver platter. You do the smart thing. You forget technicalities and go right to the kick and takedown. Your opponent's actions, as well as your immediate and long-range goals, direct you. When I teach writing, I focus students on ways to construct beginnings, middles, and ends for their stories, because that is how students best learn to write stories. In the end, however, all techniques become one: to simply tell your story. You basically do whatever you need to do in order to tell it. Life is no different. Learn technique, but don't become its slave. You are an artist, so create your story and live it.

EXERCISE

MAKE A LIST of your compulsive actions, such as things needing to be done one way and one way only. Your insistence may be on the details; timing; order and organization; past routines, designs, and rituals; the experiences of others; and the like. See how many times you carry out such compulsions in one day and how many extra steps you take. Take note of the number of times these compulsions make your actions less effective. What emotional toll do your compulsions take? On the very next day, give yourself permission to modify your set routines wherever and whenever you feel necessary. Take note of any differences between your old way of doing things and the new, modified way.

146.

Use Resistance as a Tool

USED CORRECTLY, RESISTANCE can be your friend. Muscles rely on resistance to grow, and energy uses it to intensify. In the dojo, you can train in kicks, punches, and even whole katas with arm and leg weights, weighted weapons, wooden dummies, and other devices. When you remove the resistance, your movement becomes as light as silk and as strong as iron. Stories about such "miracles" abound in martial arts. To strengthen their strikes, karate and kung fu players punch into sand, then into pebbles, and finally through wood and stone. Tai Chi trains participants to resist the urge to strike fast and hard, and instead to move as slowly and softly as possible. This practice teases your internal energy system into generating tremendous physical, mental, and spiritual energy that can be focused explosively upon demand. Life is no different. You can force yourself into passivity until you are bursting with energy. You can force yourself not to think at all, so that when you do, you'll be flooded with enthusiasm and clarity. A writer can have a great idea and force himself not to write until he is splitting at the seams to tell the story. No matter where you are, if it is used correctly, resistance can help you gain energy, clarity, and a more positive attitude.

EXERCISE

CHOOSE A TASK that you are getting ready to tackle. Once you start to feel the urge to jump in, force yourself to take an extra day or more off before beginning. Make sure you do absolutely nothing, no matter how strong the urge. Then go at it. Take note of what happens.

147.

Know When the Circle Is Best

CIRCULAR TECHNIQUES ARE one of the best-kept secrets in martial arts. You can use hands, fists, or feet. The movements vary, and a skilled practitioner can make them almost impossible to forecast. For example, they can be blocks at one minute then morph into strikes the next. Whether on or off the mats, circular techniques are intended to keep you in balance with whatever and whomever you encounter. Alternately, you can rely on these same techniques to break an opponent's balance, repositioning him or her in order to take control of unsafe situations. Circular movements can go over, under, and around many attacks or defenses. Remember, techniques derived from each natural element, as well as from each of the traditional animals, are capable of circular movement. They can best be applied against linear, straight-line approaches, but they work with round movement as well. Since the pattern is easier to detect, you need proficiency in changing direction on a dime so that although your trajectory may be obvious to your opponent, your final landing is not.

EXERCISE

CONSIDER A CURRENT action you are about to take. Visualize the other person's movement. Think of a variety of circular paths in to where you want to be. For example, imagine yourself in a job interview. Look for windows of opportunity to rechannel the conversation in order to interject information you regard as important to land the job. Early entries must be quick and more direct because you have less information to work with. Later entries allow more time to identify and choose your target, and thus the target may expose itself more clearly. Either way, give yourself a lot of flexibility as you approach your final path.

148.

Know When the Straight Line Is Best

STRAIGHT-LINE SHOTS work best against circular movements. On the mats, for example, if you see a round strike coming, you can beat it without even having to worry about blocking the oncoming shot. To do this you have to go right into offensive mode, identifying your target and launching a straight-line shot that is capable of beating your opponent to the draw, so to speak. Whether in the dojo or in daily routines, a straight-line approach will usually reach its target first, simply because the distance is shorter. If you need follow-up, your initial move will work as a stun, buying you a window of opportunity to position optimally for a successful finish. If you are able to land a vital point, of course, you can put things to rest right there. Train yourself to spot targets readily, but not hastily. When others take the long way, go short. Fire your best shot straight to the core.

EXERCISE

CONSIDER THE VARIOUS people and situations you are currently dealing with. Identify one that operates circularly. Visualize his or her approaches. This will help you time and locate responses. Choose a straight-line action that you can use to accomplish your goals. Proceed. See what happens.

149.

Combine Circular Techniques with Straight-Line Techniques

SOMETIMES CIRCULAR MOVEMENT works best, and other times a straight-line technique is best. You must decide which to use based on individual situations. Upon contact, however, circular movement eventually and naturally flows into linear patterns and vice versa. In the dojo, straight punches are turned around by circular blocks. But if you keep on using such blocks, a straight-line window of opportunity will open. Likewise, you can turn your failed straight-line punch into another strike by circling over the top of your opponent's block. Remember the law of yin-yang. Using the same movement your opponent uses leaves you feeling as if you are spinning your wheels. However, utilizing the principle of opposites, you will be able to reach into spaces you desire and invite what you desire into your spaces. This is true both on the mats and in daily routines.

EXERCISE

FOR ONE DAY, pay attention to the way in which the people you are in contact with interrelate. Are they direct or circular in their approach? When they are direct, be circular. When they are taking the long way around things, be short. Know what you want from the situation. As windows of opportunity present themselves, take them. See what happens.

150.

Look for the
Sudden Breakthrough

MARTIAL ARTS TEACH that breakthroughs happen when you least expect them. Recently someone told me he understood Chi, but couldn't "experience" it. I assured him that summoning Chi took me quite a while as well. Indeed, it happened unexpectedly one afternoon when I was pounding punches into my wooden dummy. Although I was exhausted and wanted to quit, I pushed myself well beyond my limitations. My hands were raw. My arms ached. I wasn't thinking about Chi. I was only thinking of throwing punches and keeping correct form. Then it happened. I felt a surge of heat in my abdomen that spread to my arms and legs and then my entire body. Instead of losing strength, I exploded with energy. I crashed my arms into the apparatus and felt no pain, only exhilaration. I slipped into a meditative mindset. The feeling was electric. When I finished I felt strong, alert, and pumped. I analyzed what had happened. Then, with a lot of work, I learned how to duplicate the experience. So much in martial training happens this way. Just tell yourself you *will* reach your goal. Focus on your skills and never quit trying. This is the Way. When you least expect it, you will arrive.

EXERCISE

SINGLE OUT SOMETHING you are attempting to achieve. Focus on the skills you need to get there. Analyze your performance and think about what you can do to improve. Tell yourself that you will stick to it no matter what, then apply your new ideas.

Act with Integrity

MARTIAL ARTS EMPHASIZE that you should act with integrity at all times. This means being truthful, reliable, and principled. To this end, martial systems empower you to live in a way that agrees with your moral vision. You are encouraged from day one to use your skill to discover who and what you are and to express yourself authentically. This doesn't mean that you don't consider what others think or feel. You must. How else can you fit in? How else can you harmonize? But, the dojo teaches, you fit in best by being yourself, by examining each situation on its own merits and flowing into it with an open heart. Moment by moment, it is you who ultimately must decide what correct action means—for you—and then do it. Act with integrity in all that you do. Use your power to live free and tread lightly.

EXERCISE

AS YOU MOVE from one situation to another throughout your day, ask yourself what honestly needs to be done within each situation to make the most of it. Consider where you and the particular skills you bring to the circumstance fit in. How can you best use your power to enhance the situation for yourself and all concerned? Do it.

152.

Reject What Is Useless and Add What Is Useful

THE DOJO EXPERIENCE teaches you to get in touch with yourself in order to know what you need. To this end, you learn to consider techniques that have led others to success, asking which aspects will work for you and which will not. You learn to embrace those concepts that flow from you naturally and facilitate your needs. Likewise, you learn to reject what is useless or disingenuous for you. This doesn't mean that you can't revisit concepts. You should. It just means that you are being analytical and honest with your current circumstances. You may see somebody scoring strikes with acrobatic cartwheel kick combinations. The last thing you need to be is acrobatic. However, you may have observed some useful footwork you can incorporate into your own. You learn to take what works and leave the rest behind. Remember, the significance of technique changes, so revisit your methods often. This is true on the mats or wherever you are.

EXERCISE

IDENTIFY WHICH ASPECTS of a person's maneuvers would feel natural if incorporated into your own. Then consider two other people and do the same with them. Take the best of what works from each person and adapt those ideas or actions into a strategy for dealing with current life circumstances.

153.

Don't Muscle Your Way

MARTIAL ARTS ARE not about muscling life. Brute force constricts energy flow and causes blockages. This inhibits flexibility, sensitivity, speed, and natural movement. Whenever you are using muscle instead of spirit to get you where you need to be, you move in a stop/go fashion, rather than maintaining a continuous steady flow. You become weak and vulnerable at junctures where behaviors begin or end—where you have just exhausted energy and yet are waiting for a new flow to kick in. Martial arts teach you not to fight against patterns of movement, but to move *with* them. Your job is to let spirit guide you, not muscle.

EXERCISE

FOR ONE DAY, use your pause button whenever you feel yourself about to apply force to make something work out your way. Early signs of using too much muscle may exhibit themselves as a tightening in the chest or neck and sometimes the outer extremities. Take a breath and relax. Remind yourself that you don't need to muscle through life. Instead, take a moment and adjust your posture to ease your breathing. Take a few soft, deep breaths. Loosen your jaw. Focus your attention on the energy center at the crown of your head and use your breath to unblock it and lighten. Feel your spirit rising. Sink your consciousness to your lower *Dan Tien*, and feel your energy coming alive. Let your whole body relax, especially your neck and shoulders. If you need help focusing, gently touch those areas. Remind yourself that it is important to feel good in whatever you do. Tension and pain are indicators that something needs to be addressed before going forward with the job. Let your Chi spread through your body and nurture it. Feel your spirit strengthening. Let it guide you in getting what you want through harmony rather than muscle.

154.

Be Ready for
What May Come Next

ON THE MATS as well as in life, being ready for what may come next is determined by your ability to maintain a high level of presence and spontaneity. You reach this point by practicing a wide variety of techniques until you overcome the awkwardness of having to think about them as you act. Instead, what you have learned now starts kicking in automatically. Even your capacity to modify techniques becomes reflexive. This is a significant mark of passage, because it means that you have subconsciously begun to mold martial principles to the specifics of your life and self-expression, which is what you have been striving for. Think less. Just be.

EXERCISE

CHOOSE A DAY to just go with whatever arises. Unshackle your mind. Don't try to *do* anything. Let circumstances unravel. Relax. Trust your reflexes. See what happens.

155.

See Wholeness as the
Big Picture

IN MARTIAL ARTS, wholeness is the big picture. In other words, wholeness is the unity of the body-mind-spirit connection, and achieving it—seeing and living all of life's actions through a lens that includes all three parts. For this reason, dojo experience guides you through five stages of awareness:

Universal Spirit, Spirit, Ego
Internal Energy, Body

Your first stops are the body and its internal energies. Next you turn your attentions to the contradictory voice of your ego, which pits itself between your physical and spiritual desires. Remember, the ego operates from fear and the need for social approval, telling you it safeguards happiness and, ironically, steering you to decisions that prevent it. Ego blocks the desire deep in your heart, creativity, and freedom. It confuses, energetically fracturing your sense of wholeness. Martial arts teach you to defeat the ego, defragmenting energy and reconnecting with your spirit to become whole again.

EXERCISE

CONSULT YOUR BODY, internal energy centers, and spirit before taking action steps you wish to refine, anything from the simplest of life decisions to those concerning interpersonal relationships, as well as physical and emotional health. If you feel contradictory emotions or ideas arise, ask yourself where they stem from. Such contradictions are a result of prefabricated approvals, expectations, or fears. Relax and center. Consider the needs of your body, mind, and spirit. You will discover that all three point to the same direction. When you see this unity, follow where they point.

Be Able to Move from Any Angle

MARTIAL ARTS TEACH you not to get stuck. In other words, you train by moving in and out of ranges until you land yourself in the best spaces. For example, your most proficient techniques may involve hand strikes that advance into takedowns. Your partner, an awesome kicker, however, is busy keeping you at bay, strategizing you out of your best ranges. This shuts down your best possible offensive moves. Consequently, you need to develop ways to defend against his patterns. In the dojo, you do this by intentionally putting yourself in situations that make it the most difficult to use your art, and then discovering what movement you need to develop to segue back to familiar territories. Life is no different. Everyone has environments that hide their best attributes. The flip side is that there are always ways to return to your best spaces. Your job is to discover these and practice flowing to them gracefully.

EXERCISE

BE ATTENTIVE TO situations in your daily routines, during which you feel shut down—that is, where you find it difficult, if not impossible, to utilize your best skills. Make a list of these incidents. Then reflect on each, asking yourself why you felt immobile. Ask what movements are necessary to put you back into spaces where you can activate your skills. If you have to, ask yourself how someone else would work through the situation. Visualize yourself employing these techniques. Try choreographing a strategy. Follow up. See what happens.

157.

Remember That the
Easiest Way Is the Right Way

ALL MARTIAL ARTS encourage taking the path of least resistance. This is a great thought because it means that if you're trying too hard, something must be wrong. There are many dojo examples of this concept, some of them quite comical. I remember a student once asking a master practitioner what he would do if someone grabbed him. The master replied by saying, "Tell me what *your* first inclination would be." The student, perhaps trying to impress his master, went on to demonstrate a complicated technique that involved several showy steps with locks, traps, breaks, takedowns, and the whole nine yards of Hollywood martial arts. "That's pretty impressive," said the master, "but too complicated." Then he said, "Here, grab me." With that he fired off one straight punch that, had it launched at full force, would have rendered the junior practitioner unconscious. What was interesting was that the target was wide open, huge, and so easy to hit that you could show a total novice how to do it in a three-minute lesson. "The easiest way is the right way," he said. Practice this simple lesson often, and you will take a giant step toward conserving time and effort in your life.

EXERCISE

BEFORE YOU EMBARK on any endeavors, actively identify the easiest way to get from point A to point B. Then take that route. Observe what happens and how you feel.

Experience

THE MARTIAL WAY is through experience. Every dojo will teach that talking about concepts is not enough. Watching masters perform techniques on the mats or on film is not enough. Reading is not enough. Thinking about martial theory is not enough. You have to get out there and do it. The anthem in martial arts is this: *Until you experience it, you haven't done anything.* Even if it means having to try a technique a thousand times, or getting a few bruises on your arms and legs, or landing yourself on your butt because you haven't quite polished your technique yet, you have to take the hits as part of becoming proficient. You learn to expect the falls as part of learning. But the bright side, of course, is that once you know you can do something, you have the confidence of being able to repeat it. You believe in the technique, the process, and yourself. You have more gusto for life and your ability to grow. This is what martial arts is all about.

EXERCISE

IDENTIFY A MARTIAL technique that you have yet to attempt in everyday routines. Consider several places in your life where you could give it a whirl. Think of how you can best implement the technique, and then try it. Don't worry if you are proficient or not. Be willing to try it out a few times. Experience it. It's okay to modify. See how it works.

159.

Don't Fear Risk

MARTIAL ARTS TEACH not to fear risk. The bottom line is that you always learn something—about concept, actions, other people, and especially yourself. For instance, maybe you always execute offensive shots straight down the centerline. Then you decide to take a risk. You fire a circular strike from a sideline. You are flooded with new possibilities. You may wind up vulnerable to a straight-line attack. Or you could knock your opponent off balance and find a wide range of new targets. You may even find the positioning for a "big throw," as they say in judo. If you get tagged, you could still see certain openings for the next time. No matter what, you are learning. It is always a risk to try something that didn't work once a second time. As you learn, however, your aptitudes shift, and what was impossible becomes very possible—but you have to risk the effort. To grow, you have to charter into the unknown, where possibility is infinite. So enjoy the risk. Learn. Do.

EXERCISE

THINK ABOUT AN aspect of your daily routine. Start with something small. Identify your typical approach to the situation. Consider a variety of tactics that are completely different from your usual approach. Then take the risk and try one of these tactics. For example, if you're use to getting up at 7:00 AM regardless if it is a weekday or not, try sleeping in one day on the weekend. If you always eat in on Sundays, try going out. See how you feel. See what happens.

160.

Fit In, Wherever You Are

EVERYTHING ABOUT THE dojo experience emphasizes cooperation. If your partners need to practice a certain takedown, you non-
combatively give them the shots they need to take you down. If you
need to learn how to block a roundhouse, your partners will launch as
many as are required to get you up to snuff. That's the martial Way.
Remember the law of yin-yang. It is only when you break harmony
that you put yourself in harm's way. Does this mean you are selling out?
Absolutely not. You offer what is genuine. Likewise, similar energies
will attract. The best way to bring peace and resolution to your own
life is to help someone else achieve it. Outside the dojo, you find that
the same lessons apply. Cooperation feels good. It's natural. You grow.
You move more easily. You are happier. Positivity comes your way.

EXERCISE

IDENTIFY SOMETHING YOU need in your current life. Find someone else
who has a similar need and help that person achieve it. The martial mind is
not always out for itself. Watch what happens.

Recharge Often

HOLISTIC MEDICINES AND self-healing are areas of rising interest, and martial arts is a way to plug in to those ideas. From the ancient Shaolin monks straight to present-day practice, all martial artists have trained various methods for unblocking and boosting their life force energy and recharging it often. This is because they have all discovered that whether in the dojo or out, an abundance of such energy sharpens every aspect of human life—from the biological to the emotional and spiritual. Higher-level energy intensifies the body's immune system, providing you with greater physical strength. It enhances your capability to heal yourself, as well as others. It increases your presence and sensitivity. It gives you a sense of clarity, wholesomeness, and charm.

EXERCISE

TEST AND RESTORE the quality of your energy frequently. Does your mind feel innocent, light, and clear? Look around in your environment. Are you able to select an object and focus on it at will without being bombarded by a barrage of interfering thoughts? Can you simply be present without focusing on anything in particular? If not, take a few moments and practice doing so. Start by regulating your breath and centering. Keep your focus uninterrupted. With each attempt you will feel an immediate surge of clean energy, even if only slightly. But this will have a cumulative effect as you test more regularly throughout the day.

Are your emotions open, light, and flowing freely? If not, clear your energy centers. Unblock affected areas (see secret 70).

Does your body feel stress-free, responsive, and supple? If not, where is it tight? Where do you feel pain? Touch those areas with your fingers to give you focus. Center and regulate your breathing. Concentrate your Chi and send it to those areas. Release blocked negative energy with your out-breaths.

162.

Be Patient

SOMETIMES YOU HAVE to wait until you have mastered at least the basics of a technique before you can take it out and show it. Getting antsy on the mats might just land you on the floor. On the other hand, when you first start training, you feel your oats relatively fast. You feel remarkably safer and more confident. Then one day you start thinking you'll never be as proficient as your seniors. You feel you have come as far as you can. This is like hitting the wall to a marathon runner. But you have to get over it. The really good stuff is about to happen. For example, you start to discover the connection between techniques—how one is able to enhance another. Have patience. A fellow martial artist recently told me that after twenty-five years of practice, he was most excited about having discovered yet another way to use Chi to heal and ward off sickness, in himself and in others. And, of course, that's just the tip of the iceberg for all of us. Mastery is never-ending, and so are its rewards.

EXERCISE

FILL A CUP with water, all the way to the brim. A wide, shallow cup works best. Then extend your right arm (if you are right handed, left if you are left handed), with your palm pointed downward, fingers extended. Holding the cup with your other hand, place it at mid-arm, just over your elbow. Continue holding it in place, and walk from one end of your home to the other a few times, trying not to spill the water. Walk as smoothly and quickly as possible. If the water spills, slow down. Have patience. After you do this a few times, you will realize what needs to be done to move more quickly and efficiently through the house, and you will pick up speed. Apply what you learn from this lesson to larger areas of your life.

163.

Know What You Can Sustain

PART OF SELF-DISCOVERY is learning just how much of a strike you can withstand. Muay Thai practitioners, for example, train in sustaining sideline kicks. Then they invite these as part of their fighting strategy. By taking the kick, they are able to knock opponents off balance and gain the offensive. Knowing how well you can process certain pain is important in daily life as well. A friend of mine recently endured a specific elective surgery for a second time. Apparently there are no permanent guarantees to the procedure. The surgery is rough and requires physical therapy. However, she explains, even if it is temporary, she can continue playing a sport she loves—until the next time. What's important, she says, is that she already knows she can get through it. Sometimes in order to reach your goals, there is no way to avoid pain. Knowing how much pain you can endure and training to take even more, when necessary, will help get you through.

EXERCISE

IDENTIFY SOMETHING IN your life that you have been putting off because it will cause you pain. Assess the pain. Ask yourself if you can withstand it. If so, follow through and do it. Don't deprive yourself of something that will bring joy to your life because you fear a pain that you can endure. Sometimes to get where you want to be, you have to strike through things. If you feel you can't withstand the pain, create a training program for yourself: talk to others who have successfully made it through a similar situation, acquire literature, take a course, or talk to experts who can help you gain the necessary skills and mind-set to reach your goal.

164.

Know Your Limits

MARTIAL TRAINING GIVES you the power to transform. However, if a situation puts you or others at high risk and cannot be changed, the martial Way is to accept your limitations, at least for now. Plenty of masters have been afflicted with severe illness and had to close the doors to their dojo, some temporarily and some permanently. Novices need to accept that they must learn breaking techniques before punching through bricks. If you are on certain medications, you cannot wield weapons. If you are incapacitated by injury or other personal ailments, you cannot put yourself or others at high risk. Sound familiar? Daily life is no different. People want to do things despite sickness, lack of necessary knowledge, and other debilitating personal problems. Local and national media report stories every week about the tragic consequences of such behaviors. Many things in life are beyond your control. Don't fight what you cannot change. Don't punish yourself or others. Accept uncontrollable circumstances until such a time when you can make a difference.

EXERCISE

IDENTIFY ANY STRESSFUL aspects of your life that you deem beyond your control, at least momentarily. Don't punish yourself for not being able to deal with matters just yet. Don't analyze. Look in the mirror and tell yourself that warriors aren't fools! Instead, take time to eat well, connect with others, and watch a good movie. Tell yourself that when the opportunity arises, you'll be strong enough to make the most of it.

165.

Push the Limits

THE MARTIAL WAY is to go for it—when the time is right. It's good to break out of your prison. This is how you grow. Everything in the universe grows this way. Everything changes. We've all seen it: the junior high school weakling enters a dojo and sculpts his body to look like Zeus; the skinny, shy little girl comes to look like Xena the Warrior Princess; and kids from the "wrong side of the tracks" become CEOs and best-selling authors. The dojo teaches you to keep your mind open to possibilities. If you catch yourself saying, "I can't do that," ask yourself why you feel that way. The good martial artist will accept what he or she cannot change, at least for the time being, and will respect individual needs as well as those of others. On the other hand, you train to set goals and see what will happen—to break away from your past and attempt to improve your future. When you say you can't do something, you simply mean, *Well, not for today, anyway.*

EXERCISE

IDENTIFY SOMETHING IN your life that you would like to change. Ask if this is something within your control. If not, you may have to shift your approach to see if you *can* put things in your control. If the answer is yes, make a list of ways that you can begin: do you need to do research, collect related literature to inform yourself, consult experts, enroll in a workshop or a degree program or the like? Visualize yourself having already made the change. The more detail you can see, the better. Stay positive. Start right away.

Expand Your Knowledge
of a Concept

THE DOJO TEACHES that knowledge of martial concepts evolves as your experiences evolve. Of course, just as in all other walks of life, there are people who already think they know all the answers. Some of these people are well educated and well trained. However, martial arts teach that its concepts have hidden meaning. Some are intentionally secretive. In fact, it is common to learn technique, practice it for years, and then discover a whole new dimension to it. Lots of masters teach this way intentionally. Other concepts remain "secretive" only until you grow into them. Some participants, however, enter the dojo with their cup so full they are unable to withstand instruction, even for a short time. Others reach a rank—often around black belt—and plateau, choosing instead to believe that now they know all there is to know and experience. This closed-minded attitude is in opposition to the Way. Whether in the dojo or in daily routines, you should make a habit of revisiting the basics often and look for the hidden meaning in old tools.

EXERCISE

SEEK HIDDEN MEANINGS. Think back to an earlier martial concept. Consider combining it with other concepts you have learned. Think of as many new ways as you can to use these concepts in daily routines. Try them out.

Alternate: Identify a tool that you previously used aggressively, like kimi (explosive focused power) and use it to create peace or to create a tool to center both yourself and another. Try identifying an everyday tool that you use aggressively such as your power of persuasion, writing, or retailing and use it to create peace or to center both yourself and others..

Don't Insist on Dominating

WHENEVER YOU TRY to dominate martial arts drills or exercises, you cut yourself short on benefits. Domination energetically fuels disharmony—not to mention that it feeds the falsehood that aggression and winning are the most important results of your endeavors. This mind-set is shunned in the dojo. It is driven by fear of loss rather than joy. As such, it is aimed at outcome rather than process; it is conditional rather than free, because bliss is dependent on a successful outcome. These are all ideas that your art is designed to break through. Martial arts emphasize cooperation over dominance. Even if you are in a tournament, testing your skills and scoring points, your competitor is still your friend, both during and after. Regardless of the results, your primary objective is to learn from the experience so that you can improve. I recently observed a wonderful cooperative effort. At the college where I teach, several faculty members who were up for tenure got together and helped whip one another's credentials into shape. No one tried to dominate. At the end of the day, their tenure portfolios had all been edited many times. No one could have raked these so clean on his or her own. This was a win-win situation, regardless of outcome. Everybody shined!

EXERCISE

IDENTIFY AN AREA in your life where you have been trying to dominate another person. Try a different approach. Think of a way to be a better friend to the person. See if you can partner up and share what you each do best. If you both excel at the same thing, share differences in strategies and techniques in an effort to improve each other's performance. Complement each other. Martial arts teach that like energy attracts, or that "what goes around comes around." This is known as the law of Karma. Be a karma team.

168.

Listen to Challenging
Points of View

A YOUNG MARTIAL artist of high rank whose favorite lead move in the ring was a flying front kick met an equally ranked Tae Kwon Do player at a community get-together. The TKD player was in trials for that year's Olympic team. "That kick won't work with just anybody," the Olympic hopeful said. "In fact, I've seen some guys get kicked out of midflight because the 'other guy' could see it coming." Instead of simply making conversation, the first martial artist argued his position. Back in the dojo, he told his teacher what the TKD player had said. The teacher shrugged and called a senior student over to spar the young kicker. As advised by the teacher, the senior player kicked his junior right out of the air like a soccer ball when the younger student tried the move on him. "I wanted you to see for yourself," the teacher said. "See what?" asked the student. "Let me put it into words for you," the instructor said. "You can learn a lot from people who don't agree with what you say." The lesson spoke to me as well. That day we were all wiser than the day before. As for the junior student, he went on to become a fully seasoned warrior.

EXERCISE

THE NEXT TIME someone challenges your point of view, enter a dialogue with him or her about it. See if you can identify weaknesses in your thinking. Keep an open mind. If you find vulnerabilities, set up a training plan to strengthen them.

169.

Remember That
Reason Is Limited

THE DOJO TEACHES that our ability to reason helps us survive. Consider this typical sparring episode: a hook punch is coming at your head; you move; you survive. In this situation, *reason* tells you to retreat. Logic ignores your intuition (spiritual voice), which thinks it can beat the punch, coaching you to take offensive. True, there is a certain survival rate to reliance on reason. But it is not infallible. Just consider some of the most valuable discoveries in history. Nearly all were initially deemed "unreasonable," starting with the discovery of the western hemisphere. Columbus could have *reasoned:* "It's just too much trouble. Who knows what will happen out there? I'd be better off sleeping in." Reason is a good preventative; it ignores heart and conscience. Those who want to avoid the work of bettering themselves always have a good reason—for example, "I'm driving intoxicated because there is no other way home." Indeed, some of the most bizarre actions in history have been perpetrated as sensible. Reconsider the above sparring scenario. Instead of doing the logical thing, you decide to *override reason.* Following your intuition, you fire off a series of blistering punches and win the match. Logic can give you plenty of good reasons for not pursuing the full potential of your heart and soul. Be careful.

EXERCISE

IDENTIFY AN AREA of self-improvement you have been attempting to launch in your life but keep finding excuses not to pursue. Take a fresh look at what you desire. If you still think that it is in line with the life you want for yourself, go forward and pursue it.

Just Do It

ONE OF MARTIAL arts' major anthems is "Just do it"—quit talking about it and get the job done. There are certain dojo personalities that can't stop questioning procedures. They want to reason out every little nuance of every technique. You usually see these players poised on the sidelines, inundating the instructor with questions, while all the other practitioners are scattered about the mats and busy playing the game. They would talk through the entire session if they could. In the dojo, however, this kind of activity is discouraged. There are some legitimate questions regarding set-up logistics for a technique. But unless you have experienced a technique several times, considerable and constant questioning is seen as suspicious—that is, as an excuse for not getting in there and discovering for yourself. The martial Way teaches there is no such thing as failure. There is only success or not trying. The choice is yours. You can wait until you're on your deathbed looking back and regretting not doing all the things you wish you had tried in life, or you can find out *now* which are true to your heart and purpose on the planet.

EXERCISE

IDENTIFY SOMETHING GOOD you have been procrastinating over doing. Then do it.

171.

Be Sensitive to Energy
Flowing toward You

HAVE YOU EVER felt like someone is looking at you, and when you turn around, you find that they really are? Perhaps it's someone in a car next to yours. Maybe you're in a restaurant, at a concert, or in some other public place. Energy flows toward you from everywhere in your environment. Sometimes it is so strong you can't help but feel it. Other times it's subtle. This energy is Chi. Science calls this element of Chi "information energy" and says it travels at the speed of light. This face of Chi is a quality and capability of consciousness. Part of the information it carries is *intention*. Remember, sometimes intention surfaces from a person's subconscious, even though he or she is not aware of it. Martial arts teach that Chi flows through your feelings, body, and actions. Thus, you train in reading, responding, and sometimes redirecting this energy. All of this interaction heightens your awareness to energies flowing toward you outside the dojo, too. You become more attentive to how it affects your living, and you realize that you have a lot more to do with the way things are turning out than you used to think.

EXERCISE

GO FOR A walk in a shopping mall. Relax and center. Keep your mind open and attentive. Wait to feel energy coming to you. Have patience. Use your in-breath to help you focus. Bear in mind, you're not waiting for Chi to come to you. It already is. You are trying to *feel* it. When you do, feel it flowing through your energy centers. You may feel warmth or pressure. Try to read the energy. Focus your attention on which centers are most affected. What images come to mind? What emotions? Let your intuition guide you. Ask yourself what significance this information has to do with your current life. When something strikes a chord, consider ways to use the information.

172.

Don't Confine Anything

ONE OF THE greatest gifts of the dojo is self-actualization. You are constantly encouraged to ask yourself, "What kind of person am I going to be? Am I going to live free of conflict and emotional trauma, or am I going to let myself be poisoned by these?" Martial arts steer you away from the notion of having to endure problems until they break you down or you lose yourself. You try not to let debris pile up in life. You learn not to confine anyone or anything. Protecting your own, as well as others,' freedom of thought, action, and spirit holds the greatest advantages for all. In the dojo, whenever you attempt to confine a movement—for instance, when you force an armlock—you risk something snapping. Instead, when an opponent pushes, you ease up and simply pull or push him in the direction he is already moving. You do nothing to inhibit the flow of energy, and you keep every advantage. Whether in the dojo or out, with every attempt to confine, you give up your advantage—sometimes a lot.

EXERCISE

WHEN YOU CATCH yourself ready to start piling up conflicts into your life, pause, ease up, and see where you can exert a little pull on things so that you are out of harm's way or perhaps even gain advantage. Do not oppose anyone's strength. Try lightening up enough to get behind conflict and stressors, and gently push them out of your way. Wait for opportunity to become its own design.

Alternate: Have a partner toss a large ball or pillow to you. Instead of batting it away, try sidestepping it and using your palms to gently push it along to where it is already headed. What can you learn about moving oncoming energy out of your way? Add these skills to your toolbox.

Increase Sensitivity to Repeating Patterns

RECOGNIZING PATTERNS MAKES you a better fighter. Likewise, becoming sensitive to patterns off the mats has great benefits. For example, your partner misses breakfast, doesn't make it to the bank on time, and now says you must eat dinner quickly because of commitments for that evening. You see the pattern, but your partner doesn't. The martial Way is to cooperate by remaining supple, slowing down, not adding more weight, and picking up some of the slack to help open windows of time for your partner. You do this out of compassion and love. Remember the law of Karma. This restores balance. Often, objectivity can make you aware of others' patterns before *they* are. Sometimes patterns are subtle. You choose something colorful to wear. Paradoxically, that same day, you overdraw the checking account. Your bank fines you. You worry about finances. At work, your attention is drawn to a discussion that autumn foliage is in full bloom. On your way home, your attention is drawn to the bright colors. A terrific garden catches your attention. All day long a pattern has been occurring. Despite your troubles, Life has been sending messages of brightness. You simply didn't see them. However, a few days later, you are offered that higher salaried job you've been seeking. Now you wish you hadn't wasted your time worrying about finances. *But life was telling you all along not to worry.*

EXERCISE

MAKE A LIST of patterns you notice in your life. Consider what the message might be in light of something that you are trying to do to improve yourself. Use this information to plan action that will help you reach your goals. Look for patterns in a friend's life. How can you complement these to help this person achieve a current life goal?

174.

You *Can* Change a Behavior

MARTIAL ARTS ARE all about transformation. Maybe you simply want to quit leaving your highline open to close-range attacks. Or more importantly, maybe you want to become a better listener in your daily relationships. Life will send you lessons. They can be lovely. But sometimes they are hard. You feel like you're making one mistake after another and getting hit with failing grades. However, such lessons are part of training. If you choose to ignore them, the lessons will keep coming. They may emerge in a pattern of dysfunction, pain, and sickness. Sometimes life needs to get dramatic to get you to notice. On the flip side, whenever you learn a lesson, old behaviors change. Difficulties go away. Each of us is on this earth for a special series of lessons. Trust the universe. Have you ever noticed that somehow people always come into your life, out of nowhere, when you need them most? If you don't see answers, patterns will emerge until you do. Take note, learn, and change.

EXERCISE

IDENTIFY A BEHAVIOR you want to change in your life. Relax and center. Imagine looking at yourself from outside your body. Let that consciousness drift a distance away, as if you are watching the script of your life playing on a movie screen. Through that mind-set, ask the universe for guidance with the behavior you have identified. Consider recurring events, situations, or feelings in your daily life that are linked to that behavior. Analyze the patterns. Consider what methods of change they suggest. Visualize making the changes. Watch yourself living with these new behaviors. Try them out in a few scripts you can visualize. Then give them a test run in a real-life situation. See how this works.

175.

Stay Connected to
Your Energy Source

REMEMBER, MARTIAL ARTS teach that your body is a vessel that holds energy. Your job is to get rid of negative energy, take in as much high-quality energy as you can, then process and release it in positivity. You have three energy sources: the Chi that you are born with, the Chi that you gather from everything around you, and the Chi that you summon from the Infinite. Basic level dojo practice tells you to always stay connected with your center and to move from that mind-set as much as possible. This powers, stabilizes, and frees your actions. Intermediate dojo practice tells you to identify and connect with those elements in your environment (people, places, things) from which you can receive positive energy. At this level, your job is to cycle Chi through your energy centers and empower every aspect of living. Advanced dojo practice plugs you into Universal Chi. Some call this the "mind of the Infinite" or the "Universal Body." Your job here is to enter this mind and literally feel its "thread" through both of the other two. The advanced martial artist experiences this connection in every action.

EXERCISE

SINK YOUR CONSCIOUSNESS and center. Visualize something in your environment, perhaps a tree outside. Feel the radiant energy within it. Let your consciousness drift beyond your body, through the tree into the sky, into space—far into the horizon, beyond all stars and galaxies until there is just light and vastness. Put your consciousness in the middle. Feel the presence of light (and your consciousness) in every particle of space trailing back to where you began at the center of your own body. Use your breath to guide you. Let your mind travel back to your body. Create a memory of where you have been. When you want to speak to the universe, go there.

176.

Contemplate the Impossible

IF YOU ARE reading this book, you are already a warrior rising above life limitations. You are in good company. Conquering one impossibility after another is the martial Way. Consider the Shaolin monks performing push-ups, not only with one arm, but with one finger; picking up red-hot iron rods with bare hands; balancing their entire body weight, stomach down, on the tip of a razor-sharp spear, or standing on one leg for a half hour, the other lifted over their head and wrapped around their neck like a scarf; or withstanding a three-foot steel pipe whipped across their abs like a baseball bat and walking away unscathed. Imagine the guts to contemplate what in 1932 Albert Einstein deemed impossible: "We will never obtain nuclear energy; the atom would have to be split at will." Yet that is exactly what Otto Hahn and Lise Meitner did, splitting the atom in 1938. Consider the unemployed J. K. Rowling contemplating a character named Harry Potter in a British coffeehouse. Impossibility is in the eye of the beholder. Perhaps it is unfathomable for someone to consider escaping an abusive relationship, getting out of a dead-end job, or quitting a destructive habit. Contemplate the impossible to make it possible.

EXERCISE

CONSIDER AN IMPROVEMENT in your life that seems utterly unfathomable. Begin to contemplate steps you can take toward this goal. Start by gathering information. Maybe you want to get a college degree but can't afford the cost or time because you are a single parent and need to keep a job. Do your research. You may find colleges offering courses or entire degree programs online or in alternative time frames. Others have free daycare. Others offer credits for life learning. See yourself already there. Think of how good you'll feel. Now, get going. Take joy and pride in the process.

Allow Growing Pains

DEALING WITH GROWING pains is part of martial training. Maybe you're learning a new block, but you mess up and walk around with a black eye for a few days. Some practitioners quit right there. Most, however, will shake it off and take the shot as part of learning. Rarely does anyone perform a technique perfectly the first time, or even the second, third, or fourth for that matter. The best thing you can do is accept that mastery will take time. The same is true off the mats. You practice keeping yourself balanced with an irate colleague, and instead you mess up and send your colleague right off the charts. You wish that you had called in sick that day. These are all growing pains. But you learn that surviving them isn't all that difficult. You have experienced them before, and you will again. What's important, whether on the mats or off, is good effort and repetition until proper technique sinks in. Knowledge *will* eventually become action and cultivate wisdom.

EXERCISE

THE NEXT TIME you use a technique to enhance a life situation, allow yourself the grace of making mistakes. Remember that mastery takes time. Instead of getting down on yourself, try to take things lightly and laugh. Then evaluate the situation, see where your use of technique could improve and go from there. Repeat the technique often until you see improvement.

178.

Attract Abundance

MARTIAL ARTS TEACH that abundance is not the exception. Indeed, it's the rule. If you require an abundance of strength to perform a certain technique, summon it. If you require an abundance of presence, clarity, energy, whatever—the martial Way is to invoke what you need. You learn to see the universe as an enormous oceanic well of Chi to which you can swim, dip your pail in, and bring back all the abundance you need. You become comfortable at taking abundantly, using your Chi to create the life you want, knowing it will ultimately pass through you, returning to the well again and again. Your job is to supercharge it with your history and return it with interest! If this sounds like the water cycle or homeopathy, it should. Remember, water is the guiding symbol for spirit in holistic arts as well as spirituality. As Wayne Dyer says in his book *The Power of Intention,* "The Infinite doesn't care how many times you dip in." The universe wants you to succeed. It wants you to be happy. Take what you need. All will be replenished. Visit the Infinite frequently.

EXERCISE

WHAT DO YOU need most? Be honest with yourself. Visualize yourself as having gotten what you need. Revisit the meditation exercise in secret 175. Put your consciousness through the void, centering it in the vastness of the Universal Body. With practice you'll be able to hold this mind-set for about twenty minutes. Toward the end of this part of your meditation, imagine having all you need. If you cannot maintain the whole scene or picture, don't worry. The Infinite already knows. You don't have to ask for anything. Don't worry about wanting abundance. It doesn't matter to the universe. It is plentiful. What matters is your happiness. Finish the meditation. Don't be concerned with how your needs will be met, just believe that they will.

Win without a Fight

YOU HAVE REACHED the level of expert when instead of fighting, you are able to walk away, confident that you would have overcome your opponents if you had gone into battle. Martial arts icon Ed Parker says this attitude "will be communicated to your antagonist, who will realize that he narrowly escaped defeat." Fellow martial artist and writer Joe Hyams shares in his book *Zen and the Martial Arts* that such confidence can be defined as "presence" and is a by-product of "self-confidence, [that] it is, instantly recognizable in any situation." People fight because they feel someone is taking away their dignity. They feel insecure. They need to regain face. When you're sure of your ability, however, you convey your confidence. No one can take it away. You don't need to prove anything. In a classic movie, *Enter the Dragon*, Bruce Lee is staged on a boat with an adversary who wants to fight. "What martial art do you practice," the adversary asks. "I practice the art of fighting without a fight," Lee responds. His opponent smirks. Lee suggests fighting on an island in the distance. To get there, he and his opponent must take a tiny rowboat. His opponent jumps in first. Lee stays on board and pushes the row boat out to sea. His adversary, realizing he's been duped, starts yelling that Lee is chicken. Lee laughs heartily. The lesson is the same lesson as that taught by Sun Tzu in his legendary book, *The Art of War*. "The best success is always winning without fighting."

EXERCISE

IF SOMEONE WANTS to fight today, simply don't—under any circumstances. Later on, pat yourself on the back and tell yourself that you have done well. You have nurtured and protected yourself. Feel secure in your ability. You have reached a higher rank of proficiency. Smile. Give yourself a promotion.

Use Your Skills
Outside the Dojo

MARTIAL TRAINING IS about getting to know who and what you really are. This means understanding your capabilities in the Earth dojo *and* your spiritual dojo. Science tells you that in order to command nature, you must obey its laws. To this end, all martial skills are intended to put you in touch with the way things move naturally. *Any technique used on the mats can be used in daily situations.* Additionally, and perhaps one of the better-kept secrets of martial arts, these same skills apply to the spiritual realm. On the mats, you complement a partner's forceful technique with softness. In daily routines, you learn to relax and listen when someone speaks, and vice versa. The same is true in your spiritual dojo. When you feel the forceful presence of spirit, soften your energy, relax and listen. On the other hand, you can aggressively activate your energy to a higher velocity and "speak" or draw more spiritual presence in your life.

EXERCISE

WHATEVER YOU ARE doing—at work, home, driving in your car, and the like—think about martial technique. Pick one and use it to enhance the activity. Do the same with spiritual matters. Experiment often and on all turfs. Whether you pray; seek the presence of one who has passed on; try to unite your energy with that of the universe; or seek peace in nature, a temple, a church, or the Infinite, consider what martial concepts apply and try them. See what happens.

181.

Attract Ideal Relationships

IN THE DOJO, you're job is to perfect skills for yourself. You must forget about nitpicking others. You use sensitivity to gently harmonize with another person's needs—without criticism or a need to convince anyone of anything. You seek and gratefully receive the help of others when you need it. You praise others for their good work. You become a doer. Your job is participating in the fullness of the dojo experience with your self, not your ego, at point zero. You try the widest variety of techniques: if you are a grappler, you try trapping, boxing, and kicking; you learn how to adapt to pain, joy, giving, taking, and the like. Wasting time criticizing makes no sense. Remember the law of karma! What goes around certainly will come around. The point is that your focus is on discovering who you are and improving what you do, and doing it. Indeed, this is how every cell in your body, as well as the universe, operates. Martial arts teach that you attract others by quietly believing in yourself. When you are content with yourself, others will be content with you. When you accept yourself, others will accept you.

EXERCISE

MAKE A POINT today of refusing to criticize. Focus all of your attention on doing whatever you do well. Believe in your skill as well as your ability to gather help from those around you if necessary. Stay relaxed and centered. Concentrate entirely on yourself. Delight in the proficiency of your actions. Enjoy your unique energy.

182.

Don't Use Others for Personal Gain

THE DOJO SHUNS using others for personal gain: to show off personal laurels, for vengeance, or even promotion. I could describe countless examples of such behavior that I have witnessed, even in my own studio. However, suffice to say that everyone, including myself, has had to fight off these urges. It's at times like these, however, that you have to reach way down inside and make yourself clearly see the motives and intentions that are steering you. If you use someone for personal gain, you have gained nothing but another dilemma to deal with when that energy comes back your way.

EXERCISE

THE NEXT TIME you get the itch to use someone, press your pause button and refocus. Take a good look at what is driving you. Spend your energy defeating those urges. Do not accept anything but total victory. Observe how you feel in the short run *and* later on.

Allow Others Freedom to Organize Harmoniously

MARTIAL ARTS TEACH that you gain freedom by allowing others theirs. Everything in the universe exists for a reason. The martial Way is to trust this concept. Your job is to allow everything in your environment the freedom to organize harmoniously. This, of course, means you, too! You are most useful and harmonious when you are most yourself. If your partner needs extra time stretching before going into drills, the dojo emphasizes cooperation. There is a reason you are with someone who needs extra time. Your job is to figure out why. Sometimes the explanation comes quickly. Perhaps you may need more time practicing kicks, and your partner will have to be patient with you. Other times reasons come slowly. Maybe life is asking you to cooperate with someone every time you turn the corner. You may even feel like a doormat at times. Then three months later there it is— as big as a billboard. Your lessons have paid off. You cooperate on something important at work, and *that* leads to a promotion. Peace and harmony always come back. Always.

EXERCISE

THE NEXT TIME you feel like interfering with someone's plan of action, use your pause button to help you stay out of it. Instead, observe exactly what he or she is organizing. Don't resist. Then participate, using whatever skills are appropriate. Consider how the experience creates you as much as you create the experience. Of course, if someone is trying to harm you, you will use your skills to protect yourself. Ask yourself, why did life put you into this situation? What is the lesson? Watch for the experience to come around again.

Generate Better Family Communication

BOW TO THE presence of Divinity under your own roof. Each family member is a special gift from the universe that is intended to energetically vault you to greater bliss and discovery. Indeed, you have probably already found that all martial concepts work with your relationships at home. As in the dojo, they dissolve conflict and stress and create a more positive, joyful environment. At the top of my list of favorite techniques are increased attention; calm, centered, and empty mind; balance; energy scans; and harmony. I start here because as with all improvement, you need to begin with yourself and move from there. This is not always a simple road, but it doesn't have to be bumpy either. The more you train, the more reflexively good habits kick in— and the greater the payoff. Better family communication yields more cooperation and trust. In turn, this helps family members better look out for one another and ward off problems before they occur. Make your own family life more fluid and nurturing. Start today.

EXERCISE

ENCOURAGE FAMILY MEMBERS to fully express themselves. Stress to them that the more informed you are, the more skillful you can be. Try to gently listen and speak *from the heart* first, without a hardening of attitudes. This creates a more sensitive emotional understanding—the language of one's deeper desires—as opposed to intellectual comprehension that listens primarily to just words, without recognizing the feelings behind them. Harmonize. Use your energy and emotional scans. Try to put yourself in the other person's shoes. Stay attentive to body language and facial expressions. Try to pick a detail and softly ask for more information. Put their feelings into words by repeating back to them what you've heard. This will make you sensitive to red flags and keep energies flowing warmly.

Match Speeds with Your Partner's

MARTIAL ARTS TEACH that speed depends on the person and situation you are dealing with. Your primary job is to stay in synch. Some people naturally move fast. Others are slow. Others are somewhere in between. When you are sparring and there is a punch coming at you, you have choices: retreat, block, or rechannel. Matching speed is important; otherwise, you may move too soon or not soon enough, missing your target altogether, destabilizing yourself, and risking another attack. The principle applies in daily life, too. If, for example, you're driving down a city street, it's impossible to have much of a relationship with someone who is walking. If you're walking side by side, you can interrelate more complexly, taking more information in, sending more out—making better judgments. This is true in every aspect of life. Spirituality is the experience of Divine energy in the world around you. However, just as you can't feel the earth soaring through space, there are many other aspects of your world that evade perception because they're moving way too fast or slow to register through your senses. Matching speed makes invisible things visible. It makes relationship possible where there was no relationship. It increases success on all levels.

EXERCISE

USE A LIGHTWEIGHT jump rope. Either you or your partner can do the jumping; the other will step inside the path of the rope and lightly tap the jumper (using fingertips or the palm) without getting hit by the rope. Good targets are the abdomen and breastbone. This drill teaches how clumsy things can get when you ignore rhythms in your entries and retreats. Additionally, it doesn't take a rocket scientist to figure out that the same problems occur when we don't pay attention in the pace of our daily lives.

186.

Move with Rhythm

GOOD RHYTHM IS essential to all martial arts. Sensitivity to your own internal rhythms and those of others will help you move appropriately and create opportunities with all of your actions. Feeling and using rhythm is a three-step process. First you have to identify the rhythm. For example, a fighter may move on a three count:

1. Low kick (to annoy)
2. Low kick (to annoy)
3. Back-fist (the one that counts)

Once you sense the rhythm, you can move away or enter with an attack of your own on any of the half-beats, often called pauses. Sensitivity to half-beats works magic on or off the mats. They allow you to enter, alter a partner's action, retreat, or launch your own action.

EXERCISE

THE NEXT TIME someone begins a conversation with you that you absolutely don't want to participate in, listen for the pauses in his or her rhythm(s). Perhaps the person is trashing a friend or colleague or the place where you work. In any case, when you hear a pause, smoothly enter, throwing a decoy—that is, mention something extraneous to the conversation that the person cannot resist responding to. It helps to know what really triggers the person. You may have to let the cycle repeat a few times, waiting for pauses, until you think of just the right thing to say. Then fire away and see what happens.

Flow the Yin-Yang of Space

INCREASE YOUR SENSITIVITY to the yin-yang of space, and move with more grace, efficiency, and power. Yin is energy coming at you; yang is energy pulling away. On the mats, as well as in everyday life, this concept immediately translates into the way that people move toward or away from each other. There are, however, more hidden levels to this concept. You can segue into these levels by first asking yourself the purpose of the movement. For example, you might just be trying to stay in harmony (remember the candle flame exercise from secret 114); you simply empty space as your partner fills it and vice versa. On the other hand, you can clear space offensively—intentionally positioning someone in order to better execute a technique—because people naturally gravitate into empty spaces as you create them. This is true on or off the mats. The concept applies to physical, emotional, and spiritual movement. You can apply it to yourself, internally and externally, as well as to others.

EXERCISE

FOR A WHOLE day, pay special attention to the way people move spatially—that is, watch where they begin and end their actions, whether this means the way they walk from the desk to the other side of the room, stand in line, pass through entrances, move conversationally, or even emotionally. Try not to collide or trip up. Look for the empty spaces in physical actions before you enter. Do the same with emotional responses. Do the same in meditations. Observe what happens.

188.

Consider It Done

AS SOON AS a martial artist makes up her mind to get a job done, you can consider it done. When you tap in to the Universal Energy Field, you experience time, space, and mind as a single thing. Your consciousness and the "big picture" are one and the same. The martial goal is to live with complete and reflexive presence from one moment to the next. In sparring, you don't think about takedowns. You just do it. And you have that feeling, before even making contact, that your opponent is headed for the mats. What a great feeling—to actually sense success before it happens and to be confident beyond all doubt (as you are when you are in complete synch) that it is going to happen. That's the way to live.

EXERCISE

THINK ABOUT A project you are about to begin work on. During your meditation, consider this action the only action in the universe. Visualize the project going smoothly and successfully. Let yourself feel the happiness of success. Repeat your meditation often throughout your day. Relax and consider it done.

Use Conscious Nonaction

MARTIAL ARTS TEACH that at times you must consciously do nothing. If you are sparring, this means that you let your opponent come to you. There are advantages to this technique. You can use your pause button to recharge. You can also better see your opponent's strategy, disarm the attack, and fire back with your strongest shot. A more hidden tactic, however, is to let yourself enter an ultraconsciousness during moments of nonaction. This state of awareness is your magic wand. It will allow you to keep your opponent from dictating your actions. By studying his or her reactions to your movement, you can keep your opponent reacting to you. Daily routines are similar. Incorporate conscious nonaction into all of your movements.

EXERCISE

INCORPORATE MOMENTS OF ultraconscious inaction into all of your movements. Use these energetically attentive moments of pause to do a quick environmental assessment, looking for others' reactions to your activity and deciding on your next move—considering where you want to position others in line with your goals. Take into account your own and others emotional, as well physical activity. Use this same process internally with meditations.

Set an Example

EVERYONE IS A teacher. All martial artists throughout history, from the highest ranked on down, have been expected to set an example for one another, including modeling self-respect and respecting others. Setting a good example also includes areas such as illustrating precision in technique, as well as sustaining high-quality energy, balance, centeredness, harmony, confidence, and goodwill. Lastly, it includes humility. The dojo teaches that no matter how confident you become, there is always more to know. The greatest martial artists are great, not for what they know, but for realizing all that is yet unknown and for their willingness to humbly pursue such knowledge. These principles apply outside the dojo as well. Others learn by watching you. Always do the best you can at the moment. Do it humbly, honorably, and spiritedly.

EXERCISE

PICK A DAY. Whatever you do, do it with the notion that you are providing an example for someone—even if no one is watching. If you see someone watching you, don't show off. Be humble. Smile. If no one is watching, smile for yourself. Honor yourself, honor what you do, and honor the universe for giving you the opportunity to participate in this life.

Alternate: Check the local papers to find a lecture or workshop to attend, and invite some coworkers to go with you. A forest develops better than an individual tree, no matter who is watching and amid all conditions. Be like a forest.

Turn Your Workspace into a Happier Place

THERE ARE PREDICTABLE work-related stressors. The most common of these are working long hours and personal conflicts. Sometimes the tasks we perform become stressful—writing, computing, sitting, standing, talking on the phone, conferencing, or lifting things for long periods. All of these activities can increase tension in muscles, bones, and joints and result in toxins that poison your system, which when recycled, can put you on a toxic roller coaster ride. However, you can fight back stress wherever you are. Your body sends cues whenever your tension levels are rising. You might feel fatigued or catch a cold, or you might develop digestive problems, headaches or other body aches; back, ligament, or joint pain; or depression. Ignoring these signals can result in even more serious prompts, such as high blood pressure, respiratory and heart disease, and even cancers. Your job is to alleviate tensions before they become chronic. This will keep your mind and body charged, positive, and comfortable.

EXERCISE

AS WITH ALL attacks, the best way to avoid conflict is to just step aside. Do nothing more. This creates a position of strength. Then evaluate. Consider what techniques will best lead to your goals and follow through.

Alternate: Try this three-step stress buster. (Three minutes max.) In a seated position, adjust your posture and regulate your breathing. Center, massaging each energy center with your breaths until you feel a slight tingle as your breath passes through each center. Make a *whhh* sound with your out-breath, and place your consciousness there in its center, outside of yourself each time. Feel your body restore itself.

Combat Fear at the Workplace

MANY PEOPLE TAKE on extra work at their jobs because they don't feel like dealing with the consequences of saying no. Some fear asking for guaranteed personal or sick days, even when they need them. Workers most commonly fear losing their job or backlash from callous management. Fear in sparring is usually related to losing—opportunity, points, or a match. It can sometimes be spurred by a fear of others—an opponent or even an instructor's criticism. Regardless of what setting you are in, fear contaminates performance. It makes you self-conscious and adds to all the other stressors. It can be your worst enemy, because it paralyzes. On the mats, it makes you do brainless things, such as freezing when a punch is coming, tripping up during your best move, or becoming unnaturally and inappropriately aggressive. Indeed, these same tendencies occur at the workplace. Dojo concepts teach you to conquer fear through self-awareness, self-confidence, and trust. You may worry, but it's worry about your *own* performance, not about the performance of others. You learn to focus on participating in the game instead of shying away. One of my coaches always used to say, "Force yourself to address these fears. Watch yourself grow."

EXERCISE

THINK ABOUT HOW conflict at the workplace is similar to sparring in the dojo. Consult the most important player in this matter—yourself. Meditate. Ask yourself what you need from the situation. Wait for a response. You may need to meditate on this more than once. Is your desire a legitimate and reasonable goal given the protocol of your employment? If yes, begin choreographing a strategy of techniques that will lead you to your objective. Allow room to modify once you have initiated action. Trust that the universe has put you in this position to help you grow. Follow through.

Retune Your Power of Perception

IF YOU SEEK the truth, you must retune your perceptions. We receive data through our senses and transmit that information to our brains. Our perception of reality is usually based on sensory records as reviewed by the brain. Of course, the brain's analysis is only as good as the information it receives and its ability to understand it. Both martial arts and science say the senses are limited instruments. If, for example, our sensory information were accurate, we would see one another quite differently. Instead of solid mass, we would see 99 percent empty space. This is science speaking, not philosophy. Deepak Chopra explains, "In just the last three weeks one quadrillion atoms have gone through your body that have gone through every other living species on the planet. So think of a tree in Africa, a squirrel in Siberia, a peasant in China, a taxi driver in Calcutta, a child in Afghanistan—and you have in your body the raw material that was circulating there just three weeks ago." At the atomic level, you are constantly exchanging memory and consciousness with everything else in the universe. If you could see yourself as you really are, you would see flickers of energy and information moving at the speed of light, energetically connected to all else.

EXERCISE

ATTUNE YOUR CONSCIOUSNESS with the Universal Body. Allow yourself more completely into this point. See yourself as that point. Let it fill your meditation. Allow your deeper awareness of this point to center into your daily actions. See the point in everything. Pick a person, a creature, or an element of nature and see it in that. Become the consciousness that you experience in that point. See how strongly connected to all things you feel.

Expand Your Ability to Heal

MARTIAL ARTS SAY that you are empowered from birth to take care of your own body, a position sustained by Eastern medicine. Both disciplines hold that immediate causes for disease can range widely— anything from climactic conditions to blood stasis. What makes you susceptible to illness and pain, whether it is physical, emotional, or spiritual, are the life events you create that disturb your flow of Chi. In contrast, when Chi is stable and strong, you ward off disease. Thus, the dojo teaches you to seek balance and harmony wherever you are. You can also tap your mind's natural ability to maintain and restore health by accessing its cosmic energy. Practices such as meditations and visualizations that center your Chi within Universal Consciousness allow you to tap in. You can learn to use this larger energy source to unblock damaged energy centers, strengthen muscles, and knock out colds, infections, and other ailments. You can feel your body restoring itself almost immediately.

EXERCISE

ATTUNE YOUR CONSCIOUSNESS with the Universal Body. Place your intention, that is direct yourself while in this mind-set to locate, align, and open unblocked energy centers or relieve pain or illness. Feel your body start recharging almost immediately. Practice this skill often. Take note of what happens.

Expand Your Ability
to Be Healed by Others

IN THE DOJO, you first see the cause/effect relationships of energy within a technique: you push, and your partner moves; you punch, and a board breaks. You then see how emotional energy affects reactions in those around you: your high-quality emotional and physical energy lifts a partner from down in the dumps, or your energy strengthens or weakens a partner's strikes or muscles up his or her immune system to ward off oncoming illness. This is a "felt" sense. It is tangible. Partners will say they need to do energy drills to shift their mood or restore their health. They know the "cure" will come from you. They seek it. You feel it, too, and enjoy participating—another example of yin-yang. Remember, such energy moves at very high speed. Thus, it travels vast distances in seconds. Effects appear almost immediately, whether in close or long ranges. This last principle is what allows you to send energy to others, relieving blockages and negative energies, even from miles away. From wherever you are, you can use your energy tools to influence family, friends, and whoever else. You can help them recharge, balance, relieve pain, and stress.

EXERCISE

THINK ABOUT SOMEONE you want to send energy to. Focus your consciousness in the Universal Body. Feel your energy centers beaming. Use a visualization to scan his or her energy centers, sensing blocks and weak or negative energy. Remember, thoughts are energy. Where your thoughts go, your Chi follows. Use your breath to fire up and extend your Chi. "Think" it to where your recipient needs it. Visualize the person as being restored.

Emotions are energy actions. Rather than strategizing, you can let your emotions do the "thinking" for you. Try sending someone thoughts of love. They work even better.

196.

Do Not Fear the Darkness

DARKNESS IS ASSOCIATED with yin energy and is necessary for all creative acts. A senior master used to like saying to me, half in jest, "What we all need is a good *endarkening*." He was referring to the idea that everyone could be more imaginative, creative, and intuitive. Planning is okay and somewhat necessary, but if you are ruled by it, you may limit your potential. In the dojo, you are encouraged to get comfortable in the dark. The exercise is not only a lot of fun and exciting, but it can also lead to significant discovery. To this end, many practitioners train their students to execute katas blindfolded. This helps you place more consciousness into the movement. It helps you see what is otherwise invisible in the light. Darkness heightens your physical awareness and the flow of energy moving through you to create your intentions. You sense blocks. You sense where you need to channel more energy and how much. These notions apply to emotional and spiritual intention as well. Darkness expands possibilities. It nurtures. It is as necessary for growth as light.

EXERCISE

START WITH SOMETHING small. The next occasion you have to make a decision "in the dark," tell yourself something good is about to happen. Ask yourself what you want from the situation. Follow that path. See where it leads. Try taking a shot "in the dark" emotionally. Try taking a similar shot in meditation.

197.

Honor the Beginner

BEGINNERS ARE ANOTHER of the universe's Zen blessings. First off, someone has come into your life to improve his or her life. This is the Wheel of Life in action. It is your opportunity to participate and bring more goodness into life. Beginners let you empty your cup while filling theirs. They are life's way of vaulting you to higher consciousness and better living. Your job is to discover the lessons. Here's an example from my own life. Some time ago, while grappling, I sustained a serious injury that kept me from performing at full capacity for months. One year later I took a new student in Chinese Kenpo. At first I was reluctant, concerned that my injury might be aggravated. I soon learned this would not be the case. My student already had a black belt in another system and was proficient. Thus, our emphasis easily turned to takedowns, throws, locks, and other various grappling techniques. His need became my opportunity to reintroduce techniques into my own training. Life will keep sending you opportunities to start anew. Take them. Everyone who enters your life is there for a purpose. Honor the process.

EXERCISE

LOOK FOR OPPORTUNITIES to share your expertise with others. Treat each opportunity as a learning experience for yourself. Ask yourself why life has sent you this particular person at this special time. What aspect of sharing your expertise is connected to your own current needs? Treat every such incident as a blessing. Look for your lessons. Observe what happens.

Remember That Good Things Come in Small Packages

SOMETIMES WE DRIVE to our destinations so quickly that we forget to enjoy the ride. Martial training is no exception. Early on, your biggest accomplishment might just be leaving your workplace even though you're tense, tired, and hungry, feeling it's a miracle that you're still sane, and mustering enough stamina to get to the dojo. In fact, there are days you can't believe you made it. A little thing like showing up at the dojo when you're not necessarily in the mood might look easy, but it's not. You do, however, get better at it. A month later you're focused mostly on technique. You earn your first belt. The month after that your focus shifts to fitness, health, and overall stability. Each of these stages carries a nugget of enlightenment. And in the end, the ultimate purpose of martial skill is to successfully lead you to spiritual enlightenment—that is, to see and experience Divinity from this side of the fence. Deepak Chopra calls this experiencing your "life as the miraculous expression of the Divine—not occasionally, but all the time." Inside the big package are all the smaller ones. Thank the universe for each one. Know that each of them was sent in love.

EXERCISE

HOW DO YOU define success in your life? How has it changed over the years? How has it remained the same? Make a list of all the various successes you have had in the past year. Send your gratitude to the universe for these.

199.

Do Good
without Thinking about It

LIKE MANY DISCIPLINES, martial arts reward good behavior and celebrate accomplishment. In fact, in the dojo you are taught that every single movement is a celebration—as is all of life. Another major tenet of martial training is to do good without thinking about it. There are two important points here. The first is that good action becomes so ingrained that it is automatic, a natural response of a reflexive mind. The second is that you are not thinking about any rewards to goodness. Nor are good deeds performed based on fear. Proper action is simply your modus operandi. Of course, you will experience more peace in life and less conflict, deeper and longer periods of contentment, more happiness, and more success at all levels. However, martial teaching says that this is the way life is *supposed* to be. This is another example of the law of paradox, which says that when you are most in synch, you are most automatic. When you are most automatic, you are most free. You are most creative. This is true everywhere in life.

EXERCISE

WHENEVER YOU CATCH yourself thinking about the good you are doing for others or yourself, smile. Begin training to act reflexively. Substitute the word "right" for "good." When things are right, they are in tune; and when things are in tune, they run smoothly and contentedly. Focus more on your feelings about an accomplishment than on the accomplishment itself. These feelings—not the badges for your deeds—are what lead to physical, emotional, and spiritual wellness.

200.

Let Yourself Shine

LET YOURSELF SHINE! Martial arts tell us there is more to this idea than just lip service. It is the basis for all healing. Many martial programs incorporate Chi Kung exercises to help boost energy. Basic practice begins with centering, tapping in to the lower *Dan Tien*, and moving Chi to those parts of the body that need immediate strengthening. However, there are levels to this practice that are so high that many basic training programs don't have the luxury of time to go there. These higher levels link elements of Chinese medicine, martial healing, and spirituality. This is where the fun really begins. Remember, Chi Kung was developed in China over three hundred years ago, with the purpose of affording warriors a way to maintain health even in the most devastating conditions. Some dojos teach this method of health maintenance by showing you how to channel Chi outside your body like a protective shield of white light. In addition, the ancients believed that this process of channeling Chi not only protects you from ill health physically, but emotionally and spiritually as well. They also believed it could be used to heal and generate deep mystical experiences. Here's how to begin.

EXERCISE

SIT, CLOSE YOUR eyes and interlock your hands placing them, palm up, on your lap. Raise them to chin level and rotate them outwardly, extending them, palm up, fully above your head as if lifting something heavy. Center. Visualize your lower *Dan Tien* radiating white. Reverse the movement, bringing your hands to your lap. Do this ten times. With your hands back on your lap, center and visualize yourself completely on fire, the flames intensifying until you can't stand it anymore. Will your Chi to hover over your skin. Visualize the white light protecting you. Sit calmly, feeling safe and radiating light.

201.

Choose Your Words Well

MARTIAL ARTS TEACH you to vanquish negativity, including downbeat language. The words you use transmit your intention (often unconsciously), even throughout the atomic structures of your cells, thus generating alterations in your body chemistry—and in the body chemistry of others as well. I recently overheard the following conversation: "This weather sucks; it's going to be a rotten winter," the first person said. "I don't know how _____ gets away with it. Everybody hates the guy." "I agree," his companion finally replied. "I've had it, too. Maybe _____ ought to retire." Then the first person said, "I don't have anything against older people. It's just that . . ." You could literally feel the negative energy filling that part of the room. Your body always listens to you, even though it may not agree. If you want to drink more alcohol than you should, your body will build a tolerance for you. It is there to serve, even if what you want is catastrophic. If you send your body messages of hate and frustration, it will do its job to depress you and lower your energy so that you can tolerate more. It will get you sick, and worse, in order to shield you from surpassing your threshold. Choose your words carefully. Send messages to create health and well-being.

EXERCISE

WHENEVER YOU SPEAK, listen to your words. Keep track of the destination of your negative words. See how they make you feel emotionally and physically. See where conversations go when you use negative words. Ask yourself, *Do I feel better or worse? Do I have higher energy or lower as a result? Do I feel more confident or less? More empowered or less?* Try to use positive language to generate positive experiences. Keep track of the destination of your positive words. Where do they go? How do you feel?

202.

Be at Peace

THE MARTIAL WAY is to be at peace. Buddha said, "Wisdom appears through a pure and peaceful mind." When you are not at peace, your ability to hear life's messages dwindles. No matter where you are, it's difficult to see your next move through a noisy mind. One major dictionary defines *peace* as a "state without war," as "accord," "calm," or "serenity." The hidden value of peace is conveyed in the term *accord,* which means "in agreement," and most importantly from that word's Latin roots: *ac* (in), *cord* (heart). Extreme emotional reactions to negative *and positive* emotions disconnect us from our heart. Indeed, many fatalities have occurred from people celebrating in ways that their heart would never desire if consulted. By embracing what is, from the heart, in quiet serenity, the peaceful mind reads life's messages moment by moment. It may see a rainy day as an opportunity to slow down, look for that new job, and begin writing that book you wanted to write, or to take a break to accompany your partner to dinner. The peaceful mind hears. It sees what to do and grows wiser.

EXERCISE

SPEND A DAY at peace. Agree to be wherever you are all day long. Silence your mind. Look for life's messages. *Consult your heart with every decision.* Act from there. Ask what was to be learned. See what happens. Love your peace. Let it nourish you and others.

203.

Transfer Energy from
One Person to Another

PERHAPS THERE IS a morsel of truth to the adage *One bad apple spoils the bunch*. Martial arts teach that energy, both good and bad, can unconsciously transfer from one person to the next. I once saw a demonstration of this concept. A master martial artist, a woman of integrity whom I admired, had volunteered to participate. My friend and her husband were invited up on the stage of a large lecture hall. The artist who was giving the presentation asked my friend to extend her arm and open her hand. The presenter pushed his hand into hers with considerable pressure, but she remained balanced. Her husband didn't fare so well. The presenter collapsed his arm with a single finger. My friend's energy was diagnosed as high, but her husband's was weak. They were then instructed to extend their arms and hold hands with each other, and the presenter collapsed them both with one push of a finger—using no tricks. The point was that my friend's husband was draining her energy. She was instructed to perform figure-eight movements with her arms to heighten her energy Then they repeated the tests and no one collapsed. My friend's heightened energy transferred to her husband. I have applied these principles outside the dojo often, especially in issues of classroom management, and kept many potentially rough days at bay.

EXERCISE

TRANSFER ENERGY IN groups. The next time you identify someone whose energy is draining, shield your energy centers by visually "zipping" them closed. Then apply a quickened version of secret 200, letting yourself shine by channeling your Chi outside your body. This will protect you and increase your Chi. Focus your attention on someone else in close proximity. Work to boost this person's energy. Once it gets going, use visualization and words to transfer your positive energy to the other person.

Learn to Give and Take Energy

HAVE YOU EVER had someone take your energy away with a stare? Or energize you with a glance? The notion of giving (and taking) energy in martial arts is important. Many dojo drills consciously transfer energy from one person to the next. These drills are usually carried out through physical exercises. Martial arts, however, have more hidden ways to accomplish this. You can learn to give and take energy with your power of intention, simply willing it. In the same demonstration of transferred energy referenced in secret 203, other participants were dramatically strengthened or weakened just by thought. Here's how. A person whose energy tested strong was invited on stage. The audience was asked to collectively think that the person was growing weaker. The presenter pushed him to the mats with a single finger, despite his attempt to resist. What happened in this demonstration puts a different light on the notion of self-fulfilling prophecies. Group thought will transfer energetically to individuals. It can be used to strengthen or weaken—in the dojo, at home, at work, or wherever.

EXERCISE

THE NEXT TIME you are in a situation with someone whose energy is overeager or perhaps destructive, visualize the person's energy channels. Examine the quality of each channel. Identify which of them release coarse, unstable light. First use your thoughts to heighten your own energy, and then to deplete the negative energy. See how this works.

Alternate: In a group situation, try to shift the group's mind-set toward a particular person you are attempting to detoxify. See what happens when everyone is thinking positively in that person's direction.

Watch Others
and See What Works

YOU LEARN A lot in the dojo by watching others. The hope is, of course, that what is good rubs off and what is not good teaches you what to avoid. It's common for instructors to ask you to observe several players execute the same technique, even with techniques you already use, so that you can see different variations and add them to your toolbox. Sometimes you see effective actions that are radically different from yours. For example, maybe your idea of countering a kick is with another kick and some punches. Then you see someone use a flying scissor kick that evolves into an effective takedown. When you try it, the technique winds up becoming one of your favorites. Watching others works in everyday life as well. Witnessing is energetically part of evolving.

EXERCISE

TREAT YOURSELF TO a lecture, course, manual, or other instruction in order to watch others attempt to achieve some of the same goals you have. This may involve skills you can use to enhance any aspect of your life. You choose. But observe how someone else goes about trying to reach the goal. Keep an open mind and you will walk away with good information. You will either add to your tools or learn what to avoid. Sometimes, thinking out of the box will guide you along yet another path before you can acquire what you need. The process can get kind of exciting. Don't be surprised if something you at first thought was useless—information, technique, or the like— winds up being most effective somewhere down the line. These blessings occur often.

Help Others
Achieve Their Goals

MOST MARTIAL NOVICES are self-conscious when asked to partner with someone for the first time. Your thoughts race: "What will my partner think when he sees how bad my technique is? What will my instructor think when she sees how much more proficient my partner is? I feel like a stick next to him. I feel clumsy next to her." But most of us get over these hang-ups. Once you feel yourself increasing your energy, confidence, and general skill, you bond with your partner. You learn to show your weaknesses because you know your partner is there for you. Asking for help becomes easy. You become a better listener. You start to sense your partner's needs intuitively. You help him or her without being obvious. At first you may help as a sort of payback. Then you make a quantum leap. You help because if simply feels right and good.

EXERCISE

MAKE A GOAL of listening to your partners more closely. If they ask for help, give it the best you can. Try to facilitate without their asking, without being obvious, wanting nothing in return—simply to enjoy the process.

Know Your History

MARTIAL ARTS EMPHASIZE historical lineage. This emphasis on history preserves ancestry, but it also provides root concepts—without which it is difficult to put technique into action. Here's an example. I was sitting in a coffeehouse when I heard three people discussing what they would do if someone pulled a knife. One fellow said, "I'd raise my arm and block it." A woman sitting at their table asked, "Where did you learn that?" He chuckled, "From old martial arts movies." "I study martial arts," the woman said. "I wouldn't do that unless we were both wearing armor—no one fights that way anymore." She was right. I hoped the "movie warrior" would never have to test his thinking. The technique he'd seen was historically trained with armor as well as learning how to "take a cut." So, you would think, *Well, that won't work anymore.* But the root concept is still functional: defend your highline, and strike your opponent's mid lines or low lines. Many families, coworkers, and others pass down models for behavior without rooting them in concept. So what do you do? The answer is to *reroot the concept.* In the dojo, you tap elders, old texts, or very carefully and authentically reenact techniques—a process that is necessary in daily life as well.

EXERCISE

IDENTIFY AN ISSUE you are having difficulty resolving. Ask yourself what skills you are using to help. Identify their source. Are the concepts adaptable to your current situation? If not, how are things different? Try this:

- Interpret the original concept.
- Practice using it—in real time or through visualization.
- Reinterpret the technique so it works for you.

Check Your Baggage
at the Door

WHEN YOU ENTER the dojo, you check your baggage at the door. If you don't, you are reminded. The word "baggage," of course, means more than personal belongings and other physical items. It means that you are not there to discuss business, a coworker who is bothering you, a diet that is not working, or other personal concerns. Pollutants of this sort contaminate good effort, anywhere. Some practitioners take awhile to get used to this mind-set. Everyone, of course, can fall back to old patterns from time to time. But you eventually learn to transform and strengthen your focus. You realize that by participating in behaviors that create patterns or guides for positive energy, your weaknesses go away much quicker and easier. So you relentlessly try to make your next move positive—and the next move, and the next, and so on. Thus, your first move is to start clean. Outside the dojo, you can resolve daily problems the same way. Check your baggage at the door, and watch dilemmas dissolve.

EXERCISE

CREATE A NEW pattern for entering, whether at home, at work, or wherever you go today. Put all preconceptions, problems, assumptions, urges, and so on in a mental bag, and leave it outside before walking in. Take note of what happens.

209.

Defeat Ignorance

IGNORANCE IS NOT bliss; instead, ignorance keeps you from achieving bliss: "I got pinned because *my opponent* knows ground fighting." *"My employer* is making my life miserable." *"My family* is exhausting me." *The warrior defeats ignorance by looking in the mirror.* I was ruffled the first time I heard this martial anthem. But it is so. Ignorance is a trickster. It makes itself seem advantageous. It makes you feel safe. Defeating it makes you reclaim what's real. For example, you may want a happy family life, but your pattern is exhaustion—wherever you go. Exhaustion keeps you from having to find leisure time for your family, and that may require confronting your employer, but you fear doing that. So you send your body, family, and the rest of the world false messages that you're okay. Doing so, however, readily creates protective patterns (as does your family) to depress you, so that you won't lose more energy or trips into bizarre overactivity, so that you appear burnt out. You blame your family. But you are electing to stay ignorant to the actual cause: what's making you behave this way is a fear of your employer. In this example, blaming your family only distances you from the life you really want. Ignorance steals bliss.

EXERCISE

RECLAIM YOUR BLISS! Consider something you really want but are struggling to attain. Look at your behaviors. What is really keeping you ignorant as far as finding a way to achieve your goal? Once you identify the source of ignorance, use your martial skills to create a strategy that will lead to its defeat.

210.

Understand Desire

FOR OVER THREE millenniums martial arts have taught what scientific research is now beginning to support—that you can affect daily events from the quantum level, what we call the Universal Body. Key to channeling quantum energy is your understanding of desire's two faces: specific and general. For example, if you're hungry and suddenly crave a doughnut, that's a specific desire. Or perhaps you get into an argument, and later you want to apologize. So you invite the other person over for dinner, but it doesn't work. That's also specific. General desire is: *I'm hungry. Let's eat. Where? I'm open.* Or, *I want peace. How? I'm open; show me.* Either approach energizes a situation into action. Desire creates intention—consciously or unconsciously, your choice. Intention activates energy at the quantum level (the Universal Body). Remember all those atoms you're exchanging with the planet? These atoms generate actions that lead to results. The martial Way is to remain open and *let specific solutions emerge.* Your job is to silence your mind. Place general desire(s) in the mind of the universe and watch with awe as it happens. The better you get at this, the more fulfillment you will find.

EXERCISE

IDENTIFY WHAT YOU generally desire: abundance, health, employment, and so on. Don't concern yourself with specifics. Do, however, remain present to windows of opportunity as they begin opening to you. Take advantage of them. See what happens. When your mind is open, all things are possible. Make this your daily mind-set.

211.

Use Memory

HAVE YOU EVER inexplicably become skillful at something—as if out of nowhere? This phenomenon can be related to your internal energy system. Chi is energy and carries information. Science tells us that when subatomic particles rub together, they exchange this information—in fact, they exchange their entire history. Thus, the entire quantum field, or Universal Body, is alive and growing in experience and information, just as we are. It's as if your being's "computer" were automatically updating its hardware and software every millisecond of the day. This happens so quickly that you can't see or hear it, although the process occurs every day, all day long. When you're lucky, *the unexplainable calls the updating process to your attention,* which means that life is speaking to you. Within you, there exists very ancient memory that you can tap at will. Martial arts teach you to use this memory. Remember, your brain's energetic reactions are the same whether an experience is imagined or real. Memories, recent as well as ancient, are guides for biological, emotional, and spiritual functions. When you use memory, you energetically invoke a specific guide to achieve what you want. This is what it means to be master of your own fate.

EXERCISE

CONSIDER A GOAL you are struggling to attain—anything from warding off sickness to establishing or maintaining good relationships. Ask yourself what memories you have that will empower you. These can be experiences that have happened in your daily life or to your acquaintances, things you've experienced in reading, movies, television, songs, hikes—anything! Don't think too much about the process. But do take a good inventory. Look more for an overall empowering energy emanating from each memory. Call that energy forth. Feel it to achieve your goals.

Don't Let Memory Use You

WHEN MEMORY USES you, you are not in charge. Your actions are being triggered for you. For example, if someone confronts you, you bristle. If you miss a favorite television show, you instantly become angry. Or if you happen to meet someone you are immediately disappointed. Such reactions may stem from previously remembered experiences. Harmful and sometimes hidden templates or patterns of behavior trigger such actions. These are created by a number of sources—for example, ego (what you think should be), people in your environments (remember, energy transfers memory), all living things everywhere (remember, you continuously exchange information with everything on the planet). The possibilities are energetically endless, and this is what keeps life so infinitely interesting. You can override any of these reactions, whether in the dojo or out, by consulting your innermost self. It is your weapon against anything that attempts to restrict your freedom to choose happiness over unhappiness, harm over abundance. Your innermost self will not be controlled. It will steer you toward freedom. Martial arts train you to be master of your own fate. Learn to conquer those memories that use you.

EXERCISE

CONSIDER A CURRENT goal. What memories is your life working from that are creating the outcome? Once you recognize these memories, you can choose to bypass them if they present an obstacle. Ask yourself what memories would instead empower you toward your goal. Choose to operate from these empowering memories as patterns. If you don't have any relevant memories, read literature, watch movies, do anything that will reveal information that can empower you. Use this information to generate new patterns. Think over your goal several times with your new patterns, fine-tuning them. Then apply.

Assess Your Environment

PROTECTING YOURSELF INVOLVES seeing and planning for potentially dangerous situations before they occur. This enables you to avoid harm and to increase your choices for response if a potentially precarious situation should arise. Identify where you are and what the rules are in the situation. For example, are you in a ring sparring with martial rules? Or does your opponent think you are in a street fight where there are no rules? Are you being taken by surprise? Are you outnumbered? What are your vulnerabilities? Is there an escape route? What action can you take? Certain environments allow for certain actions—and sometimes make others difficult or even impossible. For example, if the ground is littered with broken glass and chemical contaminants, you'd be hard pressed to find anyone wanting to play judo. There are some settings where threats are almost predictable. The good martial artist will avoid these settings at all cost. But sometimes incidents require more aggressive, disarming action. To this end, the good martial artists will act swiftly to prevent situations from escalating and bring them to successful conclusion. Give yourself choice. Assess your environment upon entry.

EXERCISE

ASSESS THE ENVIRONMENTS you are in on a daily basis. If you sense there are no potentially dangerous situations, it's okay to let your guard down, but not your presence. Often, threats can be dissolved simply by how you conduct yourself. Do you radiate power and confidence, or do you appear to be an easy target? If a real threat is probable, ask yourself, *What kind of predicament is most likely, given the environment? What type can reasonably be eliminated? What disarming techniques would be most effective?* Increase your defense options. This experience will strengthen your intuition. This generates the rapid judgment you need to avoid escalating a situation and end it quickly and safely.

214.

Move Like You're
the Only Motion in the Universe

MARTIAL TRAINING TEACHES you to express yourself with your choice of movement. I remember my own instructor saying to me, "Move like you're the only motion in the universe." He was teaching me how to flow more fluidly from one posture to another as I performed katas. Well, at least that is what I thought back then. Ah, the rewards of martial training are truly never ending. I don't think a day goes by when I don't thank that instructor with all I have. At any rate, his maxim worked. And then it flowered and flowered, sending my Earth dojo experiences to another level. Yes, I developed more grace, and with that came strength and proficiency. But one day the truly unexpected happened and I entered the Universal dojo. The notion of there being only one movement in the universe took on a whole other meaning.

EXERCISE

CREATE A MOVEMENT using your hands, arms, and legs. Maybe you will trace huge figure eights in the air, maybe a tree or flower, a bird's flight, your name—you create. Move as slowly as possible at first so you can see the tiniest idiosyncrasy of your movement. Visualize the smallest details. Center and regulate your breathing. Love your energy. Love the universe for sharing energy with you. Be grateful beyond words. Create an image of thanks—perhaps a flash of white light—that you can energetically release into the heavens. Make this your image, your language. Open all of your energy centers and feel.

215.

Be Plentiful with Compliments

WANT TO MIX a little energy potion and watch it work? Try complimenting someone. In the dojo, you compliment a lot. It feels good to hear praise. Compliments boost a player's energy, as well as the energy of the entire place. Team athletes everywhere know this. Coaches know this. Praise generates better performance. It is, in effect, another example of energy transfer and what you can do with it. It works because you are weaving positive energy with your words and energetically directing them to those around you. Complimenting is easy. It works magic. Everyone feels better. Everyone wins.

EXERCISE

LOOK FOR SOMETHING worthy of praise wherever you go. Share that thought with others who are around. Try to find something complimentary to say to the people you meet throughout your day. Take note of how the positive energy from your compliment moves through them. Watch for changes in their body language. See their eyes brighten, a smile emerge, their breath even, and their mood lighten. Do this often. It is great energy medicine.

Stop Bad Behavior Early On

TAKE INVENTORY OF faulty postures early on so as not to train in bad form. In the dojo, your instructor observes your technique very closely, looking for any weakness so that it can be corrected immediately. The last thing you want to do is train a liability or become proficient at putting yourself at disadvantages. But, whether on the mats or in daily life, we have all seen people do such things—and with expertise. Indeed, there isn't anyone in the Earth dojo who hasn't caught himself or herself in such a role. The whole idea behind training is to identify movement that works and repeat it over and over until the pattern sinks in to your muscle memory. Emotional and spiritual action works the same way. Repetition will create memory and generate patterns that will command future actions. Be aware of new patterns as they begin to emerge. This is your easiest time to head off weak behavior.

EXERCISE

TAKE TWENTY MINUTES at the end of your day. Find a quiet space and relax. Center. Breathe slowly, inhaling through your nose and exhaling through your mouth. Visualize a universe of sparkling energy flickering full of information and joy. Feel all of life flowing through you—things seen and unseen. Focus your attention on drawing positive energy into your body and mind. When you feel restored, reflect on your day, especially on things you tried to accomplish. Even if you reached your goals, ask if there was anything in your actions that could be adjusted next time to make things happen more fluidly. Note: Don't get down on yourself. Remember, life sends you lessons that often appear as mistakes. This is the Way illuminating your next leap of consciousness. Praise yourself as soon as you see it.

Train Alone

MARTIAL ARTISTS SPEND many hours training with others. But you also need to train alone, working on such skills as leg and hand movements or generating, summoning, and channeling Chi, meditations, or visualizations. You look for ways, some quite hidden, to connect the dots. You're panning for gold, hunting down what Joseph Campbell calls that "elite experience" that will sweeten your life even more with what martial arts call a flash of enlightenment. First flashes commonly deal with sparring. For instance, perhaps you move your arms in flowing figure eights and see how to use the same motion to block two oncoming punches with one arm. You try your technique in the dojo. To your delight, it works. Is something spiritual happening? Your epiphanies increase. They become more important. Seeing the benefits, you go to your solo "space" more frequently. And the cycle continues. You *see*, then *test*, then *refine*. Physical enlightenment never stops. Indeed, it leads to emotional and spiritual epiphany. Remember yin-yang. Alone time (yin) feeds your creative energy. Be alone. Test your visions (yang). Go back and create more (yin). This is the Wheel of Life.

EXERCISE

GIVE YOURSELF AN hour of time. Take a good walk, hike, swim, or drive— or do some inside or outside work, anything you like that frees your mind. Think about a favorite martial lesson. Don't force a circumstance to apply it to. But if a circumstance, real or imagined, comes, let it happen. Don't analyze, just let it float by, looking for nothing except the opportunity to try to perfect your martial concept. See what happens. Try this at least three times a week. Feel free to choose different concepts. Ideas will bubble up that are related to daily issues. Recall these later. Test them. See how they enhance or resolve issues in your daily life.

218.

Choose a Good Partner

FINDING A GOOD partner is important, in the dojo as well as in life. Close interaction offers you opportunity to use, refine, and grow in your skills. Partners use each other to learn how to stay balanced while responding effectively to unpredictable life actions—to power up for everyday routines and generating success. Good partners push you when you need it and know when to back off. A good partner works with you toward achieving mutual interests, never against you or in competition with you. A good partner helps you overcome weaknesses without criticism, but also without lip service. Dojo partners won't "take the fall," pretending your technique worked if it didn't. Good partners are happy when you tag them and assume you'll be happy if they stop you—exposing what's holding you back so you can correct it. Likewise, good partners adjust to each other's proficiencies. If your kicks fly at seventy-five miles an hour, you don't go full bore on a new partner. Can you imagine? Good partners never intentionally hurt you. If they do, you forgive them immediately because you know it's the last thing they ever want. Have fun with your partner.

EXERCISE

THE BEST WAY to find a good partner is to be a good partner to someone else. Do something special for your partner today.

Go Light When Your Partner Isn't "On"

THERE ARE TIMES partners just aren't "on." They enter the dojo and simply can't focus. They may botch drills, miss targets, or slip up on a technique they usually could do blindfolded. So you bring out the target mitts. But still there's no concentration. Now your own performance starts to nosedive. Flags go up. This is when you remember that you are not in combat, fighting for your life. If you were, you would follow a different path. You are, however, in the dojo. You are with your friend. It's time to slow down activity rather than risk injury. I'm not a fan of giving up your own focus, though. The way to help another person is to enhance your own strength, not to diminish it. Your job is to remain centered and balanced—especially when your partner is at an impasse—so don't force anything. Accept your partner's present performance and work with it. Focus on helping your partner to realign. You may have to take time out to respond to his or her needs. If your partner wants to be coaxed out, push, pull, and do whatever you have to do. But if not, go light. *Easy* should be the word of the day.

EXERCISE

THE NEXT TIME your partner is having an off day, rather than risk a faulty performance, take a time out. Focus on helping your partner regain a sense of balance. Follow his or her lead. If you need to be aggressive, do so. If you need to go easy, do that.

220.

Know When to Attach

ATTACHMENT IS A favorite tactic in kung fu. It means stick-to-itiveness. Many novices, however, work this concept by haphazardly grabbing their opponents any way they can in an attempt to gain position. They have a goal in mind and shoot for it, jumping the gun by acting before they should. This tactic will often land them at a disadvantage, if not on their butt. Generating your own real window of opportunity is half the battle. You do this by sharpening your attention, remaining calm, and maintaining some light contact, or attachment, as you wait, tapping away anything that isn't real enough to launch technique. Marital arts refer to this as your "bridge." Just as in life, you don't want to burn your bridge, because it is what will eventually make all else possible. Eventually the right shot comes into your centerline. This is the one you've been looking for. You attach yourself to your partner, softly at first, as if you are surfing his energy. When you have redirected the action for optimum positioning, you take your shot, powerfully and decisively.

EXERCISE

INSTEAD OF JUST jumping into conversations, wait. Stay relaxed and alert. Let your partner speak. Make yourself sensitive to how near your partner is coming to what really matters, what the conversation is really about. Until then, offer some very light and short responses to statements that catch your attention. This will create a bridge, an attachment, between you and your partner. When he or she enters the heart of the matter, make your move—gently positioning the conversation for optimum results. Then make your pitch. People's reactions are different. Thus, the more people you work this skill with, the better you will get at it.

Share Discoveries

MUCH OF WHAT we know in the martial arts had been passed down through direct experience, from mentor to student and so on. Sharing is important. First off, it's fun. It's your chance to test your discovery, see what works, what needs work, where else you can go with it. A lot of techniques stay basic until you share them repeatedly. Then one day you see their higher functions—and of course, martial practice says there are no limits to what you can do with your techniques. What's more, sharing offers you an opportunity to observe your ideas as other people interpret them. No one else will see or feel your ideas *exactly* the same as you. Interpretations often lead to further discovery. Sharing accelerates growth. It is natural. It is a win–win situation all around.

EXERCISE

THE NEXT TIME you make a discovery, regarding anything from self-improvement to office-related procedures, share your finding with someone of mutual interest. Give that person time to respond fully without arguing for your position. Remember that one of the joys of putting new information out there is to see what others do with it. Then take that information, retool your skills, and put them in your toolbox for future use.

Nurture Yourself before Workouts

YOU HAVE TO do a little mental training before a workout session begins. Motivation is key. But before you can motivate yourself, you need to drain any tensions you might have. You need to turn off the day's intensity. Slowing down is important. You breathe deeply, walk slower, and calm and relax your mind. Some martial artists like giving themselves more time before starting a session to listen to music. In the dojo, everyone does a regimen of stretches. Others, myself included, like doing katas to help shift. You ask yourself what you hope to accomplish during the session that will, by day's end, make you a slightly better player. You use visualizations to see yourself moving more fluidly, kicking faster and higher, and punching with more power. You use positive words to start revving your engines, telling yourself, *"Be strong, breathe, keep going, walk straight, shine!"* This is all part of energetically programming your body to do what athletes call "warm-up." Repetition will generate biological and mental patterns so that you will start kicking into warm-up mode automatically. Such encoding is useful in all daily situations.

EXERCISE

BEFORE ENGAGING IN any of the day's activities, tell yourself to slow down. Try giving yourself extra time to get to where you are going. Relax. Breathe in whatever way feels natural to you, but breathe deeply. Listen to your favorite music on the way if you can and if you are in the mood. Set some reasonable goals for yourself regarding the activity. Tell yourself that every little thing you do to bring yourself closer to those goals is a success. Remind yourself that you will be enjoying those successes afterward. Create your own word collection that you can use to help boost your energy and maintain your focus during your pursuit. Visualize yourself flowing through the activity with ease.

Nurture Yourself
after Workouts

DOJO WORKOUTS USUALLY end with a short meditation. You are pumped and need this time to regulate energy. Some players don't consider this time part of training, but it is and it's important. *You are training your body to restore itself.* Repeating a routine designed to rebalance will create appropriate patterns. You will program your body to know when to go into cool-down mode. This will enable you to feel refreshed after a task instead of wiped out. Whether in the dojo or in daily routines, you need to let your body tap its natural capacity to stabilize. What's more, the physical and mental euphoria you will feel by enhancing your restoration mechanisms is one of life's great pleasures—a sort of payback for hard work. Be there. Celebrate your success.

EXERCISE

AFTER ENGAGING IN any of the day's activities, take a moment to meditate, even if just for three minutes. Feel the energy that you have generated from acting in positivity. Circulate it throughout your body. Feel it nourishing you, restoring you. Use positive words to praise yourself for your good work. Visualize positive energy radiating beyond yourself and extending through your environment. Think of someone special, and send that positive energy to him or her. Smile. Go to your next destination feeling light, healthy, and positive.

Pay Attention to Sparring Dreams

SPARRING DREAMS ARE one of martial arts' most entertaining and coveted phenomenon. They even made an appearance in the popular Bruce Lee movie, *Dragon: The Bruce Lee Story*. Indeed, Lee keeps having a recurring dream in which he is pitted against a masked challenger. He uses martial skills to defeat his opponent, but he never quite has the right moves. Of course, he has no idea why he is having this dream. And unless you have begun training in martial philosophy, such dreams may appear to be truly fictional. But once you start, you find yourself in just the kind of dream sequence that Carl Jung and Joseph Campbell would have loved. Here's why: dreams eventually expose the very information that is keeping you from being everything you want to be. This is necessary information, according to both Jung and Campbell, for living free and blissful lives. If you are having these dreams, pat yourself on the back. You are about to make a quantum leap of consciousness.

EXERCISE

WHEN YOU HAVE a dream in which you are in danger, notice where the dream is set. What emotions do you encounter within the dream? After? Visualize the characters. Do you see any emotional parallels between your dream's set and characters and your own daily routines? What did you fear in your dream? What made you feel good? It is important to replay this dream in your memory, calling on appropriate martial skills to help you overcome any adversities. Repeat this process until you feel confident of a strategy that will lead to your goals. *Repetition will successfully create your pattern.* Tell yourself that more success is just around the corner.

Pay Attention When Sparring Dreams Go Away

GET PSYCHED. YOUR warrior skills are working just as they should! Your inner warrior has learned to, in effect, conquer aspects of your personal life that have been keeping you from soaring. What I liked about *Dragon: The Bruce Lee Story* was that the movie addressed the hidden meaning of such dreams. Psychologists and mythologists call these hidden meanings elements of your ego—that part of you that wants to keep you small, fearful, and dependent. In the same spirit, *Dragon* shows that as Lee defeats his inner fears and dependencies, he immediately becomes freer and stronger externally. This, of course, is the martial Way. Be attentive to sparring dreams that go away. *You are winning the battle to which all martial training ultimately leads. You are defeating your own inner fears and dependencies. You are taking control of your life.*

EXERCISE

DO SOMETHING TO celebrate. You have just done something terrific. You have defeated the worrier inside you. Enjoy your freedom.

226.

Don't Chase a Decoy

FEINTS, OR DECOYS, are nice, as long as they aren't being used against you. Feints and decoys are intentional *offensive* moves, one of the oldest and most effective sparring tactics for controlling others. Feints open opponents' defenses and position them right where you want. For example, if your partner is standing in front of you, you can just whip both your arms out to the sides, palms facing out, and most partners will raise their hands, thus opening and completely exposing their centerline. This principle also holds off of the mats. For example, a college student of mine recently asked for exemption from a test (while it was in progress), saying he had had insufficient funds to purchase the textbook—two months previously. Meanwhile, the book was available for free in the college library and in my office. I paused until I saw the vulnerability in his thinking. I took my time explaining it to him. There were two separate issues: his finances and his poor judgment. He agreed. If I had chased his decoy, he wouldn't have learned anything and I would have been duped. We came up with a plan to acquire the book and complete the course in very good standing. That day we both won and learned.

EXERCISE

INCREASE YOUR ATTENTION in conversations. Notice how many feints people throw your way in an attempt to posture themselves and you. Pause whenever you see one of these feints coming. See the decoy for what it is. Then choose your next action. Now you're calling the shots. After you make your move, vary your timing—that is, pause more often, whenever you need it, but also randomly, to prevent other decoys. When someone can't recognize your patterns, he or she can't launch as many effective feints.

227.

Know Your Aptitudes

APTITUDES ARE ANOTHER way life talks to you. They tell you who you are and what you are here to do. The dojo is rich with stories of people recognizing their aptitudes. For example, players come in thinking their whole game is going to be punching. Then one day they realize they are terrific grapplers. The only reason they didn't see this before was that they feared sparring on the ground, so they never tried it. Daily life happens this way, too. Say you were very good at math in high school, but you are also drawn to athletics and fine arts, such as music and literature. You wonder which of these disciplines is you. You go to college to pursue studies in science and math. You play in an orchestra to finance your education. You begin to feel drawn more toward literature, so you switch and earn a degree in English. Based on your communication and math skills, you end up working for a steel company. Who would have thought? This finances another degree, in writing this time. Years later you see that math has always played a role in your successes. Now you welcome it into your life. You go on to write a best-selling book. It is such an extension of who you are that you would have done it for free. Just don't tell your publisher that.

EXERCISE

TAKE SOME TIME to list all of your aptitudes. Thank the universe for these. Map how each strength has surfaced in your life thus far. Consider a variety of fun projects that can draw upon all of them. Pursue one of these projects. Watch what happens.

Know Your Opponent's Aptitudes

A GENERAL RULE of sparring is to identify your opponent's main game and stay away from it unless you can outplay him at his own game. If a player is twice your weight, don't get into a situation where he or she can use weight against you. If he or she is fast, take the person through territories where speed becomes secondary. You certainly don't play peek-a-boo with this player, unless you're looking for someone to knock the water out of your ears. Indeed, you scan your mental hard drive for techniques to help you counter your opponent's speed. In the ring, you try to maintain a high alert for ways to keep "Speedy" at bay and on escape routes if he or she should come at you. You look to create or discover opportunities to employ your speed-disabling techniques. You spar scientifically, as they say. Knowing an adversary's aptitudes off the mats helps you create advantage as well. Stay safe. Generate opportunity. Spar scientifically.

EXERCISE

THE NEXT TIME you sense a rival in daily life, consider your opponent's aptitudes. Don't spar where these strengths can be activated. Say you are competing for a position at work and your opponent is a good public speaker. Don't ask your boss to observe an oral presentation unless your skill is superior to that of your competition or you can get some fantastic preparatory training. Perhaps researching is part of the new job description. This is an area where *you* excel. Consider sharing a current research project with your boss. You have choices. You can extend your credentials by beefing up and updating skills in which your rival currently has an edge. Perhaps you have untapped aptitude here. Maybe you just need a workshop or class in a particular area. It's good to find out. Or you can move the play over to where your best shots are.

229.

Remember That a
Little Knowledge Can Be Useful

JUST AS IN LIFE, the dojo is filled with wonderful irony. I can't tell you how many times I have seen players get out of a potentially disastrous clutch situation at the last second by using a concept they only knew a little about. Everybody has been this player. You have an enormous martial arts demonstration and you are coming down with flu. You have never tried using your internal energy center for warding off illness, but have heard that if you can discover and eliminate blockage, you can sustain health. You have heard about using visualization and tapping blocked areas. You're not 100 percent sure how to do it, but you go with what you've got. It works. Having the nerve to try something you don't fully grasp has made all the difference in the world for people in all facets of life. In health fields, such thinking fuels self-examination and early detection of what can be serious illness. At times, even a little knowledge protects.

EXERCISE

TRY THIS EXERCISE the next time you're in a pinch situation, especially if you have been there before and not been happy with results. It can be an area of conflict or an area of pleasure you would like to enhance. List the obvious concepts to achieve your goals. Then consider related areas of good information you may only know a little about. Center. Ask yourself which of these you have a good sense about. Pick those that intuition tells you will be best, and try them. See what happens. Consider training in those areas that work for you and adding them to your full-time toolbox.

Remember That a Little Knowledge Can Be Harmful

YOU HAVE TO be careful when acting on partial information. Minor dojo injuries often occur this way. In Kali, a martial art that uses rattan sticks, many instructors start you off with cardboard replicas of the weapons until you've mastered postures. In other arts, you practice certain katas for years and then one day are handed swords and instructed to complete movements as though the blades were an extension of your hands. You are pleasantly surprised because without knowing, you have been mastering a beautiful dance of swords. In everyday life it is important more often than not to have competency in an action before attempting it. Sometimes there are exceptions. For instance, if you're under attack and your life is in danger, you may *have to* pick up a sword and protect yourself even if you haven't mastered the technique. Yet, when risk is low, you stand to gain by waiting until you acquire sufficient knowledge. This keeps both you and others safe.

EXERCISE

CONSIDER AN IMPORTANT endeavor that you will be embarking upon in the near future. List the best skills you can employ to see the job to successful completion. Are there any skills that you could further hone? How can you acquire more information? Can you consult a colleague? Read a text? Attend a workshop or lecture? Do what is necessary to gather as much information as you can. Then follow through.

Celebrate Your Achievements

MOST MARTIAL SYSTEMS offer some means to mark a person's achievement. Traditionally our various levels of accomplishment are marked with different colored belts or sashes that range from white (the lowest level) to black (the highest level). The number of colors depends on the school and instructor. Some schools use a myriad of rainbow colors, while others use only white and black, and still others use white, brown, and black. Some systems use patches or stripes instead or in addition to belts or sashes. The point is that awarding people for competence in technique and self-development is common. Overall, there are three levels to the martial journey: *basic,* where you seek to improve your life and the techniques that will get you there; *intermediate,* where you seek to employ your skills and see results; and *advanced,* where you seek the highest levels of presence, spontaneity, and joy by learning to conduct your actions not only without any strain, but also without any expectation. Ranking is intended to encourage you to forge toward higher levels of achievement and to offer occasion to pause and celebrate.

EXERCISE

CONSIDER THE LEVELS listed above, from basic to advanced. Mark your own achievement in terms of belt color or some other way as you progress toward your black belt in life. Give yourself feedback on how you have progressed and how you can continue on to even higher levels of living. Celebrate well. Do remember all the smaller achievements that have led to these major ranks along the way.

Celebrate the Achievements of Others

IS THIS A private celebration, or can anybody join in? In the dojo, the answer to this question is easy: *celebration of one is celebration for all.* There is a practical element to this attitude. By taking pleasure in the joy of others, you encourage further successes and assure more positivity in your immediate environment and beyond. Celebrating the achievements of others is also a natural part of the Wheel of Life. It is your way of creating harmony and the best way of assuring that celebratory events will occur for you, too. This is also true in daily life.

EXERCISE

REFLECT UPON THE achievements of several people you know. This will give you insight as to how you can best interrelate with them. It will help you fit in and create harmony. Indeed, we can learn from those who have greater expertise than we do in areas we wish to explore. Likewise, we can gently assist others toward their goals when we are the holders of expertise in which they are interested—the objective, however, is purely *their* success. Try to make any assistance you offer as selfless and invisible as possible.

Encourage Others to Express Themselves Authentically

IMAGINE A ROOM full of karate, kung fu, aikido, Tae Kwon Do, and judo players. This is what most martial art expositions look like. Martial arts teach that life itself is a continuous flow seeking self-expression. It is 100 percent natural to want to put your real self into every action. One of the best things you can do for others is encourage them to do the same. It's simple and healthy; when others think you know where they are coming from, they feel good. You don't even have to agree, just try to understand. This helps others gain confidence as well as discover their higher potentials. When you don't try to understand others, they won't trust you. This makes tasks twice as difficult, because people begin contributing less enthusiastically. They may even stop listening. Going with the flow means that people cross paths for a reason. By encouraging others to express themselves fully and genuinely you achieve the best of possibilities from each of life's moments. Paradoxically, guaranteeing another person's freedom is how to sustain your own. Such environments are good for physical and emotional health, reducing stress, lowering heart rate and blood pressure, and warding off a variety of other stress-related illnesses. Bowing to life is accepting the diversity of Divinity within each of us.

EXERCISE

MAKE A DAILY contribution to your personal health and well-being. Help others express themselves authentically. See how you open the range of positive input from others both at work and at play. See how much more you will accomplish. Observe how smoothly things get done.

234.

Always Do Your Best

THE MARTIAL ATTITUDE is to go for your best—at all times. But in the dojo, this isn't always easy. You have your goals. The session starts. Circumstances take on whatever nature they will have for the day. Doing your best redefines itself moment by moment. While you're stretching out, you discover that a shin splint you developed while jogging the day before is still haunting you. You do your best by stretching longer and slower. You ask if anyone has special stretches you can try. Someone shows you one. You do it. It helps marginally. You are scheduled to perform a kata that day for the class. You're sore and tight. You remember the last time you had a splint—you couldn't even finish the kata without stopping. You assess your goals. Your new goal is to finish without interruption and make things look as painless as possible. You hurt, but you do it and end with a smile. You've done your best. You know you wouldn't have been satisfied any other way. You radiate. Fellow practitioners applaud your radiance. Remember the law of karma: when you do your best, you receive the best. This is true in the Earth dojo as well.

EXERCISE

TAKE A MOMENT-BY-MOMENT scan of things. When unexpected incidents, people, and feelings emerge throughout your day, let your goals shift accordingly. This may mean ignoring the unexpected, addressing it and moving on, or changing your goals entirely. Decide what is best for each circumstance. Deliver. Radiate. Smile. See how you feel.

Avoid Self-Abuse

CHALLENGE IN MARTIAL training is good; abuse is not. Indeed, training is aimed at defeating those behaviors that are abusive to either yourself or others. The "no pain, no gain" anthem has some merit, but not to an extreme. Nevertheless, every dojo encounters people who push themselves irrationally. This is a psychological condition in athletics that is comparable in scope to anorexia or bulimia. Abuses range from practitioners training so hard they pass out from dehydration and fatigue to drug and hormone abuse. I recently heard a story of a tennis player who worked himself so far beyond his physical capacity that he tore holes in his lung tissue. The dojo is not immune to such tragedies. The irony of using tools intended to lead to self-improvement and enlightenment as a means to your demise is unacceptable. It violates a core principle of the martial Way: whether in the dojo or in daily routines, your body is a temple of Divine energy. Treat it with respect. Treat it well.

EXERCISE

CONSIDER YOUR LAST week. Did you make any attempts at self-improvement that you feel were headed to an extreme? List them. When you do things to an extreme, the tendency is to lose sight of the big picture. For example, what good is taking steroids to improve a game if it destroys your family or takes your life? I don't know of any martial artist who would intentionally cash in his life to gain an inch of muscle in his or her bicep. Start where you feel comfortable, and begin pulling back extreme behaviors.

236.

Avoid Regret

WHAT YOU MAY perceive as a missed opportunity is part of life. Martial arts teach you to let go and keep moving forward. Regret will only get you stuck and generate stress. Your job is to keep flowing, accepting what comes your way, and acting decisively when you make your moves. Consider the law of gain–loss: where there appears to be loss something else simultaneously opens up. You just have to look. *When you regret something, you are not present to opportunities that arise as a natural part of the cycle.* In the ring, if you didn't miss a shot every now and then, you would most likely lose interest in the game. The adventure is the best part. Your attitude is "Ouch, I missed that shot, but wow look at this one! And this and this and this! Oh, wow!" Any martial artist will admit that the possibility of missing is what keeps things interesting. You accept things not because you're "sucking it up," as they say, but because now you are in the epicenter of incredible action, where all things are possible—again and again.

EXERCISE

TAKE NOTE WHENEVER you use phrases like "should have," "would have," "could have," "wish I had," and such. At the end of the day, list these phrases on a piece of paper and carry them around in your pocket for a week. Take the list out every now and then and read it. Let the energy of these words enter you. Feel it. Pay attention to what emotions are sparked, where in your body you feel tightness or pain (neck, shoulders, chest, and abdomen). Feel the toll this negative energy takes on you. What words would you use to describe this toll? The next time you tell yourself to suck it up or to regret or feel guilt over something, remember your list. Say no to those negative thoughts. Choose to move forward where positive experiences are infinite.

Redefine Growth

MARTIAL ARTS TEACH that you exchange energy and information with everything in the universe. Science maintains that such growth happens at the cellular level and is inevitable. Awareness to this process of exchange is a choice. When you enter the dojo, you may be looking for self-defense or fitness skills. You soon begin to notice better physical and emotional health. Then you begin to experience energy in a new way. You realize that you can use personal energy to influence others and your environment, and vice versa. You may call this a spiritual feeling. You now intentionally summon and welcome the universe's energy. You get better at defending yourself. Daily life becomes easier. You're more content. You can do less and accomplish more. Perceptions change to include what you can see and what you can feel. You begin to sense a connection between the two. Your concept of what is real shifts. You become attentive to the energy you release and its influence on everything around you. You become attentive to how the energy you release returns. You begin to sense the radius of your influence. You gain and enjoy a newly discovered responsibility to all creation. You look one day and see how far you have come.

EXERCISE

CHART YOUR PERSONAL growth by marking improvements (fair, good, excellent) in these areas: Interpersonal skills, physical well being, emotional well being (including the ability to de-stress), capacity to use your energy to influence others and your environment, capacity to draw energy from others and your environment, overall outlook on life. See how far you have come.

Imagine Perfection in Stages

WHEN A GREAT martial arts master performs, it is hard to believe that he or she wasn't just born with that level of expertise. You don't have the benefit of seeing the incremental development of skill, unless you've had a sideline seat in that person's life. All greats remember witnessing their notion of perfection earlier in their lives, too. But we must also remain present to each progressive stage of our own path. The martial Way imagines perfection at whatever stage you are at. There is a practicality to this concept: by perfecting the angle of a strike, you hit with more accuracy. Body mechanics come next. When you perfect these, you hit with more force. Now you have accuracy and force. Likewise, if you are learning to play a violin, you learn how to hold the instrument, read notes, play notes and scales, play simple melodies, play with other musicians, and so on. By perfecting one stage at a time, you enhance your capabilities at all stages. There is a philosophical element to this. Remember that every motion contains the informational history of every other. Thus, in the simplest motion you can reach the depth of enlightenment contained in the most complex. This is important to remember in the dojo and in daily life.

EXERCISE

CONSIDER THREE ASPECTS of your life—for example, work, home, and recreation. Imagine what these would look like if they were perfected. List what skills are required for each aspect. You can begin by visualizing someone you know who has already mastered those skills. Eventually, however, visualize yourself employing each skill. Revisit these thoughts often. Let this influence and gauge your daily actions.

Imagine Perfection for Others

PART OF TRAINING is being attentive to your partner's notion of perfection. For example, perhaps you're an expert kicker, and your partner, a judo player, is attempting to become proficient in kick-boxing. You help her achieve her vision—to harmonize, to do well, not to manipulate. If, however, you know that your partner is asking you to demonstrate techniques for the purpose of avenging someone, then you can approach that scenario differently. Knowing another person's idea of perfection helps you realistically gauge your relation-ship—at least for the moment. Perhaps you will demonstrate only nonviolent postures from that point on, emphasizing the historical, philosophical, and legal origins of violent actions. Depending on how that works, you may terminate instruction all together. Your participa-tion (and responsibility) transmits energy and information from the personal level to everywhere else that energy touches. This is true in daily life as well. Note: Lise Meitner deferred from having her name on the Nobel Prize for her work with Otto Hahn in splitting the atom, because she sensed its inevitable violent destination. Knowing another person's image of perfection helps you make more authentic decisions, heighten joy for yourself and others, and circulate positivity.

EXERCISE

CONSIDER SOMEONE SPECIAL in your life. Think of the next time you will see this person. What is the occasion? What would that person's vision of perfection be for this situation? Think about ways you can harmonize with this vision. Follow up. See what happens. Use this same concept with people at work, family, friends, and so on.

If You Hurt Someone, Apologize Right Away

BECAUSE ACCIDENTS HAPPEN often in the dojo, you learn to apologize for mishaps immediately. For example, you may be trying a new technique and forget that your partner agreed not to block. You accidentally strike him. Dojo etiquette tells us not to waste a second and apologize immediately. Your partner usually says it's all right, because he knows full well that mistakes occur easily. You think about what happened and identify what went wrong so you can avoid hurting anyone in the future. Maybe you were too anxious. The incident, however, becomes a nonissue. These good manners promote good teamwork. They keep spirits high. They help bond participants, because everyone acknowledges that people can slip up sometimes and relationships will still be okay. No one demonizes you. The best policy is *Don't withhold. If you've hurt someone, apologize.*

EXERCISE

IF YOUR ACTIONS hurt someone, apologize right away. Don't carry the apology around. This will only stress you and your relationship with the person you've hurt. You will feel better and so will your partner.

241.

Look for Patterns
That Result in Harm

MARTIAL ARTS TEACH you to keep your eye peeled for patterns of harmful behavior that need to be disengaged before they escalate. For example, when you execute an armlock, you notice that your partner struggles to recuperate. So you address the problem. The consensus is that your partner needs to tap out (ask to withdraw) sooner. You try this approach, but the problem repeats. Flags need to go up. This doesn't necessarily mean that you are the cause of the problem. But ignoring the flags could lead to injury. You may notice that the same technique elicits similar results from multiple partners. This still doesn't necessarily mean that you are the cause. For instance, you may be working out with people who don't know when to tap out or whose skills have yet to reach full-contact level. On the other hand, you may have yet to master the lock, or perhaps your movement is too abrupt or aggressive. Whatever the case, you need to act responsibly. This means disengaging action as soon as possible, as well as discovering the cause and making necessary corrections where necessary. Harmful patterns speak volumes, whether on the mats or in daily affairs. Pay attention. Disengage until you can reactivate behaviors safely.

EXERCISE

MAKE YOURSELF ATTENTIVE to patterns of harmful behaviors that are repeatedly placing you or others in harm's way. If you discover any such behaviors, immediately remove yourself from scenarios that might spark the behaviors. Look at the situation from your perspective, from the other person's, and objectively—that is, from the perspective of a total stranger. What conclusions might you arrive at from information gathered from all three views? Use that information to help identify what is triggering the behavior. Use this to alleviate or avoid such situations until you are able to eliminate the cause.

242.

Play Someone Else's Game
Once in a While

PLAY IS IMPORTANT everywhere in life; the dojo is no exception. Thus, martial arts encourage you to not only play your own game, but to play someone else's game every now and then as well. This keeps things invigorating, interesting, and fun. In addition, keep in mind that most dojos encourage you to work with as many partners as possible. For example, launching any technique is one thing against someone a little smaller than you and something entirely different on someone twice your strength and size. Techniques against boxers, karate players, judo players, and Tae Kwon Do players also call for some adjustment. Schools are notorious for inviting people of other disciplines to workshop and spar with practitioners. This is a great way to sharpen and expand your skills. Additionally, every player has something unique to offer. Playing someone else's game is a good way to pick up new skills, techniques, and strategies that you can add to your own repertoire. It furthers your understanding and allows others to shine.

EXERCISE

TAKE A DAY and put yourself in someone else's shoes. Spend some time at work with a friend. Pay attention to how they do what they do. Watch a video or read a book that deals with an occupation different from yours. Learn how others do what they do. See what skills you can pick up that can assist you at your job. Send your thanks—if only with a quiet blessing of gratitude.

243.

Don't Play into Someone Else's Image of You, Unless . . .

ON THE MATS, players are always sizing up each other. The idea is that if they can figure out where their opponent is coming from before he or she does anything, they will have some advantage over the opponent. Perhaps you have a reputation for fast, high kicks. You step in the ring. You know your partner is looking for this. So you surprise him. You train yourself to fire a series of low shots. If your partner thinks you are Mr. or Ms. Aggressive and are going to come charging out like a maniac, you train to take your sweet time. Your strategy is not to play into your partner's strategy—unless you're positioning him for your next move. This concept works well in daily life as well. Here's a good example. A student of mine recently told me he had apprehensively attended a college "tour day" in northern Vermont. He was reluctant because he didn't want to sit through a sales pitch. However, he was quite surprised and pleased when college personnel emphasized that the school was not for everyone and claimed that 100 percent of its students knew exactly what they would be doing after graduation. "Most people were turned away," he said. He left with a favorable impression of the school, saying, "They cared about more than just your money."

EXERCISE

THINK OVER WHAT needs to be done today and with whom. Choose a circumstance. Then think about the other person involved and what image that person may have of you. Pick an element of this image and change it. For example, if it's your habit to let other people do all the talking, walk in with a plan and speak first. If you are usually indirect, be direct. If you don't usually offer alternate solutions, do some homework and offer plenty of them. How might you strategize your change to lead you to your goals? Use this idea to troubleshoot or to increase joy in pleasurable situations.

Always Play Fair

DOJOS HAVE ALL kinds of rules regarding fair play. In general, all activities must be conducted in proper etiquette and friendship. More specific rules serve as guidelines for sparring and combative drills. For instance, certain attacks—striking the arms, throat, joints, groin, instep, and face—are illegal. Behaviors such as failing to obey a referee or faking personal injury are banned. Making a partner feel inferior is also shunned. Intentionally perpetrating injury on anyone to prove something is a major offense. You don't break someone's nose or purposely try to make someone feel like they are less than they are in order to win a match. The underlying concepts are also true in life routines. Far too often, people take unethical and dangerous shots at each other. Some people try to make themselves appear superior by making others seem inferior. Then there is always the bully who uses excessive force for unprincipled gain. These behaviors pollute an environment and come back to you. Fair play circulates positivity. It makes people feel safe, creative, free, and happy.

EXERCISE

BE ATTENTIVE TO your overall maneuvers toward achieving your goals—what skills and tactics do you use? Ask yourself, *Are these maneuvers being conducted in proper etiquette? Am I playing fair?* If you think any of your tactics are unacceptable, abandon them immediately. They will only lead to negative returns. Scan your martial tools. Put together a new strategy that flows down a higher road. See how this affects your overall returns.

Remember That Others Watch and Learn from the Sidelines

SOME OF THE best skills you learn in a dojo come through indirect observations—that is, watching from the sidelines. My one-year-old, for example, hears someone say an unfamiliar word two rooms over and starts repeating it. Writing students hear classmates read stories, and suddenly these styles trickle into their own work. I watch a professional painter balancing himself on a roof and burn that into my memory so that I can do it later. Much of what we learn in life comes from sideline observation. We receive very little formal instruction. As a parent, writer, and teacher, I have to remind myself of this often. Whether I am in my home, dojo, or on the pages of a book, an awful lot goes down peripherally. What's amazing is all you can do once you make yourself attentive to this constant learning. You don't have to see where information (energy) "downloads" are going. Just being attentive to this natural process helps you gain control over a major, perhaps untapped way of affecting your environment—people, incidents, circumstances, and other aspects of your life. The best part of this approach is that you appear to be doing nothing!

EXERCISE

BE ATTENTIVE TO your overall actions so that you eventually see them as ways to influence the behaviors of others. Be persistent. Shoot yourself a smile when you identify a pattern of conduct you feel you generated. Affect your environment with positivity.

246.

Help Your Partners
Train Their Skills

ONE OF MY favorite dojo anthems is, *It's not always about you, but it always comes back to you.* The dojo teaches that part of working with others is being sensitive to what they are attempting to train. The easiest way to do this is ask. Perhaps your partner says she needs to get her energy up, and asks if you would mind doing energy drills for the day. You may have entered the session hoping to iron out the kinks in a new kata. You let her question sink in. Intuition tells you to go her way. It doesn't take long before you realize you have forgotten about rehearsing your kata. The energy drills heighten your partner's spirits—and, to your delight, yours as well. When you leave the dojo, the energy you generated follows and ripples into other pleasantries. You have a more exhilarated night out with your domestic partner, who de-stresses and has a better next day at work, and so on.

EXERCISE

ASK OTHERS WHAT they hope to achieve from various circumstances of the day. Or ask them what upcoming incidents they are preparing for and help them. Watch what happens.

Use Your Mirror

MANY DOJOS USE mirrored walls to help the people training there to sharpen their skills. Kata training is a good example. Everyone watches the mirror as you go through the movements with your instructor, making sure you have all the right moves as well as the correct sequence. You start paying more attention to form as you go along: Are your arms angled properly? Shoulders down? Are your kicks clean and on target? The more you watch yourself, the technically better you get. This is akin to the violinist watching herself in the mirror to fine-tune everything from posture to bowing. Mirrors help you notice idiosyncrasies and eliminate bad habits. They train you to place your attention outside yourself as you work. This helps gather information you can use to refine technique and strategy. The mirror is an easy coach. It identifies weaknesses without analyzing you.

EXERCISE

AT THE START of your day, consider one important activity you will need to address before your day is over. *Use those activities you encounter as your mirror.* Make yourself attentive to the way you appear in their eyes. Remember, mirrors don't judge. You do. So you analyze your actions—not them. See what you discover. Identify what you'd like to improve and generate a plan for follow-up. Consider also what you do well. Compliment yourself.

Don't Let It All Hang Out

THE DOJO TEACHES that critical statements and their intensity are subject to purpose. Your goal in offering opinion is to facilitate others in achieving their objectives. If a novice asks you how his roundhouse kick is looking, you're not going to scrutinize the kick as you would for a more experienced player who is about to test for her black belt. At the moment, just getting the angles right may be enough for the novice. The senior will require feedback on body mechanics, strength, and power. Likewise, you will be more intense with someone, say, who is training for life-and-death military operations. Time and place weigh in, too. For example, the dynamics of private comments would differ from what you'd say in front of a player's instructor, friends, or family. Outside the dojo, medical, educational, and other practitioners are subject to new laws that govern what they can and can't say—as well as when, where, and how. Remember that even when everything isn't perfect, it's still okay to compliment.

EXERCISE

MAKE YOURSELF ATTENTIVE to the circumstances under which others ask your opinion. Consider their purpose, the time and place. Remember, you don't have to "let it all hang out." See what happens.

Don't Offer False Praise

THE DOJO TEACHES that honesty doesn't mean just letting your thoughts pour out like water from a faucet. This applies to compliments as well. For example, if a novice asks how his snap kicks are looking and they look good, you don't need to exaggerate and tell him they are the absolute best you have ever seen or that he is a prodigy—unless, of course, these things are true. Sometimes a performance peaks your emotions and you can't help having strong feelings about what you've seen. However, letting someone think he or she has reached a pinnacle if that is not the case may be regressive in terms of training. It may also be damaging to your credibility and significance as a confidant. All seekers, that is, those of us looking to improve their lives require accurate information in order to advance. Whether in the dojo, the classroom, the office, or what have you, inflated assessment risks creating an artificial barrier to someone's true potential. Remain credible.

EXERCISE

BE ATTENTIVE WHEN you are offering praise. Make sure that your comments are accurate and balanced. Don't withhold. But don't go over the top.

Share Spiritual Experiences with Your Partner

SPIRITUAL SHARING IS important in the dojo experience. You speak freely of harnessing internal energy (Chi) and manifesting it in external ways—for example, focusing energy into a punch or into your capacity to take a punch. As you begin sharing deeper spiritual encounters with your partners, you may find them opening up to you with an assortment of stories. The most popular dojo stories are about using Chi or Universal Energy to stay healthy or to overcome pain and illness. Others tell of a wide variety of out-of-body encounters, using Chi to enter the mind, and powers of nature and the Infinite. Such conversations are important. If you have had any of these phenomenal experiences, you discover that you are not alone, which leads you to consider your skill in an entirely different light. Such conversations create a history to which new information is contributed daily. This generates a road map to higher consciousness for us all.

EXERCISE

THINK ABOUT SOME of the clearest examples of spiritual experience in your life thus far. Consider premonitions you had about serious or light matters that came to pass, or power that you summoned from an outside source without which you couldn't have resolved a certain conflict. Consider illnesses or disease you or others have encountered that somehow just went away. Consider improbabilities that occurred, despite the fact that people may have given up; i.e., pregnancies, employment opportunities, overcoming of handicaps and the like. Now choose some of these incidences, and share them with a friend. See what happens. If it feels right, share more. Also try sharing experiences from your meditations.

Feel the Strength
in Moving with Grace

YOU CAN IMMEDIATELY feel the power you have when you strike a heavy bag or lift a heavy object. This strength comes from within your bones, muscles, and tendons. You can also feel your strength drain. Experiencing massive power inside soft, graceful postures comes with a little more sensitivity and practice. But this is where martial arts points for the big payoff. Such energy is endless. The trail begins with the lower *Dan Tien* and moves to your energy pumps. But stopping there is, as my brother—a medical care administrator and martial artist—likes to say, "Seeing the ball in the catcher's mitt and thinking baseball is initiated from the catcher's position." Your job is to stay on course and go where the energy game really begins—that is, from a consciousness and power source outside the body. Slow, luscious movement, as in Tai Chi and Chi Kung exposes this energy more thrillingly, making it easier to feel Chi moving through your body. You feel it banding around you, exchanging energy with everything in the universe. This energy will survive your physical self.

EXERCISE

BECOME YOUR ENVIRONMENT. Visualize a large circle in midair about a foot in front of you. Then, trace the circle in large clockwise movements simultaneously with both palms and return to the same position from which you began. Be attentive to that part of you that is outside your body yet consciously witnessing your actions. Visualize everything in your environment, including you, as a single, conscious energy field. Keep tracing your circle, imagining the air turning to water, then mud, metal, wood, then soft as air again. Feel your body drawing nourishing, protective power. Repeat counterclockwise. Try outdoors..

Know Your Partner's Imminent Behaviors

SOME PATTERNS EXPOSE imminent behaviors. The operative word here is "imminent," meaning actions that are about to take place. For example, your sparring partner may take a right step forward just seconds before launching an attack. Or he may go one, two, two and a half steps and attack. You can learn to recognize these patterns. What you are paying attention to are the movement and the measure of time that follows before decisive action begins. This helps you avoid surprise and being thrown off balance. Everyday routines work the same. Perhaps a colleague or partner has a habit of rolling his or her eyes moments before going into aggressive activity. Sometimes words are good indicators. Maybe he or she uses more dramatic language or particular language that quickly emerges into an identifiable behavior pattern, which may be desirable or not. Recognizing your partner's imminent behaviors can also help you to better gauge your response—hard, soft, circular, straight on, and the like. Sometimes a last-minute sign allows you to ward off or encourage your partners' next moves.

EXERCISE

SPEND A DAY paying attention to the patterns people expose that predict their impending actions. Pay attention to body language, words, mood shifts, tones, and energy levels. You can make a game out of this by keeping track of just how many times you are right. At the end of the day, reflect on your experiment. Consider how you can use this information to improve your relationships with others.

253.

Watch for Off-the-Wall Attacks

WHEN YOU ARE on the mats, you are not immune to off-the-wall, unexpected attacks. You could be squared off with someone who is sparring sanely one minute, and the next thing you know, he is charging at you with every zone exposed. You wonder what's running through the guy's head, but you may never know. Sometimes you're overwhelmed with surprise, and this leaves you vulnerable. An old anthem says *Expect the unexpected*. So, you look for patterns that telegraph rash, disorganized movement. This information can help you intercept an action before it begins. For example, a player may appear extremely fatigued, disorganized, or confused, as if his mind is full of noise, before breaking into senseless attacks. He may breathe erratically, or his skin can become extremely flush. Once you recognize the pattern, you can *initiate* movements that will foil his actions and land you in a position of advantage, rather than landing you on your butt. This same strategy works outside the dojo. Look for the patterns. Divert senseless attacks before they occur.

EXERCISE

CONSIDER THE LAST time someone significant in your everyday routines pulled a surprise attack on you. Revisit the incident, considering a variety of meetings with the person for some time leading up to the circumstance. Take a close look. Can you see the patterns of behavior that might have indicated he or she was about to do something irrational? If so, list these behaviors. Have they ever been displayed before? What was the result then? Is the pattern fixed? If so, consider how you could have steered the situation in a direction that would have diverted the irrational action. Make this idea part of your itinerary for dealing with this person in the future.

Pay Attention to
Long-Range Patterns

MARTIAL ARTS TEACH you to identify life's subtler and longer-range patterns. Here's an example from sparring: *A* overwhelmingly outscores *B* in round one. *B* takes the next round slow. *A* keeps scoring. *B* hardly fights back. *A* traps her on the ropes and blasts away, scoring one point after another. *B* just raises a few protective blocks. Spectators shout for *B* to get going. They take note that *B* hardly fights back. But they aren't considering a potential long-range pattern. *A* begins to tire in round six, and by round eight, she is exhausted. *B* miraculously perks up suddenly *explodes* into action. Out of the blue, the match is over. *B* has won by knockout. This is how Muhammad Ali became boxing's world champion over George Foreman in Zaire, Africa, in 1974. The gene pool offers another example. Although we cannot see patterns of change on our own, with computer assistance scientists have learned that life will eventually clear the pool of all hereditary diseases, such as diabetes, hemophilia, and the like. Computers also show how without the introduction of "predators," or new diseases, genes naturally become lazy. Thus, life paradoxically generates its own problems into the cycle—to stay strong! Seeing long-range patterns helps you make more accurate assessments and generate more effective responses.

EXERCISE

CONSIDER THE LAST time someone significant in your everyday routines did something that surprised you. Go back in time to previous dealings with this person. See if you can identify any long-range patterns that would indicate such surprising behaviors. Think about how you would respond to the behaviors and keep that information in the back of your mind. Use what you discover to adjust your responses in the future.

Practice Humility

HUMILITY IS A great asset in the dojo and in relationships everywhere, including with the Infinite. It sustains respect and cooperation. Then again, I don't know anyone who hasn't tried to show off at various times, myself included. The effects range from humorous to catastrophic. I've seen people attempt bizarre acrobatic kicks on the mats, land face down on the ground, and then get up and laugh—what else can you do? Others have blistered their hands raw on a heavy bag, showing off how they didn't need gloves, and others have broken their own bones showing off how they could break more wood than anybody else. Injuries to self are one thing. But sometimes egos injure other people. It's common for beginners to show off by abnormally speeding up techniques on partners and inadvertently injuring them. To this, the great martial masters stress the importance of humility. By keeping your assets to yourself—not bragging, not being so concerned with image—you make it more difficult for others to manipulate you. You sustain respect, friendship, and cooperation. You absorb knowledge more easily. You grow faster. Success arrives more easily. Go with the flow and life will float you to greatness.

EXERCISE

KEEP YOUR TREASURES to yourself. Let others discover them.

Remember That Joint Goals Are Pluralistic

THE DOJO EMPHASIZES the establishment of joint goals—a compilation of personal goals along with those of your instructor, your partner, and others, as well as the goals of your art and the universe. This calls for a lot of cooperation. As such, the dojo is like a body. For example, science tells us that a cell may develop itself, but at the same time it contributes to the development of a certain organ, which contributes to the development of the entire body. Like cells, we develop ourselves at the same time we contribute to the growth of partners and families, which contribute to the development of societies and so on. In the dojo, as well as in daily life, we do well to consider joint goals at each level. You might ask yourself, *How can I better meet my goals by meeting my instructor's? How does this affect my partner, his goals, and our mutual ones? How does this affect the entire class?* The same principles apply to daily life. Increasing your awareness at each level gives you input not only into your own destiny but within the bigger picture as well.

EXERCISE

THINK ABOUT ONE or two circumstances in your daily affairs, and identify what you need from the circumstance. Ask partners at home, work, or play what they hope to achieve from your mutual efforts. Weigh that against the needs of others in your environment. For example, you and your partner need leisure time, but your partner has work obligations. Consider taking longer individual time together but less frequently. Take more time but limit the place—for instance, traveling a shorter distance.

Create New Techniques,
But . . .

MARTIAL ARTS ENCOURAGE you to create new techniques. This is how you grow. But they also encourage you to master the basics along the way. For example, you may learn three different ways to redirect an oncoming strike: using a palm, a single arm, or both arms. You later learn blocking that uses full circles. At some point, you may create a new block that uses all three. You are able to do this because you have mastered each of the original postures. Indeed, teaching your new block to someone would require you to break it down to its individual parts. This is a good lesson to remember. Our ability to intentionally create, modify, and evolve are all part of the greatness of life. Can you spontaneously evolve? Yes. We have all witnessed such incredible moments of genius in athletics, art, science, and other disciplines. Mastering the smaller elements of learning on the way, however, helps you put it all together later.

EXERCISE

CONSIDER A CURRENT circumstance that you have not been able to resolve. Identify what conventional techniques, martial or otherwise, you have already used to troubleshoot the situation. Reflect on other techniques that may be useful, even if just marginally. Think of ways you might create a new technique by combining some of the aforementioned ones. Note: You may need to retrain in the individual components in order to make yourself proficient. Design a strategy to implement your new technique. Follow through. Observe what happens.

258.

Practice Heart-Mind
to Heart-Mind

IN CHINESE THE term *Xin-Yi* means heart-mind. This is a core concept in Shaolin martial training and is enormously empowering. It is perhaps one of the most coveted mind-sets you can achieve. Here is how it works. By making yourself attentive to *Xin* (heart consciousness), you feel what is presently most natural for you. *Yi* (intention) is the mind's power for directing energy. When you combine the two, you are utilizing your internal energy system to literally transmit the desires of your heart into your environment. Indeed, the hectic moments in our lives arise from our insistence on muscling and pounding events into what we want. This, of course, is in conflict with the notion of *Xin-Yi*. Eastern and martial philosophy emphasize that personal success arises from knowing the heart's deepest desire and strengthening the mind to invoke it. When you connect with another person (*Xin-Yi* to *Xin-Yi*), you are most natural, sensing each other deeply. Intentions harmonize and become synergistic. You feel relaxed, content, and free.

EXERCISE

BEFORE YOU MEET with a loved one, relax and center. Place your attention in your heart's energy center. Consult your feelings. Be honest with yourself about what you feel and what you desire in relationship with your partner. Use your heart's energy center to feel your partner's desires. Visualize those desires. Let yourself feel them emotionally. Use your meditation to enter the Universal Body (see secret 175). Invoke its power to create your mutual intentions. See what happens. If you feel comfortable, share this technique (or a version of it) with your partner. Place your mutual intentions in the Universal Body. See how this feels. Watch what happens.

Mind over Brute Force

CAN YOU REALLY take someone's energy away with just a look? Self-defense programs begin and end with this point. Confidence is energy and information. You exude it naturally, and you can learn to issue it more piercingly. In the dojo, senior players discover they can "de-energize" beginners without doing anything more than looking at them. When someone looks at you with so much confidence and determination, it can make you feel like your energy pumps have been sapped. You sometimes encounter weakness in your extremities or queasiness in the abdominal area, where the energy you need for aggression is stored. This phenomenon can be compounded by fear. Fear blocks energy and depletes flexibility and so on. But the afore-mentioned condition is an *instant* draining. You have less, not blocked energy. This lessening of energy is being done *to* you, not by you. Perhaps you've felt your energy drain just walking down the street, as someone's eyes scan you from top to bottom. Start warding off or diminishing potential threats today. Transmit your own signals of fear-lessness, confidence, skill, friendliness, and goodwill. Be safe.

EXERCISE

THE NEXT TIME you intuit a potential problem center, stay calm. Use your mind to intercept aggressive behaviors. Draw energy from your environ-ment. Use your breath to unblock energy centers. Feel your internal power charging up. Empty your mind. Use your energy pumps to create an aura of confidence and strength. Visualize this attitude radiating. Let your positive words bubble up and float across your field of consciousness: *calm, strong, totally proficient,* and *dignified.* This aura will be transmitted to your antago-nist, who will realize he has luckily escaped confrontation.

260.

Seek Someone of Greater Skill

MARTIAL ARTS ENCOURAGE you to never stop seeking ways to improve yourself. To this end, you work with as many partners of greater skill as possible. Many dojos host a variety of workshops with masters. Both novice and senior players tighten their belts, so to speak, head for the mats, and participate. All of my teachers along the way have set terrific examples. All of them, masters themselves, have sought others of greater skill from whom they could learn, improve their own game, and pass the knowledge on. This process was never just a one-time endeavor either, but rather part of the Way. Daily routines are the same. What's key is that you regularly partner up with someone of greater skill. This will help get you to the next rung on the ladder and give you clear focus on the one after that.

EXERCISE

THINK ABOUT AN aspect in your life you want to improve. Do a search on experts in that subject. You may be an expert yourself. What's important is to find someone with greater skill. See if that person is offering a workshop in your area and make plans to attend it. If funds are available, consider traveling to a workshop or lecture. You can also consult books, videos, and other media sources. Don't stop there. Make this practice a component of your ongoing process of self-improvement.

261.

Remember That Every Technique Contains All Others

MARTIAL ARTS TEACH that every movement carries within it the knowledge of every other movement in the universe. So theoretically you could study one single martial technique and discover all others. Then why not do that? Probably because doing so requires greater focus than most of us have at the beginning of our process. However, this is why you can learn new martial art concepts and systems so quickly after you're already proficient in one. The same is true in everyday life. If you are proficient in one computer operating system, you can learn another more easily. The visionary poet William Blake wrote the often quoted words: "To see the world in a grain of sand, / And heaven in a wild flower, / Hold infinity in the palm of your hand, / And eternity in an hour." These words hold true for any of life's movements, whether you are on the beach, in a garden, or on the mats. Interestingly more than one hundred years after Blake wrote his iconic lines, Einstein and his gang "discovered" what Blake had explained by watching flowers and what martial arts had taught for millenniums: That every movement is a mini-cosmos. You just have to pay enough attention.

EXERCISE

FIND A PHOTOGRAPH of something in nature you enjoy. Consider an unresolved personal issue. Find a quiet space. Use your breath to heighten your energy. Just observe the image. Empty your mind of everything except the image. Don't analyze it. Just look at it, trying to take in its smallest nuances. Touch it. Let what you see flow through each of your energy centers slowly. Stop and feel it with each energy center—not thinking, just feeling. If what you see wants to evolve, let it. When it fades, bring your attention back to the physical image. Just let thoughts flow. Let the answer you seek come to you.

Avoid False Cravings

AS YOU BECOME a more proficient artist, you become more in touch with your body's subtler sensitivities. You feel good all over and want to keep that feeling. You become more adept at how you process energy, with your mind as well as your body. You are aware of patterns and the role they play. You know, for example, that if you come home and your newly discovered health foods are not available, an old pattern can kick in. Next thing you know, you are headed for the chips and dip—again! Although you have felt and lived the benefits of eating nutritiously, you know you are capable of falling back to old habits. So you have to be on the watch for those cravings. But there is a hidden effect here. False cravings often come in disguise. We may say we're giving a colleague advice or sending an old lover a birthday card, but underneath it all, our true intent is sometimes injurious: to upstage, brag, or upset. What's more, any kind of craving transmits intention (*Yi*). From the cellular level to the social, the universe is wired to deliver. It's vital to send it the right message.

EXERCISE

LOOK DEEPER INTO your urges. Ask yourself if there are any disingenuous intentions brewing in disguise. If so, do not act on these urges. They will only bring negativity into the lives of others and into yours as well. Instead, try to understand where these urges originate. The trail will eventually lead you to a source of personal fear. Revisit your fear. Use all of your martial skills to develop a strategy to defeat your fear and thus conquer any cravings for things that steal your good energies.

Trust Your Body

AS MARTIAL ARTIST you become well versed in reading the body's communications. This means its high-velocity positive energy as well as its aches and pains. You understand that the body's primary language is not English, but feelings. For example, on the mats, let's say your body starts charging up in the third round. It's letting you know it will take care of matters on automatic pilot. You follow the vibe and let it go all out. You win the match. Likewise, you might be at the office, working long hours on the computer, and you develop a lot of tension or muscle ache in your shoulders. Your body is asking for a break, but you override its message. The next day, you botch an important job. Students at the college where I teach talk about this phenomenon. They say they consistently do better on exams when they listen to their body rather than pulling all-nighters. Listening to your body is natural. You do it often during the day—though if you are like me, you don't do it enough. Listen more. Overrule your feelings less.

EXERCISE

LISTEN TO YOUR body's energy messages. Translate them if you must or interpret them just by simply feeling—this is good, this is not; this is something to do, this is not. Speak to your body by visualizing what you are doing or want to be doing. Wait for a response. Trust your body's talk. See what happens.

Trust Your Intuition

MARTIAL ARTS TELL you that intuition is a function of energy. It is your internal energy system speaking to you, and remember, it is subatomically connected to everything in the universe. This is what makes intuition such a powerful tool. In the dojo, you take the mystery out of intuitive movement. By practicing techniques blindfolded you learn to literally feel for your partners' Chi as it is being directed (*Chi-Yi*) to you. You feel the energy (Chi) and translate the intention (*Yi*). Indeed, all this "energy talk" comes together. Intuition is your power to translate intention instantaneously. When you try to think it through, you move at a crawl—more like trying to unscramble an anagram in a foreign language. In the ring as well as in daily affairs, this mind-set can be costly. Don't pay the price. Stay connected to your intuitive power.

EXERCISE

LISTEN TO YOUR intuition. Don't make impulsive moves such as buying or selling off all of your stocks or discarding your job. Start with small things until you get used to this process. When you get up today, ask yourself what you'd like to achieve. Make yourself sensitive to energy flowing into your body. What ideas pop into your head? Don't waste time trying to analyze. Think of a few action steps you can take that employ your newly found ideas. Visualize yourself carrying out these steps. What other ideas pop into your mind? Create an action plan and try it out in your daily routines.

265.

Visualize the Road Ahead

MARTIAL TRAINING ENCOURAGES you to take a good look at the road ahead. Yes, your focus is on the present moment; however, part of being in the present is seeing all there is to see. If there is a two-foot pothole on the ground where you are sparring, you need to know that. Visualizing what's ahead helps you be realistic. For example, if you're a novice with a goal of performing katas with flaming weapons in a touring martial arts show, you know you have a way to go. However, let's say you'd like to lose five pounds. The road to your goal is relatively short and easily manageable. You only have to discover lower-calorie foods you can enjoy and begin a program of minimum exercise—perhaps just a regular walk after dinner. There is, however, another dimension to visualizing what's ahead. Remember heart-mind (*Xin-Yi*). By visualizing what is in your heart, you plant the seeds of your intentions in the fertile energies of the Universal Body, wherein intention becomes reality. Now rather than looking at the future, you are creating it.

EXERCISE

AT THE END of your day, visualize where you want to be—in both the short and long runs. Visualize yourself having already achieved your goal. Plant this image in the Universal Body. Use your heart-mind-to-heart-mind techniques with the Infinite. Open your heart. Listen with your heart. Be open to what skills you will need to develop to reach your goals, how, where, and when. Be open to modifications along the way. See what happens.

Look for Forks in the Road

THERE ARE INFINITE crossroads in every moment of life. But every now and then one crossroad stands out. Martial arts teach you to look for these. They are considered blessings and opportunities for growth and improvement. In the dojo, you could be working on take-downs with your partner and midway through realize your positioning is better for an armlock—so you go for the lock instead. New situations always offer lessons and opportunity, whether you pursue them or not. You may have been waiting for an employment opportunity for ten years. It finally comes when you have decided to take time off to work on a personal project, perhaps writing a book. There's the fork. You decide *not* to take the job. This only reinforces your fortitude to write your book. Two years later a publisher agrees to publish the book. You think about how much easier it could have been "If I had only known when . . ." But you did know. You had it all in your heart.

EXERCISE

SOMETIMES FORKS STOP you in your tracks: Should you buy a house or live in an apartment? Should you have a child or wait? Should you go for a promotion, switch jobs, retire early? Don't let yourself feel stuck in a rut. This is when you must consult your heart and see what rings true. Think to yourself, *Where do I want to be?* Listen. Feel the answer. Trust your intuition. Then take the desired fork.

Learn Lessons the Easiest Way

ALL LESSONS IN the dojo start out as easy. Difficulty, most practitioners discover, is something you bring to the task. For example, you start training in kicks and realize that yours are flying low. Later on you notice your legs are stiff. But you are disappointed because your kicks aren't where you want them. You take aspirin, get rid of the pain, and work your body hard the next day, trying to put more altitude in your kicks. You experience more pain. You swallow more aspirin and continue the same activity. You do this for a couple of days. Then you wake up one morning and discover you can't walk. Your body is shutting down to repair itself. It has sent you several messages, starting with your low kicks, and you ignored them. Your problem is now compounded. There are several lessons here. First, you need to stretch more before training and learn some simple body mechanics. You also need to listen to your body. You need patience. You can't always speed things up by taking them into your own hands. It's not difficult to learn to kick high. People make it difficult by not listening to their own protective mechanisms. This same principle applies to all kinds of life situations.

EXERCISE

THE NEXT TIME you attempt something new, make yourself attentive to your instincts and intuitions. If you feel resistance or pain anywhere, pause. Ask yourself what these feelings are attempting to say. If you don't know the answer, try asking someone else's opinion. Don't proceed if you are receiving signals that are cautioning you to do otherwise. Remember, the ease of a task is proportionate to effective preparation. If you must proceed, peak your sensitivities, listen to yourself, and move with caution.

Be Real

OUR ART TELLS us to proceed with and through enlightenment. Nonetheless, we have all, upon occasion, been mind-blind. There is a certain protectiveness to this condition, especially in incidents of trauma—domestic, childhood, and other forms. I was mind-blind when I continued to work an occupation that was financially profitable yet was bankrupting my spirit, or when I stayed in a relationship I knew was over yet pretended everything was fine. Like everyone, I was mind-blind for as long as I could pull it off. However, life eventually reminds us of consequences. In the dojo, you learn that if you smoke, you run out of breath. It's simple. Off the mats, there are more serious consequences. Smoking can deteriorate your health or take your life. If we drink alcohol excessively or take drugs, we can pretend that these substances make us feel better, they help us recreate, they help us deal . . . we never run out of justification. But then, of course, the consequences arrive (medical, legal, social, and such). Martial arts empower you to make individual choices, to flex your freedom. Part of your freedom, however, is to realistically see and accept the consequences of your decisions. The law of cause and effect is real.

EXERCISE

CONSIDER SOME OF the aspects of your life that you are reluctant to change. Pay special attention to those things that your body, mind, or other people are nudging you in the ribs to reconsider. Science tells you that denying reality (psychosis) leads to muscle and emotional pain, as well as diseases ranging from high blood pressure to cancers. Take a realistic look at the effects of your choices. Identify the positive aspects. Then identify any negative aspects. Make your decisions in freedom, acceptance, and peace.

Watch What You Say,
or Someone Will Call Your Bluff

THE MATS HAVE a way of calling you out. Thus, most practitioners try not to fool themselves or others. For example, ancient warriors couldn't pretend to wield a sword, or they'd wind up dead on the battlefield. The dojo won't let you go around saying you can smash your hand through concrete if you can't actually do so—you will go home with an awfully sore hand if you try. Likewise, you can't say you can stop a 250-pound player's punches and kicks unless you actually can. The pitfalls of illusion are dangerous wherever you are. A professor of English can't brag about her knowledge of, say, Robert Frost, if she can't back it up. Inevitably, someone in the class will have questions. If you go around telling everyone you know all there is to know about computers, don't be surprised when someone asks for your expertise. On a less visible level, the universe also listens and calls you out. If you profess to be fair, unprejudiced, cooperative, low-key, or what have you, the universe will create situations in which you'll be called upon to employ these characteristics. Your next moment may depend on what you say now. Choose your words carefully.

EXERCISE

TRY THIS IN the evening. Find a relaxing place and revisit the major events of your day. Consider how you present yourself to yourself, others, and the universe. Ask yourself if you could stand behind your words. If not, ask yourself if these are qualities you authentically would like to achieve. If they are, ask why? Are these the desires of your heart? What are the positive and negative consequences? Or are your desires driven by hidden reasons more connected to certain fears? If this is the case, identify your fears. Use your martial skills to create a strategy that will lead to their defeat. If your desires are of the heart, use your heart-mind skills to acquire them.

270.

Tap Your Body's Absence of Belief

ONE OF THE most fascinating details of martial as well as Eastern thought is the absence of "I believe this" or "I believe that" thinking. The dojo isn't concerned with what we "think," and neither is reality. As the writer Dan Millman puts it in his book, *No Ordinary Moments: A Peaceful Warrior's Guide to Daily Life*, "While our beliefs help create our reality . . . gravity works whether we believe it or not!" Your body's consciousness is a perfect example of this notion. It doesn't believe it is cold or hot or hungry or thirsty. It just *is*. In the dojo, your body tells you: "This block hurts; loosen up and roll with the punch instead of trying to stop it dead on." In daily life, your body tells you: "My feet are cold. Cover them before I get sick." Your body is in a constant reality check. Your mind, however, can become delusional. Millman warns, "The mind sails between past and present [and future] like a ghost ship. [You] can sit cross-legged with your eyes closed in meditation and imagine yourself 'highly evolved,' while turning your back on real world responsibility." What can be done? The answer is to use your body's capacity for reality checks. Tap your body's physical feedback to your actions. Then retool your wisdom.

EXERCISE

CONSIDER SOMETHING YOU believe, like if you have a positive attitude toward a colleague, you will get along better. But when you try out your belief, your body is resistant. It tenses and bristles. Listen. It won't lie. Try to figure out why it is anxious. You may discover that while, yes, a positive attitude helps, you still feel lousy. Trailing your emotions and physical reactions may lead to a pattern from earlier days that is contaminating your current relationship. Now, however, you have the opportunity to disengage the pattern, retool your techniques, and start fresh.

271.

Use Your Body's Attraction to Pleasure

PHYSICAL TRAINING TEACHES you to overcome resistance. In the micro sense, resistance slows you down. In the macro sense, it can vanquish your goals. Psychology tells us that we are attracted to things that bring us pleasure, and vice versa. Philosophy tells us that what we imagine influences our reality. Thus, if you see an action as painful, you will naturally resist it. For example, one martial artist may see sparring someone who is twice his skill as painful indeed. He will naturally resist. He may feel pressured. Another person will see being on the platform with such an opponent as a way to gain experience or as a measure of personal skill. It wouldn't be surprising to see this person invigorated by the experience. In daily life, you may resist taking on a new hobby. But when you consider how good you will feel if you choose differently, you will gravitate toward giving it a try. What's certain is that it will be twice as difficult to accomplish the experience if you can't imagine and desire the advantages.

EXERCISE

IDENTIFY AN ACTION you have been resisting. Make a written list of any negative results of such an action. Make a list of the positive. Is this still something you want in your heart? If so, list all the benefits of having successfully accomplished the action. Imagine yourself having achieved your goal. Let this energy run through all of your energy centers. Let yourself literally feel the benefits. Then go for it.

Get Excited

THERE'S NOTHING LIKE a new toy, whether you are in the dojo or in daily life. In this regard, our mental faculties aren't much different than children's. All I have to do is take out a sticker on an old plastic cup and my one-year-old is suddenly interested. Likewise, for my birthday, my brother recently gave me a new pair of boxing gloves—the Cadillac model. I couldn't wait to give them a whirl. It must have been near midnight when I opened the box, so I had to wait until the next day to try them out. By then my anticipation had grown. I made a special trip to the dojo that afternoon. There wasn't anyone else around, so I had the place to myself. You guessed it—I headed right for the heavy bag and went at it until dark. It's amazing how much energy our body and mind will give to something when we are excited. I went home with terrifically high spirits that transferred my excitement into a good evening with my wife and daughter. Indeed, this concept works in all daily affairs. Sometimes all you need is a sense of something new—no matter how small.

EXERCISE

TAKE SOMETHING YOU are currently struggling to accomplish. Promise yourself a reward—something different, perhaps an article of clothing, a daytrip to a new place, or a visit to a different restaurant. Watch what happens.

273.

Don't Overestimate Challenges

CHALLENGES ARE GOOD. But martial training warns you to not overestimate challenges by thinking they're impossible to meet. When you think this way, you run the risk of depleting your energy. The behaviorist Ivan Pavlov explained that what keeps a person motivated is the *"anticipation* of reward." Deadlines are perfect examples. As you come closer to your destination, excitement and energy build. Mind and body start pumping you with what you need to drive you to a glowing finish. But as soon as you perceive your goal as overwhelming, you begin to grow frustrated. Your mind and body depress themselves to keep you from feeling any physical or emotional pain. Computing mishaps are a good example. I have a friend who was in the final draft of a novel she was writing. Just before finishing, she accidentally erased the entire novel—with no back up, just some earlier hard-copy versions. She held tight and saw herself not only remembering the changes, but also making a better book. She finished, and the novel went on to become a best seller. You can control your body-mind performance by imagining how good you will feel once you acquire your goal. This keeps you motivated, focused, and driving all the way to the finish line.

EXERCISE

CONSIDER A GOAL that you would like to accomplish, but that seems overwhelming at the moment. Think about ways you can break it down into smaller, more manageable goals. For example, you may want to create a professional-style landscape for your house and garden, but such a large-scale plan seems complicated. By putting things off, you run the risk of losing interest. Try landscaping a small area of your yard. Then look for opportunities to accelerate your plan as things begin to move forward.

274.

Don't Underestimate Challenges

THE FLIP SIDE of being overwhelmed by challenges is to underestimate them. This mind-set can lead to problems. No one is immune. You can, however, become more attentive to this tendency—especially if it is habitual. The sports world is full of examples. A team or player with all the accolades doesn't take the underdog seriously and gets defeated. This happens all the time, in every sport. Or perhaps it's one of those days, and despite your good intentions to get out of bed early, you have luxuriated a little longer than you'd planned. You have an important family gathering for which you cannot be late. You look at the clock, do some quick math, and decide to give yourself just a few more luscious minutes of rest. Something inside says, "Better get going," but you override it. You guessed it—you arrive late or stressed or both. This recently happened to a friend who told me she received a speeding ticket on top of it all. Sometimes we underestimate—unconsciously trying to relieve stress. In the end, however, this ploy delivers just the opposite.

EXERCISE

CONSIDER YOUR LAST week. Can you identify any stressors or unachieved goals that were the result of your underestimation of circumstances? Revisit these. You may not be able to fix a missed opportunity, but its lessons may be more important in the long run. Ask yourself, *What would have been a more accurate perspective? What could I have done differently?* Consider these elements when planning for the same or similar situations. Look for the lessons.

Create New Patterns

PEOPLE AROUND YOU often take their cues from patterns they can identify in your behavior. There are advantages to their taking such cues. Strategically speaking, this is a good way to invite specific actions. When you are sparring, opening your centerline invites your opponent to target strikes there. Likewise, sitting down to dinner relaxed and content invites conversation. The use of patterns tactically helps you choose the field of play. The strategy works well. However, if you overuse a pattern, it becomes readily identifiable, and you may not generate the response you anticipate. Or you may discover a less energetic response. Thus, martial arts emphasize creating new patterns. If I want partners to target my centerline, I can lure them by launching a slow-moving strike down *their* centerline, inviting them to intercept it. If I want to invite conversation, I might try asking questions that friends or family find irresistible. Newness will recharge everyone involved.

EXERCISE

CONSIDER SOMEONE YOU will meet. Think of how you usually initiate conversation (or work or what have you) with him or her. Create a new pattern to achieve the same response. See what happens.

Stay Committed

YOU CAN COMMIT for a minute or for a lifetime—to a partner, project, training program, sport, and so on. What's important is that you sense things are moving forward and generating a higher good. You want to feel opportunity opening, no matter how subtle. In your heart, you want to know this direction is best, for you, at the time. Most martial exercises take from one to three months before taking effect. Thus, you can't just expect things to turn overnight. You simply have to stay committed. Do you recall the classic training scene from *Rocky* where Sylvester Stallone's character finally makes it up the museum steps? It's like that. Everything eventually comes together. Commitment is a good teacher. It helps you see what you're made of and how to use it. You learn to hunker down—to energetically pool from heaven, as well as from your most primitive earthly instincts. It's exciting. But commitment isn't a test of stubborn endurance. If something cannot work, despite all of your best efforts, if a circumstance is literally shutting you down, you need to put it away, at least for a time.

EXERCISE

CONSIDER SOMETHING IN your life you have been attempting to achieve and have yet to reach. Commit yourself to seeing the issue to successful conclusion. Make a list of anything you can think of that will help achieve your objective. The list might include behavioral changes, scheduling, people, books, places, and the like. Give yourself a reasonable amount of time to reach your goal. If that doesn't work, commit yourself to letting go—at least for now.

Remember That Everything Has Its Time

HAVE YOU EVER been working very hard on a project and experienced one interruption and blunder after another until you just gave up for the day? Have you ever thrown up your hands, saying the time just isn't right? Everyone has had these kinds of experiences. What's more, when you do eventually get the job done, you often find you've exceeded your expectations. Now you are happy that life interrupted. Let's say you like to jog every morning before heading to the office. But one day, just as you're on your way out the door, you remember a presentation you had to prepare for work. You should have done it the night before, but you were exhausted. Then someone calls you on the phone. It's important. You have to answer. Bye-bye workout. Something the person says on the phone, however, triggers an idea that inspires your presentation into an unexpected direction. You go with it. Later you give an impressive presentation. That afternoon your energy is high, and you have a great workout. Things like this happen all the time. You just have to become more trusting, keep your eyes open, and go with the flow.

EXERCISE

WHENEVER YOU FEEL life is interrupting your plans, relax. Don't stress out. Instead, increase your attention to the windows of opportunity that are opening to you. Practice following the natural order of things. Watch how easily life opens up for you.

Watch Your Partner's Innermost Self Pour Through

MARTIAL ARTS TRAIN you to look closely at reflexive movements. This is because these movements tell us about who we are. For example, if I reflexively avoid close-range combat, preferring instead to kick it out from a distance, I get a glimpse of what I assume are my present aptitudes and anxieties. My actions mirror my habits and fears. Such body language is important outside the dojo, too. Aspiring college and secondary teachers are taught that students don't always say what's on their minds, but they do let you know. If you teach, you become an expert in body language—noticing who's looking down at their shoes when you ask a question, who looks up and smiles, and such. You never require a watch, because there are always enough students shutting their books at the end of class. Parents, children, businesswomen, and businessmen—all, even infants—strive to read body language. What's key is separating contrived movement from genuine. Authentic movement will be reflexive. Those brief moments tell you who others really are, and especially how they see themselves. Trust what you see.

EXERCISE

LOOK FOR PEOPLE'S reflective actions. These can be movements, voice tones, emotional responses, and the like. Ask yourself what these behaviors tell you about the way this person sees himself or herself. Reflect on your involvement with this person. How can you use this information to create a better relationship and work toward mutual goals?

Alternate: Identify body language that doesn't jive with a person's words or actions. Consider how this information may help you better relate with this person. Don't forget to examine you own body language and behaviors.

Get Back to Nature

GETTING BACK TO nature is an important martial concept. Indeed, we are creatures of both heaven and earth—higher and lower powers. The idea is that if you heighten your sensitivity to one, you heighten your sensitivity to the other. The converse is true as well. If you contaminate one, you will contaminate the other. Thus, it is important to stay close to both higher and lower powers. Nature helps us reclaim our body. It removes us from our hectic lives and aligns us with a more organic part of our existence. It teaches us how to live in harmony with natural laws and awakens our body's instinct and balance. One of its instincts is to luxuriate in Universal Energy.

EXERCISE

FIND A NATURAL setting you enjoy, and begin to frequent it—perhaps on a walk, hike, or even a drive. Spend some time with your pet or in your garden, or creating an arrangement of indoor houseplants. Interact physically. Use your senses. Let this experience restore you.

Get Rid of Chronic Tension

THE DOJO TEACHES you to use tension to relieve tension. To this end, you learn how to perform postures with what is known as *full-tension movement*. This means that you tighten every single muscle in your body to the fullest extent and then execute the posture. You can do any technique or even whole katas this way. The concept of yin-yang comes into play—that is, any movement taken to its extreme becomes its opposite. Remember that your body can only hold so much energy—positive or negative, soft or hard. Thus, you can transform tension to calmness, hardness to softness by simply taking these states to their limit. Rejuvenate yourself often. This easy process will make a big difference in your daily wear and tear. Here's how to do it.

EXERCISE

TRY THIS EXERCISE several times a day. Locate areas in your body where you feel tension knotting up. If you do typing or deskwork, it is common to build tension in your shoulders. You may feel it in your arms or legs or in your chest. Once you identify the affected areas, begin to tense them one at a time to whatever level feels good to you. Regulate and deepen your breathing. and focus your breath on the area, specifically where you feel knotted. Then release the tension with your out-breath as if you were releasing air from a tube. There will be an immediate release. You may need to repeat the process a few times to get the remaining tension out. Then proceed to the next affected area.

281.

Avoid Extremes

ANYTHING CAN BE taken to an extreme, anywhere, including in the dojo. When you take a behavior to an extreme and leave it there, you begin to see a decline in returns, even though the action is intended to be beneficial. In Kali we perform several drills and katas with rattan sticks. One benefit of such activities is that they teach you strategies for open-hand postures—that is, moves you can perform with just your hands, no sticks. Additionally, the sticks strengthen all the muscles used in open-hand applications and loosen your wrists so that you can perform these moves with lightning speed. A student of mine, whose sparring skills flourished as a result of such exercises, decided to triple her workouts. Instead of becoming faster and looser, she strained her muscles and ended up out of action for almost two months. In daily life, it's easy to see the benefits of working overtime. However, taken to an extreme, returns begin dwindling proportionately. Remember, balance works best. As they say, everything in moderation—including moderation itself.

EXERCISE

CONSIDER YOUR PAST week. Can you identify any activities that you engaged in that you took to an extreme? If so, list them. Identify the immediate benefits and the immediate liabilities. How far could you take these before returns started to shift? Where do you draw the line between where maximum performance ends and extreme begins? This is important because what is extreme for you (at this time) may not be extreme for someone else, or vice versa. Identify your limits. Use them to gauge strategies and activities.

282.

Stretch Randomly

CATS ARE INCREDIBLE athletes. And they are masters of flexibility. My twenty-two-year-old cat, Mignonne, was notorious for generating explosive energy with which to scold our family dog. Then, one second later, she would extend her back and paws into a long, languid stretch and appear totally relaxed. Cats love stretching and do so randomly all day long. This is why they maintain such dexterity even into old age. For human beings, growing older carries more responsibilities and pressures. These aspects of our lives raise blood pressure and tense muscles. If we are not mindful, we become frail. You can learn to ward off a lot of wear and tear, however, simply by taking a lesson from the cat. Stretching detoxifies muscles. This relieves stress and loosens the mind. Whether in the dojo or in daily routines, a little cat stretch will take you a long way. Stretch often.

EXERCISE

TRY THIS STRETCHING exercise several times throughout the day. Relax. Regulate your breathing. Take slow deep breaths. Scan your body. Let it tell you what part it wants to stretch. Then stretch as far as feels good and continue breathing throughout. Note: Don't push too far, or your body will just produce more tension. Imagine any tensions and negative energies leaving your muscles as you exhale. If muscles don't loosen right away, don't push them. They will continue to relax after the stretch, even into the next day.

Deepen and Measure
Your Breathing

BREATHING MAY BE automatic. Measured breathing, however, isn't; otherwise, your body would adjust breath just as it does heartbeat. Everyone can breathe more mindfully. It amazes me to watch how deeply and calmly my one-year-old daughter breathes, with virtually no tensions anywhere in her body. Her limbs are as relaxed as if they were afloat on water. Most of us adults marvel at such peace. Unfortunately, by the time you are old enough to be in a dojo, you already carry enough stressors to have to be reminded to breathe. Can you imagine? Indeed, you can be in the middle of a technique and all into yourself when someone starts yelling that you are not breathing. It's funny. This phenomenon occurs outside the dojo as well. Often while talking, your breathing gets choppy, maybe even stops all together. Muscles tighten. Tension builds. Muscles tighten more. More tension. After a while you stop feeling any of this—until it's too late and you develop more serious physical problems ranging from chronic muscle ache to heart disease. Martial arts emphasize mindful breathing. Breathing correctly is one of the best ways to beat stress, relax, and stay strong, clear, and healthy.

EXERCISE

PAUSE OFTEN THROUGHOUT your day and pay attention to how you're breathing. Are you breathing slowly, deeply, and calmly? If not, regulate your breath. Loosen the muscles in your face, tongue, jaw, and the rest of your body. Take a slow, deep breath. Then regulate your breathing. Breathe in through your nose. Hold your breath as you breathe in. Count one, two, three, four. Feel your breath going all the way down to your toes. Breathe out, counting one, two, three, four. Be conscious of how your breath is bringing positive, nutritious energy into your body and expelling tension.

Straighten Up

POSTURE IS VITAL in martial training. Just like figure skaters and dancers, you are told to straighten your lines. This makes all movement look better. Tai Chi tells you to relax your shoulders and move as though there were a taut string attached to the top of your head and held by someone from above. As you practice day by day, you begin to build and strengthen the necessary muscles to maintain this posture even throughout the day. There is, however, more to the idea than just your physical appearance. Straightening out aligns and sensitizes your energy pumps and helps open areas of blocked energy. It moves tension out of muscles you are using to hold up awkward postures. When you combine good posture with good breathing, you will feel an even higher jolt of energy. This will keep you healthy. You will look simultaneously strong and at ease.

EXERCISE

PAUSE OFTEN THROUGHOUT your day and consider the quality of your posture. Relax your shoulders. Move as though someone from above is pulling at a string attached to the top of your head and straightening your spine so that all of your energy pumps are perfectly aligned. Enjoy the difference in how energy moves through your body.

285.

Eliminate Old Assumptions

THE DOJO OFFERS you an opportunity to transform unhealthy behaviors into healthy ones. As you change your behavior, you notice that your lifestyle changes as well. As you become healthier, happier, stronger, more successful, and more peaceful, you are reluctant to want anything to do with former behaviors. You see the connection between them and the lifestyle you are leaving behind. Thus, there comes a point in martial training where you begin to vanquish old assumptions in order to better operate with your new ways of doing things. You are on the mats squared off with someone twice your size (or half) and simply don't assume anything about how the match will conclude. Your focus isn't on winning or losing. Instead, it is on participation and growing. Outside the dojo, you do a lot of physical, mental, and spiritual housecleaning as well. You dump behavioral patterns that restricted you in the past. You are a different person, and you like the difference. You are now in tune with new feelings and energies. They feel good and right. You're ready to trade in negativity for magic.

EXERCISE

DO SOME CLEAN-UP today. Whenever you feel an old assumption surfacing, hit your mental delete button. Look at it for what it is. Remember where it got you in the past. Tell yourself and the assumption that you no longer need it. You are different. The assumption is of no more use.

286.

Remain Open
to New Possibilities

ACCORDING TO THE martial Way is important to keep pushing forward into areas of new possibility. For example, you learn that you can strengthen someone's energy with your mind. The next time someone around you is downtrodden, you try this technique. You are able to make the technique work only a little, but when you share it with a partner (who is also new to you), together you get it to work a little better. You don't have to believe one way or the other. You do, however, stay open to the possibility. Such openness perpetuates the evolution of your art, life, and everything in the world around you. The universe is living energy, growing in consciousness every second. It inundates us with possible opportunities. We simply have to be there and see them. What you learn matters. What you do matters. The martial Way is to adopt a position of continuous learning and take advantage of opportunities as they arise. Your job is to keep learning, from as many sources as possible—the more diverse the better. Your mentor is everywhere.

EXERCISE

EXPERIMENT. OPEN YOUR mind to everyone you encounter. Don't impose any barriers. Consider everyone a teacher. Look for the lesson. If you feel you are in the teacher position, don't dominate. Share. Then shift. Become the student.

287.

Test Your Growth Regularly

AN ANCIENT WARRIOR who couldn't effectively use technique stood to lose his or her life. So being able to implement martial concepts has always been vital. To this end, regular self-testing is embedded in these arts. In the contemporary dojo, there are skills everyone learns. These are tested and celebrated with belts. Ultimately, however, overall progress is personal. Yes, everyone learns the same postures, but what you take from these postures and how far you can take what you learn is up to you. Self-testing shows you what's working in terms of your personal visions, and what isn't. It provides instant feedback for refining your personal skills. It tells you when you are ready to investigate higher-level concepts. I don't think you ever enter the dojo without something to test—either from a former class, another practitioner, assigned or personal readings, or what have you. The same principle applies to daily life. Self-testing is how you grow.

EXERCISE

START JOURNAL TO help you see how you are advancing in you use of martial concepts. You can place any detail you wish on it. I suggest tracking both difficulties and successes in the following areas: Balance, Energy, Awareness, Focus, Self-Discovery, Bringing _____ to a Successful Solution, Overall Contentment, Health, Relationships (itemize these). Date your entries. Evaluate your progress as fair, good, or excellent.

Alternate: Take index cards and write the name of one martial skill on each card. Then decide on a day and test your ability to use the skill in your daily routines. Leave space for several entries. Date each. Jot a few notes for each entry. Check your progress regularly.

Lend a Hand

THE DOJO TEACHES you to seek opportunities to help others through rough times. Indeed, you learn that everyone struggles with some kind of turbulence. Thus, when you see someone faltering in his or her training, you try to assist—in humility. In acknowledging another person's difficulty, you recognize your own. In helping someone else, you essentially help yourself. Assisting other people illuminates your mutual connection. You feel more like a team, because you are. You learn that no matter how difficult things become, you aren't in it alone. You generate bonds and commitments where they didn't previously exist. I have put this concept to the test in daily life many times—at home, in the classroom, with colleagues, and with business partners. What's key here is that you must act without any self-serving intentions. You lend a hand because you are trying to understand someone deeper than words can comprehend.

EXERCISE

LOOK FOR WAYS to assist others. There are many opportunities: Give a friend or colleague a call to see how he or she is doing. Visit someone. Join an organization (like the Humane Society, Leukemia Foundation, etc.). Do a walk or run for a good cause (diabetes, breast cancer, heart disease, etc.). Help out at a facility for youth or the elderly. Use your expertise to teach someone else a skill to reach a goal he or she is struggling with. See how you feel.

Develop a Sense of Compassion

ALL MARTIAL ARTS ask you to be compassionate both inside and outside the dojo. At a fundamental level, this mind-set begins by acknowledging the struggles of other people. But there is hidden dimension here. For martial and all Eastern thought, a very important concept is that *compassion is the basis for living an enlightened life.* You start out thinking, "Let me help you with so and so." Then your focus shifts. Rather than being so goal oriented, you are instead more interested in helping to lighten another person's load. You've come to see that everyone is just doing the best he or she can. Some, of course, will say you can always do better. And perhaps, virtually speaking, this is true. However, what happens is all relative to whatever is going on in your life at the time. You can train for an extra hour a day, but you can't do so if you have to be at work by a certain time. You do your best. There are creative ways around your schedule, but they have yet to occur to you. Give yourself permission to love others, even if their actions are riddled with what appear to be mistakes. Look to the big picture. Remember, everything has purpose. Love is compassion in motion.

EXERCISE

TRY TO SEE everyone you meet as doing his or her best. Don't personalize their behaviors. Instead, if you see mistakes, look for the opportunity to help lighten their struggle. Follow through. See what happens.

290.

Don't Punish Yourself

IS THERE ANY truth to the idea of self-fulfilling prophecy? Martial arts say there is. Cause and effect applies not only to how you see others, but how you see yourself as well. If you make a mistake, you don't punish or victimize yourself. If you do, you are using your energetic power (*Xin-Yi*) to create circumstances in your life that will fulfill your beliefs. A greater problem here is that you generate an ongoing cycle of hazardous situations. In the dojo, most practitioners eventually recognize the relationship between self-image and outcomes. When you feel on top of your game, you do well. When you feel less, you perform at a lower level. If you go into the ring punishing yourself for your last performance, you will only make things more difficult than they need to be. Learn to give yourself a break. Remember, the law of karma assures that the world will mirror your beliefs. When you feel good, you are healthier, stronger, and more alert. If you feel you deserve more, life will create opportunities for you to achieve more. Then it's up to you to take advantage of these opportunities.

EXERCISE

TAKE A CLOSER look at behaviors that give the impression of being mistakes. Consider what life might be trying to tell you to help move you toward success. Tell yourself you have done your best. Then look at what actions impeded the performance you preferred. What caused these actions? What can be done to troubleshoot them? Feel good about your effort. Follow up. Watch what happens.

Check Your Ego at the Door

EGOCENTRICITY, INSOFAR AS the dojo is concerned, is the epitome of conflict. Martial philosophy favors harmony and respect. If you try to act superior with others, you will eventually attract someone who will seek to humble you. Using superior power to deal with others is as good as your supposedly superior power lasts. The martial Way is to eliminate conflict altogether and follow oneness and wholeness with everyone and everything. In other words, check your ego at the door. This avoids conceit and keeps everyone in balance. Some people try to project an appearance of superiority. This will only lead to internal and external conflict. Seek oneness with others instead. Harmony dissolves conflict and gives you strength. Stay balanced.

EXERCISE

MAKE YOURSELF ATTENTIVE to how you attempt to work things out with others. The next time you catch yourself trying to get the job done by one-upping, put the brakes on. Don't force issues. Work, instead, to remove conflicts or obstructions from the beginning. Consider all of your martial skills, and use those that will assist you in achieving harmony. Pay special attention to scans and other sensitivity-boosting techniques. Remember yin-yang. Then work from there. See what happens.

Observe, Personalize, Functionalize

EARLY HUMANS GENERATED fire by rubbing sticks. This progressed to using stone, flint matches, glass, and other materials. Similarly, the early Shaolin monks, through intimate contact with nature, generated systems of natural movement to improve health and spiritual power. Later these were tested on untrained people and their responses studied. This feedback helped refine the original movements and create techniques for a system of self-defense. Transported further—this time into ordinary life situations—these techniques were refined, again through natural feedback, and established as a way of living. The dojo experience is similar. You objectively observe a technique. Usually it is illustrated on a fellow practitioner. Then you learn the technique by executing it yourself. You then try it on a general population of practitioners, modifying as you go along to as many different natural reactions as possible. In the end, you learn to deliver a single technique in an endless variety of ways. You have not only discovered how to adjust to other people's idiosyncrasies, and your own, but more importantly, you have learned how to relax and alert your mind so that it is capable of such adjustments. Whether in the dojo or daily life, the process is the same. Observe, personalize, functionalize.

EXERCISE

CONSIDER A SITUATION you are currently attempting to resolve. Identify what martial techniques will assist you to achieve resolution. Imagine someone, not you, effectively using the technique on another person. Then imagine yourself using the procedure with a diversity of people who offer the widest range of reactions. Modify the technique with each person and reaction. Lastly, visualize yourself applying the technique to the circumstance you have in mind. Make all necessary adjustments. Follow up.

Don't Try to Liberate from What Is

IN HEAT YOU sweat. In cold you shiver. Martial arts encourage you to live with nature's ways. This prevents stress and keeps things flowing. Judo says *don't resist the fall*. But don't resist executing the throw either. Martial arts are all about right movement and nonresistance. You move at the right time, in the right way, with the right intensity—each gauged by what *is*. *This means being honest. For example, are you falling or are you executing the throw? Of the techniques that you could employ, which are most natural given the circumstance? What is your skill in these techniques?* You learn to go with what is most natural *at the time.* If there's a high-flying kick coming for your head, the book may say you should bend back or step away. But what may be most natural at the moment is to drop into a very low stance, explode upward, and fire back. Next time, you might just step back. Similarly, taking an extra two hours today to train a technique you haven't worked on for a while can leave you in pain tomorrow. You don't become resistant and end up doing the same thing again. You let yourself heal. Likewise, if you want acknowledgment at work for good deeds, be sure to celebrate those of your colleagues. Remember, an institution's way of doing things is not necessarily based on what's natural. Resisting what's natural is dysfunctional to all. Sometimes you have to step outside the box.

EXERCISE

BE ATTENTIVE TO circumstances when you bristle, come to a standstill, or try to force circumstances into an unnatural direction. Liberate yourself from these tendencies. Pause. See where things are naturally headed. For example, if a colleague is upset and on a roll, don't interrupt. Try to listen with all of your relaxed attention. Move *with* the flow until a window of opportunity opens. Then make your move to bring the situation to your advantage.

Don't Look for
Someone Else's Approval

MARTIAL ARTS ARE about attaining ultimate freedom. Needing approval is seen as a toxin of the ego that keeps you operating on false motivations. Indeed, the martial Way is intended to liberate you from the ego's shackles. What's key here is that the martial mind isn't focused on winning the game, so to speak—as is the ego. Instead, you are zeroed in on playing the game and taking pleasure in the refinement of each single move. Your interest is in making that action your best. You don't need anyone's approval. You have but one consultant—your innermost self. When you call the shot from here, you have moved correctly. The future you were born to live is a composite of such shots. Your job is to take each one at a time, see where they land you, and enjoy the thrill of the journey. Don't concern yourself with the approval of others.

EXERCISE

WHENEVER YOU FEEL the urge to seek someone's approval for a *personal* action, focus your attention inward. Center, relax. Look at the circumstances. Consider all possible moves. Know where you'd like to end up, but detach and just focus on the action you are about to take. Scan your emotions, and consult your body. What do these tell you? Consult your heart. Then make that move your best.

Accept Yourself

DO YOU SPEND excessive money on health supplements, fashion, diet, and beauty products? Exercise excessively? Work out when you are injured? Use alcohol, food, work, or drugs to feel better? Are you content? If you aren't comfortable with yourself, you won't live to your full potential. For example, a short, husky karate player loses his first sparring match to a tall female who outscores him with long, graceful kicks. He angers and attributes his loss to size. Someone reminds him that Bruce Lee was a little guy. But, he says, at least Lee was handsome. He suffers more defeat, blaming the gods for his problems. In another dojo, there's someone with nearly the exact same body style—but with different mind. She has realized that tall opponents can't hold technique on her very extensively and has thus perfected escapes. She has also perfected devastating kicks to all lower targets. She is graceful, unself-conscious, and confident in her movement. She is accepted as one of the best martial artists in her dojo. Indeed, life outside the dojo is disappointing to the first player above, yet exciting and enjoyable to the second. Whether in the dojo or out, when you accept yourself, others will accept you.

EXERCISE

STEREOTYPES AS PERPETUATED by others and ourselves have contaminated what we see when we look at ourselves. Look in the mirror. Really see yourself. Identify your attributes. You have plenty. Consider what successes these can open for you later. For now, simply see that you are worthy. Use your heart-mind energy. Watch as life opens opportunities for you. I once watched a dying martial artist blast every stereotype out of the sky and perform one of the most beautiful katas I'd ever seen—just months before her death. Don't undermine yourself. Just keep shining.

296.

Don't Damage
Another Person's Spirit

THE DOJO IS not immune to people who attempt to take advantage of others. It's not just those in power either. Everyone has seen the more experienced player flattering himself by pushing the novice around. This is like faulting a baby who is just learning to crawl for not being able to walk. You see bullying in every occupation. Sometimes we see it in our families and extended families. A child paints a portrait, and the parent analyzes it as though he were an art critic or an economist questioning the monetary value of amateur art or the financial probabilities of becoming a successful artist. Perhaps someone enrolls in a dance class, takes violin lessons, or creates a stock portfolio, and his partner offers only harsh commentary—oblivious to the fact that life is offering an opportunity to see deeper into someone else's innermost desire. Such behavior is in direct opposition to martial philosophy. There is no good reason to put a dark cloud in someone's sky, even if your job is to help refine his or her technique.

EXERCISE

THE NEXT TIME you catch yourself about to say something to take the wind out of someone's sails, push your pause button. Don't take yourself so seriously. You can radiate positive energy at will. Consider the circumstance as an opportunity to see deeper into the person's character. Ask what the circumstance tells you. Perhaps the person sees himself as artistically inclined or athletic, in need of becoming physically fit, or wanting to help with finances. Depleting this energy will leave your partner lifeless. The worse someone feels, the more difficult it is for him or her to accomplish goals. Everyone needs to start somewhere. Find ways to tap this person's interests and dreams to everyone's advantage. Watch for this energy to come back.

Don't Allow Yourself to Be Easily Discouraged

ADVERSITY IS LIFE'S way of calling you to grow. Indeed, dojo training often intentionally puts you in turbulent situations to see if you can work your way through. You are even encouraged to script your own scenarios. For example, say you believe you are too reactionary. You can choreograph a drill to have a partner flurry you with attacks from various distances, some posing actual threats and others not. You use this scripted situation to make you a bit less trigger-happy and perhaps move more advantageously. Sometimes adverse situations occur spontaneously. You're trying out a new technique and your partner shuts it down completely. You don't get discouraged. Instead, you use this as a double opportunity: first, to iron the kinks out of your maneuver, and second, to learn your opponent's counter. This is true outside the dojo as well. In all of nature, adversity is required for growth. The human gene pool is a good example. Science tells us that good genes prevail over all harmful ones. The more they do, the stronger they get. But without some turbulence they weaken. Disruption promotes growth even at the cellular level. This is life's way of raising your horizons.

EXERCISE

WHENEVER YOU ENTER an adverse situation, remember that life is pushing you to discover personal capabilities you didn't know you had. Don't be surprised if you, or someone you know or will soon coincidentally meet, will sometime require your newly found skills. Don't allow yourself to be discouraged, even if the lesson repeats. In the dojo, as well as in undergraduate and especially graduate education, you repeat things a lot. This repetition or practice creates expertise. It creates patterns for fast recall. It creates strength. Trust the process. Be present for the gift.

298.

Don't Give All of
Your Energy Away

DON'T DEPLETE YOURSELF. Martial arts caution not to issue more energy than you can simultaneously generate. If, for example, you can fire off five kicks at full bore without diminishing your energy supply, doubling an attack might leave you fatigued. This, of course, is no problem if you succeed in taking out your opponent. However, if you don't succeed, you become an easy target. You have to hold on to something. If your opponent knocks you down, you'll need energy to get back up. If your opponent counters with kicks, you'll need energy to move. If you get tagged, you'll need energy to move on. This principle applies off the mats as well. If you're up late planning a presentation for the next day, remember that you'll need energy to deliver the presentation. Use as much energy as you need to get the job done, but don't give it all away.

EXERCISE

BEFORE BEGINNING ACTIVITIES, assess how much energy they will require. Make sure you leave enough in your reserves for whatever comes next.

Cloak Firmness with Gentleness

BE DECISIVE. BUT act with compassion. This is the martial Way—to be both powerful and gentle. You move with confidence and resolve, yet remain soft and flexible enough to sustain harmony, reading your opponent's intentions as you go, evolving wherever and whenever necessary. But there is a hidden meaning to this. It epitomizes the warrior mind-set, sometimes symbolized in martial philosophy as *water and iron*. This means the mind should always be soft and flowing like water (*Xin*), and the will or intention (*Yi*) should be determined and iron hard. If you can stay soft, you can harmonize with wherever your opponent goes, rendering him powerless. Underneath, your will stays solid and focused until it reaches its destination. The concept also holds true in daily life.

EXERCISE

BE ATTENTIVE TO your mind-set as you go through your daily routines. Consider how science tells us that if an atom were the size of the Empire State Building, its nucleus would only be the size of a grain of sand. Center and relax. Empty your mind. Visualize your consciousness as being expansive—as boundless as the sky. Then compress your will to the size of a grain of sand, as if it were the nucleus of an atom. Then reverse the meditation. regulate your breathing. Feel the power of your intention. Reverse again. Breathe deeply. You will feel a surge of relaxed energy. Take this mind-set into your daily affairs.

300.

Don't Become Spaghetti

SOFTNESS DOESN'T MEAN listlessness or lethargy. If your movement is lifeless (in the dojo, you use the image of spaghetti) and apathetic, you won't have the necessary internal power to guide actions to where you want. You won't have the protective internal strength to ward off and rechannel opponents. They will cut right through without anything energetically keeping them from their destination. If my arms are like spaghetti, punches will fly through. Opponents can push them flat against me and open targets at will. Disinterested, lackadaisical, droopy action can quickly leave you vulnerable. You need enough determined energy to get a job done. You can't be totally passive on the mats or in daily life.

EXERCISE

SCAN YOUR MIND-SET and physical drive as you enter your daily situations. If you feel weary, sluggish, or listless, push your pause button. These are indications that your movement may not be as effective as you need. They also flag vulnerability. Use your meditations and visualizations to strengthen and focus your internal energy. When you feel refreshed, follow up and continue what you were doing, but with increased energy.

301.

Be Panoramic

THE MARTIAL MIND is panoramic. In the basic sense, this means not giving so much attention to yourself that you are blind to the actions of others. At a higher level, this means that you can fix your perspective so that it is infinitely wide (meditative), with no borders, and yet sharply focused, detecting the slightest motion on a select target. Such capability is easily observable in the behaviors of cats. They can simultaneously take in the whole skyline, sense that the heat just went on across the room, and detect the tiniest movement two inches in front of them. Remember, information energy travels at very high speed. Opportunities and targets reveal themselves first through your sensitivity, internal energy channels, and intuitions. Train simultaneously to see the big picture along with the tiniest ones that make it up. Here's how you can do it.

EXERCISE

EXPAND YOUR ATTENTION. Use an image of the sky or anything else that is boundless. Then shift your attention so that your focus is as sharp as a laser. Now, try to maintain both focuses at once. You can achieve this by creating the following anchor (or create your own). Imagine your consciousness expanding until there is no image left—simply a blank ultra-alert state. Do the same with your compressed attention.

Alternate: Imagine a blue circle on your computer screen. Then imagine a small white dot in the center. Now highlight the whole visual in white. Everything disappears, yet everything is still there. Pick a few circumstances throughout your day and try to maintain this panoramic (expanded-compressed) mind-set. Start with something small until you get more comfortable with the technique. See what happens.

Eliminate Dualities

MARTIAL ARTS TRAIN you to eliminate dualities. This means to get past the notion of opposites and instead see opposing forces as complements, parts of the same thing. An easy way to understand this is to simply see opposites as hyphenated—for instance, yin-yang, hard-soft, or here-there. This concept is well illustrated in the Chinese translation of the word "romance." Rather than one word, the Chinese translation results in an entire phrase: *winter-flower-blossom-snow-moon.* What I like about this is that the more you think about the image, the more opposites you discover exist simultaneously in what we call "romance." When you expect romance to be one way or the other, you are not seeing it fully. On the mats, you begin to break down dualities all over the place. You find that blocks can strike and that strikes can block. You learn that you can push. You learn to pull. Then you find the push-pull. You don't fall down and get up. You go down-up. You can apply this concept to any situation, on or off the mats. When you do so, you stop simply learning moves. Instead, you string all of your moves together and start dancing.

EXERCISE

AT THE END of your day, do a quick scan of the circumstances and people you have encountered. Make a list of words you would use to describe them. Try for a variety of words that appeal to the senses: sight, touch, hearing, taste, and smell. Afterward, hyphenate each word and add the opposite—for example, light-dark, bitter-sweet, hot-cold, loud-silent. How does your opinion of the day's affairs change when you consider the full spectrum of complements (hyphenated words) instead of perceiving events as one way or the other? How can this concept change the way you plan for or approach upcoming events in your life?

303.

Develop a Positive Perspective

THIS DOJO SECRET isn't about denying the existence of pain and suffering. It's about radiating positive energy from your center as you move through such feelings. On the mats, you can feel like your opponent is taking batting practice on you. But if your core is solid, you continue to emanate positive energy. Does this mean you don't feel the punches? Of course not. However, this is the time to tap your core energy, reassess, make better choices, and carry on. Remember, positive energy begets positive energy. You may not know exactly when opportunity will open, but it will open. Your job is to be there and draw from your well of positivity to strengthen and protect you. "Strong at the core" is how my wife, Elaine, and I describe our relationship. This is how we continue as a couple, recuperating from arguments and disagreements and the like, because at our deepest core we love and care for each other. When obstacles get in the way, we draw upon this mutual core energy, this positivity, and use it to bring conflicts to quick resolution. The fully seasoned warrior feels pain and then uses his or her core strength to transcend it.

EXERCISE

THE NEXT TIME you feel conflict, anxiety, or pain, let yourself experience it, but don't cling. Tap your core energy. Trust that positive energy will lead to windows of opportunity. Use your positive energy to guide and protect you.

304.

Watch Out for Some Rewards

SOME REWARDS CAN contaminate your soul. For example, sometimes martial practitioners take cheap shots and are rewarded—for instance, they "accidentally" poke an opponent in the eyes and as a result whip into a flurry of techniques that win a sparring match, while friends cheer from the sidelines. Sometimes, a player who hasn't really learned his or her stuff receives a promotion. Rewards come this way in daily life as well. Someone cheats on a college test and gets an "A." Someone falsifies a timesheet and gets paid overtime. Someone badmouths a fellow employee and doesn't get caught but later ends up taking that employee's job. These kinds of "rewards" are not tolerated in the dojo. They are like spyware surfacing up in your field of consciousness, tempting you to seek rewards for dysfunctional action. They are dangerous because if you follow them enough, you can generate negative patterns of behavior. These will have you acting to some ghost author's script, on automatic pilot. Know what you're being rewarded for.

EXERCISE

THE NEXT TIME someone rewards you for a behavior, press your pause button. Ask yourself what the reward is for. If it is for negative behavior—perhaps you just made a negative comment about a coworker—push your pause button. If you feel comfortable, apologize. Get the record straight and tell the person that you realize that speaking in such a way isn't right. If you're not agreeable to this, internally see the reward for what it is and mentally dispose it.

305.

Be a Doer

DOERS LIVE THEIR own lives. They don't live vicariously through the experiences of others. They jump in and play the game. They sample the entire spectrum of events and circumstances that life opens. This is the martial Way. In the dojo, you may see a concept demonstrated, talk about it very briefly, and hit the mats and try it as soon as you can. Then you have an opportunity to ask questions intended to refine your understanding and execution of the technique. After your instructor's response, you're back on the mats— "experiencing" the answer. This process is an important part of learning. Willingness, observation, words, and comprehension alone are not enough. You have to hit the mats, so to speak, to complete the process. At this point, you are able to run the information through your personal "software" and start applying it to the unique circumstances of your own life.

EXERCISE

BE A DOER. As you go through the events of your day, try to find something in each event that will put you in the role of doer. For example, if a coworker formats a word processing document for you that you have unsuccessfully been trying to set up, don't stop at having the job done for you. Ask your partner to walk you through the task. Then try it yourself. If you see or hear about something interesting—from a good new recipe, to good ways of saving more money, or dealing with relationships—try it. Something attracted you to the idea. See if you can discover what. Keep an open mind. You may have to modify or explore further before you can generate benefits. But this is natural. Sample the full spectrum of events, circumstances, people, and emotions in your life.

306.

Embrace Diversity

THE MARTIAL ARTS club I advise has attracted players from around the world. We have recently had members from Africa, Russia, Indonesia, Afghanistan, China, Japan, Korea, India, and several other countries. It's simply fascinating to see how no matter where they are from, players have been exposed to the same core elements of martial art styles as you. It's like sharing an ancient language. However, embracing differences may in the end prove equally as useful. These differences show what others have been able to do with this important primal language. Diversity exposes you to information that has the potential of advancing your ability—sometimes fast and extensively. It inspires, challenges, and improves your play. It reminds you that knowledge is active and grows. It reminds you of your bond to others and to the world.

EXERCISE

CONSIDER SOME ELEMENTS of your life that would be interesting to explore globally—for instance, your occupation, a sport you enjoy playing, or a concept (religious, political, social, medical, or what have you). Conduct a search on the Internet, in a bookshop, or at the library. Don't be afraid to directly contact experts and ask for them to make recommendations on people or places to continue your search. The more diverse you make your search, the better. Approach each juncture with an open and positive mind. Ask yourself what there is to learn. How can you apply this information to your own life?

307.

Don't Force Your Routine

CAN YOU IMAGINE forcing winter to start early or late? But we all know that sometimes it does so on its own, regardless of the dates we establish for this routine. This is nature's way. The idea is that even when things become routine, there is still natural spontaneity to them—a certain unforced timing. Martial training teaches that you shouldn't mess with this timing. Simply put, you are where you are. As your life changes, so will routine. For example, if your routine is to perform katas at daybreak and your newborn child has been awake all night with teething pains, you may start a little later. If it is your routine to travel on the evening before major holidays and news networks are broadcasting severe storm warnings, you may change your routine. If it's your habit to always be the one to try to fix things after you have had an argument and your gut feeling says to wait, the warrior will defeat the tendency to act first and will wait. The warrior is free.

EXERCISE

THE NEXT TIME you find yourself trying to force an issue under the justification of being "routine," push your pause button. Ask yourself what the best action is, given the circumstance. Then take that course of action.

308.

Move On

ON THE MATS, if you take a shot and someone catches it and knocks you down, you don't get up and immediately take the same shot again. You first have to figure out what went wrong. Maybe you just slipped up. So you roll with it, regain your balance, and try again when you have the chance. But maybe you haven't mastered the technique enough to make it effective. Or maybe your opponent has perfected defending and countering the technique. If either of these scenarios is the case, you don't want to try it again anytime soon, at least not with this person. If you don't know the solution to a problem, martial wisdom tells you to hold off if you can. Daily situations are similar. Say you request a salary raise based on years of service. Your request, however, is shot down. The reason, you are told, is that raises are based on college preparatory work or field experience. You don't get up and fire the same ammunition. Nevertheless, you now have clear targets. You can roll into a place of advantage. For instance, you can figure out how to acquire the necessary *moxy* or fieldwork and take your shot. Or you can walk on to new and better employment.

EXERCISE

THE NEXT TIME you unsuccessfully try to achieve a goal, pause and identify what techniques you have applied. Try to see why they are not functioning. If your evaluation is that these techniques will not work in this situation, give them up, at least for the time being. Ask your heart what you want from this situation. Then strategize another approach that perhaps has more promise, given both your analysis and gut feelings. If you feel you just slipped up, roll on until opportunity again arises, and try your approach again.

Follow a Barrier,
Don't Lay into It

A KARATE PLAYER is in the ring. There's a hard, straight punch coming right for her head. Taking it is not an option. Unless you have extensively trained in bone-to-bone technique, challenging it head-on, fist to fist, is something that only works in cartoons. She decides to throw out a block. She stops the punch but doesn't try to muscle it. That would only dull her tools as if she were trying to push a sharp knife through concrete. Her iron-hard block morphs, now lightening and cutting alongside the obstacle, lifting, sliding, and rolling it away. Then she takes her shot. Martial arts teach you to follow barriers in daily life as well. Taking them head on can de-energize your best tools. The idea is to stay sharp and close to the bone, so to speak, until harm is out of your way. Then make your move.

EXERCISE

WHEN YOU EXPERIENCE conflict, stay with it. Name it. Say to yourself, "____ is a barrier." This immediately takes some stress away. If the barrier is a conversation, meet it, but don't try to pulverize it. Instead, relax, lighten up, and keep close to the issue by following the direction it is naturally going, gently applying just enough input to keep you from harm. When the opening eventually surfaces, shift. Make your move.

Regularly Ask Yourself
How You Can Improve

LIFE IS CONSTANTLY flowing and changing. Ultimately, everyone needs to ask on a daily basis, "What can I do today to improve myself?" In the dojo, for example, needs shift repeatedly. One day things are tame, and the next it seems everything is ballistic. Certainly, each scenario calls for different improvements. The more aggressive things get, the more attune you have to be to improving energy levels and focus. Thus, before entering the dojo it is essential to ask yourself what skills you will require to facilitate a successful session and what you can do to enhance them. Your objective is to make the most of that day. You can also include a general assessment of things. For example, if you've been doing a lot of conditioning activities, you might consider switching to sensitivity drills. If you've been training in long-range techniques, you might consider switching to closer techniques—but again, depending on mutual and individual roads ahead. Daily routines work the same. Check in with life every day. Seize each day!

EXERCISE

BEFORE ENTERING YOUR various day's events and circumstances, reflect on what you will be doing and what skills you will require to reach your goals. Ask yourself what you can do to improve yourself. Can you utilize other skills? Modify existing ones? What skills will you need to remember to emphasize? Is there anything you can do to remember these skills? To enhance them? Enter each situation relaxed and confident. See what happens. At the end of the day, see what your quest has told you about yourself. Reward yourself for all of your good actions. Consider adjustments or new techniques that can be added to your repertoire to improve your performance next time. Follow up.

Don't Go Around Proving Yourself

THE DOJO TEACHES that people who pose challenges are one thing, but the way you react to those people is up to you. You can't stop others from wanting to fight or cause trouble. But only you can decide to treat matters intensely or to stay laid-back. Such behavior is evidenced in professional sports all too often. A pitcher hits a batter, intentionally or not, and in the next inning the opposing team's pitcher hits a batter. Players from both teams jump off of their benches, and a fight ensues. In the dojo, someone gets a little aggressive with a technique and lands a partner on the mats too hard. Then the next thing you know, the aggressive person is getting the rough treatment and ducking for cover. In daily routines, one driver cuts another off and a chase ensues, with all the toppings of good old, traditional road rage. One partner criticizes, so the other now feels the burden of having to prove something. When this occurs, you lose your free will and give up your control to someone else. Martial arts emphasize not letting such things get to you. If you are secure and self-confident, just treat things lightly; if you are not, you have another problem. *Why* aren't you secure? You need to try to overcome your insecurity. But don't try to prove something, especially when your fear is warranted.

EXERCISE

THE NEXT TIME you catch yourself heading out to prove something, put the brakes on. Don't do it. Ask yourself, *Is there any doubt in my mind that things will turn out safely and successfully?* If not, just let the situation go. If there is doubt, ask, *What is causing this doubt?* Maybe you have to give a presentation for work. You feel your communication skills are weak. Try purchasing a CD or video that provides creative tips on public speaking. Improve your skills and replace doubt with confidence.

312.

Be Free

MARTIAL ARTS SAY that you don't become free. You *are* free. What's more, your freedom is expressed in the choices you make. Ultimately speaking, choices are infinite. Thus, you are free moment by moment to create the life you want. When you know you are free, you realize your reactions belong to you. They are episodes you paint on your life's canvas. Early in dojo experience, everyone tends to freeze with indecisiveness. Or you parrot actions just to get by. You don't typically see the tremendous range of choices before you. This is because things are happening too fast. Someone throws a punch, and you think of one possible response—a block. A month later you see a dozen alternate responses. This continues until your choices seem virtually infinite. Now you begin to realize that it is entirely within your power to create your next slice of life. Blocking the punch now excitingly shifts to *What do you want your next moment of life to be?* This is freedom. It's no longer the punch that is driving your future. *You* are driving it. Training in freedom is training to see choices. Here's how you can do it.

EXERCISE

PUSH YOUR PAUSE button often. Ask yourself what you want your next moments of life to look like. Consider and respond from the heart.

313.

Don't Think One Style
Is Better Than Another

FROM THEIR INCEPTION, martial arts have been a means to enlightenment. They are not an end in and of themselves. Indeed, martial philosophy emphasizes that no one art is better than another. Like different dances, each is a specific mode of expression. *Wushu,* for example, is a Chinese art characterized by graceful, athletic movement. Capoeira is a Brazilian art that uses a lot of gymnastic technique, such as cartwheel kicks, one-handed back flips, and the works. Aikido is all about rechanneling energy. There are hard systems like Tae Kwon Do and the karates, soft systems like Tai Chi, and hard-soft systems like Wing Chun kung fu. You choose which of these systems you want to pursue based on how you feel and depending on what you want to articulate. You can also look at each art as a complete set of tools to help you reach and enhance goals on your path to enlightenment. You may prefer one to another given a particular circumstance, but this is based on individual creative expression more than the art. They are all capable of getting the job done. You can apply the same sensibilities to life. Here's how.

EXERCISE

THE NEXT TIME you feel like nit-picking someone who is after the same goal as you, but is following a different path, press your pause button. Instead of criticizing, use your observations to better understand that person.

Alternate: Identify others who currently express the same life values and goals as you, especially someone whom you admire. Consider the idiosyncrasies of their Way; that is, their educational background, occupation, philosophical orientation, and so on. Explore the differences. See what happens.

Practice *Wu Chi*

WU CHI IS a practice with roots in ancient kung fu. It was developed in China over three thousand years ago and consists of nothing more than standing in an upright martial posture anywhere from several minutes to hours. *Wu Chi* is used to strengthen the muscles and cleanse them of toxins. It follows the yin-yang concept that anything taken to an extreme becomes its opposite. Stillness, then, taken to an extreme becomes quickness; immobility becomes mobility. This principle, at the basic level, refers to physical movement. However, hidden in the concept is an excellent way to quicken the mind and spirit as well. This is driven by the ancient notion that the material world intoxicates your energy. Stillness puts you into a cleaner, more organic mind-set in which you trade off materialistic desire and demands for a more relaxed and energized physical and mental state.

EXERCISE

YOU CAN PRACTICE *Wu Chi* anywhere. Stand with your hands in front of your lower *Dan Tien*. Imagine yourself holding a balloon the size of a basketball—your left hand on the bottom, palm up, fingers slightly cupped and aimed to the right—your right hand on top, palm down, fingers slightly cupped, aimed to the left. Imagine the skin of the balloon disappearing, but the air pressure maintaining its circular shape. Feel this pressure in between your hands. Extend your Chi. Feel the pressure between your hands strengthen. Stay in this position without moving for five minutes. Let your mind drift wherever it wants to go. Don't let any thoughts stick. Do this daily. Try to work your way up to ten minutes.

Know That the Best Help Is Self-Help

ONE OF BRUCE Lee's favorite lines was, "The best help is self-help." This applies to all activity both inside and outside the dojo. Ultimately, no one knows better than you what you need and when you need it, and when you have reached your goal and when it is time to move on. Simply put, no one else knows what it's like to be you. The dojo experience helps you discover more about your goals, capabilities, self-expression, and other personal aspects. Part of such discovery is learning to sharpen your skills and coordinate them with your goals. The martial axiom is to be the master of your own destiny. Even warriors need help. The master initiates and guides this process—and on a regular basis. A teacher of mine used to always say, "You can buy fish to satisfy you hunger, or you can learn to fish and you will never go hungry." Practice fishing!

EXERCISE

TAKE A LOOK at the details of your life. Make a list of what you like and what you'd like to change. Identify some ways you could enhance what you already like. Ask yourself how you could achieve what you would like to change. Pick one from each category and carve a path to reach your goal. Get your energy going by imagining yourself having achieved your goal. Visualize how good you feel. Follow up by trying to make the necessary changes to achieve your goals. Do this often.

Learning Is
More Than Imitation

IN MARTIAL ARTS, seeing and even imitating are not enough. You have to feel a technique before it is yours. When you see a take-down, you try it and feel all of its quirks. You have to run it through your own internal energy system. You live with it for a while, and once you get it, you repeat it over and over until it and all of the peculiarities you have encountered are committed to your body's memory. Essential here is the notion of quirks. These can emanate from your own experience, and are thus not always conveyed by your teacher. They can result from the time and place of performance, or from any people involved. Additionally, martial philosophy says that learning is a living process. As situations change, so does the function of what you know. You tune in, modify, utilize, and commit to memory. You live, learn, and grow.

EXERCISE

TAKE A METHOD of doing something that you have seen a family member, friend, or colleague use. This might be a way of organizing, saving, working out, or any other task. If you feel comfortable, ask for advice on how to use the technique. If not, try to break it down into smaller elements. Follow up by trying the technique, feeling all of its quirks, and then modifying it to fit your needs. Watch what happens.

Remember That You Are the Ultimate Creative Artist

MARTIAL ARTS TEACH that life is one great act of creativity. Your job is to paint your own canvas. Martial training helps free you to paint originally and from the heart. Yes, you train in a style or styles. Concepts are fundamental. What you do with them is up to you. You could critically examine all styles of punching, kicking, blocking, and other moves and discover that each is designed to do a similar job. The real differences are subtle at best and intended to make the shot more functional. Other, perhaps larger, differences are the result of self-expression for a particular circumstance. Similarly, the rules to writing or speech are fairly simple. Yet, you can go into a bookshop and see 150,000 ways to use these skills. All of life works this way. Techniques help you become more functional. Where you go with them is endlessly up to you. Remember, your job is to paint your own canvas.

EXERCISE

NEXT TIME YOU find yourself trying to decide between one proven way of doing things and another, consider which better fits your personal mode of expression. Go with that. See what happens.

Alternate: Next time you see someone spontaneously choosing between two styles of reaching a goal, consider it an opportunity to see deeper into the person's character. Instead of looking at the technique, look at the picture he or she is painting. What does this tell you? What does the canvas say that you wouldn't learn directly from the person?

318.

Don't Accept Less Than 100 Percent

MARTIAL ARTS TEACH that you must act in honesty. This includes emotional honesty. Remember, emotions are energy. When they flow unobstructed, you feel them, let them inform you, let go, and act. When they are ignored or minimized, they block up. Have you ever set out to do one thing and then, being emotionally driven, done just the opposite? For example, you go to the dojo to feel good. You're angry with your partner for being late. Your drills are sloppy. Someone gets hurt. Your partner has no idea what has motivated these actions and thus reacts to whatever fictional scenario she assumes. Maybe you're afraid of disappointing your life partner that you spend money you need to save. Maybe you're so happy to see someone and celebrate that you break a diet or sobriety. Listening to emotions can protect us from doing things we shouldn't or give us the go-ahead to do things we should—for example, an Olympic figure skater opts to include in her routine a more difficult technique than planned and wins a medal. You may not always get what you want from a person, circumstance, or event, but acting with emotional clarity sends the right message. This leads to greater self-discovery, integrity, and opportunity to refine actions. It offers others something real to react to.

EXERCISE

NEXT TIME YOU enter a situation, scan your emotions. Let yourself feel them 100 percent. Remember, you don't have to act on a negative emotion, but acknowledge it. See where it is coming from. Let it inform you. Look for ways to use the information positively. Then process the energy, letting it leave your body in positivity. Take action, and watch what happens. See how others react.

Don't Use Emotions to Manipulate

MARTIAL PRACTICE TEACHES you to avoid using emotional manipulation. It's not easy however because it's a way of acquiring things that has been ingrained in us since early childhood. We quickly learn that showing sadness or fear can get us what we need. Such manipulation happens in the dojo as well. Some beginners notice that if they show fear, for example, partners generally take it easy on them for a while—until, that is, their partner sees through the manipulation. The danger is that if you keep it up, you will not acquire the benefits of martial technique, only emotional exploitation. Colleagues, family, and community members use expressions of anger, sadness, and even joy this way, too. You see this in statements like, "Back off," "Let's get this lousy job done," "*You* do the heavy work today," or "Can't you see the kind of day I am having?" Such tactics surface everywhere but have rapidly diminishing returns. Not accepting your emotions, letting them tell you about yourself, and letting new behaviors evolve will keep you blocked and disempowered. Here's what you can do.

EXERCISE

NEXT TIME YOU find yourself trying to control someone with your emotions, press your pause button. Scan your energy centers to see which are affected. For example, perhaps you are using your fear of superiors to push coworkers to work harder. To them, your behavior may seem disproportionate to the task. It generates chain reactions that are based on incorrect assumptions. Exploring your fear, you discover it's all about your upcoming promotion, which you don't want to mess up. You need the additional money and also fear what would happen without it. The better approach is to just outright ask your coworkers to help out. If you want something real, offer something real.

320.

Take Care of Basic Needs

THE LONGER YOU stay with a martial training program, the easier it is to follow it. Additionally, you become much more adept at taking care of basic physical needs: relaxation, meals, hygiene, and sleep. You are experiencing firsthand how each of these affects the quality of your energy and your ability to use it to achieve goals. You are, however, never immune to falling into old, less desirable patterns—especially in terms of basics. You feel more solid all around, so you think, *Why not push it?* But the rewards of doing so deplete quickly. Just a few days of neglecting your basic needs can put you into a downward swing. In the dojo, you retain more tension and tire more easily. You run the risk of injury or taking time off. The pattern can become habitual. You see this often with well-intentioned people in after-work aerobic and other athletic programs. Training that neglects basic needs doesn't last. Treat your body well if you want it to work for you.

EXERCISE

STOP FOR A moment and consider your basic needs. If there are any that are not being met, resolve to address them today.

Abandon the Idea
of Conclusion

THE WAY HAS no conclusion. You see this in katas as each posture morphs into the next. Remember, beginning and end are next-door neighbors. The same is true of meaning. As soon as you discover meaning in any concept, you are already headed toward the next level of understanding. As soon as you grasp the meaning, you are already letting go. Such is the Wheel of Life. But there is hidden information here as well—that is, *beginning* and *end* are just words we need to talk about and share ideas. They are terribly limited. When you consider the two most dramatic notions of beginning and end, birth and death, you see the limits of language in full bloom. What were we before we were born? What is memory? Science tells us it is likened to little electrical currents moving at the speed of light. Science tells us this energy cannot be destroyed. What happens after the body dies? What happens to this energy? Martial arts, science, and all of Eastern thought say that all such energy continues to live and grow. The problem is that we have trouble sensing it. Remember the mantras of Einstein and Watts: beginnings and endings are only illusions. There is only and always *now*.

EXERCISE

CHART HOW YOUR actions flow from one to another. Examine particularly the transitional moments. Ask yourself what you can do to move through your next day's actions with more attention and precision. Look ahead to what your heart desires. Be attentive to how your shaping of things now will help create those moments in your future.

Alternate: To add information to a past situation, recall it in your memory. Bring the scenario to whatever new places you wish. The next time you open the memory, look for the download of new experience.

Keep Moving Ahead

MARTIAL TRAINING ENCOURAGES you to move ahead without wavering. In sparring, a single moment's flinch or hesitation breaks harmony and can cost you the match. Indeed, you train to read such actions in your opponents as flags indicating an open target. Early in your training it is important to understand and execute techniques properly, so you tend to move slowly most of the time. Eventually you build speed and your actions become reflexive. However, even at advanced stages, you must slow down whenever you are being introduced to new techniques. The idea is that once a technique is committed to memory, you can flow from one posture to another, nonstop, adapting to the particular situation. On the mats, this means that you don't throw a punch or a block and stop or hesitate. As soon as the motion begins, you keep cutting forward until the job is done—and even then you see the finish as another beginning moving into whatever comes next. This is true of life as well.

EXERCISE

BE ATTENTIVE AS you leave one set of circumstances and enter another. Ask yourself what you can learn from the situation you are leaving that will enhance the state of affairs you are entering. See the whole day as different movements within a single song. Consider how that song will continue the next day and so on. This, of course, is the song of your life.

323.

Be Everywhere

THINK ABOUT THE lusciously relaxed, open, yet responsive awareness you experience just moments before falling asleep. This very common and normal sensation is vital in your journey to enlightenment. In fact, this meditative mind-set is coveted in martial training and is intended to transfer into all daily routines. It keeps you tuned to the big picture and protects you from compulsions and reaching for mirages. On the mats, this mind-set will prevent you from becoming preoccupied with any single point on your opponent. Your vision broadens to the point of being nowhere, yet maintaining a vibrant awareness that puts your consciousness everywhere. It enables you to deal with even multiple opponents. There may be a barrage of actions coming at you, but you are not transfixed to any *one*. You train to take them all in—like images reflected on a lake that has been sensitized with very high voltage electricity. Your awareness is expansive, calm, and radiating. If you don't want to be bogged down, analyzing this or that, always debating, or driven by compulsions, practice broadening your vision. Here's how you can do it.

EXERCISE

CENTER. REGULATE YOUR breathing. Imagine how fully relaxed you are just moments before a great night's sleep. Scan your body to feel all of your muscles becoming less tense, softening. Feel your mind unknotting. Be aware of your breath. Imagine your field of vision widening and widening until it is as big as the sky. Increase your awareness as if it were an electric current you could run through the air itself. Feel everything—words, images, movement, and the like. But don't grasp for any of these. Let them float through your consciousness, responding softly, efficiently, and only when necessary.

Watch for Innocent Bystanders

THE DOJO TEACHES that all practitioners need to be mindful of innocent bystanders. It is far too easy to execute a technique, either for purposes of exhibition or practice, and make a mistake, putting observers at risk. You literally have to fight off the urge to just jump into things and troubleshoot your environment first to identify any possible hazards. For instance, players can trip up while attempting techniques and unintentionally injure observers. Of even more concern is a player wielding a weapon—a knife, sword, nunchakus (more commonly known as *nunchucks*), and the like—while others watch close by. All glass fixtures pose safety hazards as well. Moreover, an enthusiastic player may demonstrate a technique that is too advanced for others in the room. Indeed, someone is bound to try it, putting himself and others at risk. The martial Way is to act responsibly and place peoples' safety before urges.

EXERCISE

ASSESS YOUR ENVIRONMENT before acting. Consider how your actions will affect others in the room. If liabilities are high, consider an alternate approach to things. At the end of your day, review your actions. Ask yourself how they may have affected sideline viewers. Could you have done anything differently to make better use of your peripheral audience? Use this information to help tighten your actions toward future successes.

325.

Reject What Is Useless—
For Today

IMAGINE HEADING TO the dojo once, twice, or even more times a week, year after year, and learning new techniques almost every time you go. You're right—that would be a lot. I remember when I first began studying Chinese Kenpo. I asked my instructor how many takedowns he had learned. "Hundreds," he said. He paused and then added, "For every angle imaginable." This, of course, translated to *thousands* of takedowns. I thought, "I have a lot to learn." Then my instructor said, "But they are not all useful right away. You have to discover what's most functional for you at the moment and use it. Then put the rest on the back burner." What he was getting at was that if something doesn't work today, you simply reject it and opt for another technique. You use your ability to reject. But don't totally discard techniques. There is a time and place for everything, and a concept that seems to have no use today may be your best friend tomorrow. This principle is true of daily situations as well.

EXERCISE

MAKE YOURSELF ATTENTIVE throughout the day to the skills that you, and those you encounter, draw upon to lead situations to success. No matter what, set your mind on walking away with something useful. At the end of your day, revisit these circumstances. List the skills that worked. Consider other scenarios in your near future where those same skills may be of use. Add them to the top shelf of your toolbox. Don't discard the other skills. They may become useful at a later date.

Get Rid of That Chip
on Your Shoulder

MARTIAL ARTS TEACH you not to harbor anything toxic. Such contaminants corrupt your performance and make all actions more difficult. If, for example, you have something against grappling and that's what your dojo is training, you can't keep participating without getting rid of the chip on your shoulder. This is true for many reasons: you're not having a good time, and this generates low-grade energy, which leads to energy blocks that infect other aspects of your performance and transmit into your daily life. Additionally, this is the energy you pass onward and further cultivate inwardly. Carrying a grudge also falsifies your actions to others. Perhaps someone interprets your behavior as a sign of having a personal problem with him or her. They react to the facade, creating the beginnings of a history of events that are rooted in pretense. This is the way it works in daily life as well. If you hate your job, find out why. The best way to escape a problem is to fix it or move on. Don't complain to your wife, family, coworkers, or others. A chip on your shoulder will grow if you give it the opportunity. Your best bet is removing it completely.

EXERCISE

IDENTIFY ANY CHIPS you carry into your daily activities. Tell yourself that these are shackles and that you intend to free yourself of them. Consider your last week. Write a list of all the circumstances your grudges leaked into. Scan your emotions and tune in to how you felt in each situation. How did your grudge complicate things? What things were left unresolved? How does it feel to still be carrying this information? Who else did it contaminate? What were the results? How did this make you feel? Consider what is causing the grudge. Make a list of possible solutions. Try them.

Do One More

SOMETIMES YOU DO one more repetition of a move or technique just to do it. These are special moments of high, confident energy. Every performance has its peak. You can feel it. Sometimes, though, you set out to do a ten-repetition kicking drill, and when you finish, your body is telling you it is ready, willing, and able to do more. You make a game out of it and go the extra round. This keeps routines fresh and interesting. You push through with a heightened sense of achievement, confidence, and well-being. On the other hand, there is a more subtle aspect to this concept. Often during these extra moments, something special happens: you perfectly execute a posture you've previously been unable to grasp, or you discover an energy you thought yourself incapable of. Such things happen in the Earth dojo, too: you put twenty extra minutes into a report you're writing and suddenly burst with the inspiration you've been waiting for all day, or you spend one more hour with your child and energetically bond in a way you never expected. These are gifted moments. Seek them. Take advantage of them.

EXERCISE

THE NEXT TIME you feel you feel conditions are right to extend the amount of time you are devoting to a situation, try taking it one more round. If you are at the dinner table and engaged in conversation, sit awhile longer. If you are engaged in a project with a colleague at work, try staying with it a little longer. When you are out on a walk, stay with it a bit more than you planned. Don't be surprised if something special happens.

Be an Amateur Again

WHEN YOU ARE starting out in martial training, you are eager to be with people who are advanced. Then, with time, *you* become the advanced player and it's time to become an amateur again. Remember the story of the white belt becoming black and becoming white again (see secret 23). Once you reach the level of expert, your job has traditionally been to share what you have learned, going back to basics with the next generation. By putting yourself in this role, you too reenter the mind of the amateur, searching all of your techniques for truths they convey and taking more from them each time you do. Indeed, this exhilarates you and vaults you to yet another rung up the ladder of progress. This is true in all aspects of daily life as well. Every skill that has gotten us to where we are can be reopened for more learning.

EXERCISE

MAKE A LIST of life skills acquired either through formal or informal education, such as communication, interpersonal relationships, mathematic, psychology, theology, and so on. Make a second list of skills you have achieved from your own searching that have enhanced or deepened your aforementioned list, such as self-improvement, history of religion, science, sports, and so on. Now, put the two together. For example, ask how you can create a single tool of mathematics, psychology, and science to deal with a current life issue. You may discover a need to not only to revisit but also to update information from formal instruction. Likewise, you may expand information from personal schooling. Recycle by sharing with others. See what happens.

Remember That a Goal Is Not Always Meant to Be Reached

IT'S WINTER AND you feel like you are in a rut. This affects your training as well as your overall mind-set. You struggle with depression. There doesn't seem to be anything exciting in your future. Your state of affairs is beginning to take its toll on your health. You have a difficult enough time just getting up enough enthusiasm to get to the dojo. You think of a friend who recently earned her black belt in Tae Kwon Do, remembering that she had to create an original kata as part of her test. This is something you always wanted to do—in fact, you have been thinking of putting together a kata with music. You feel a jolt of excitement just thinking about the possibility. Out of desperation, you decide to do it. Your goal is to have it ready to perform by spring. You feel a little better immediately, and your mind-set steadily improves. But by spring, you have moved on to other things. What happened to the kata? It served its purpose. The dojo utilizes some goals that are not meant for achieving. Sometimes you just need a target to aim at.

EXERCISE

IF YOU'RE FEELING stuck or in a rut, consider something you always wanted to do and make plans to pursue it. Maybe it's acting lessons, a martial arts class, or a cooking or pottery class. Perhaps, it is part-time work at something very different from what you do full-time. Maybe it's joining a community organization or other group. Just create a target for yourself. Sometimes that's all you need to pull you through.

Think Optimistically

MARTIAL ARTS TEACH you to think optimistically. If, for example, you're going to be able to execute a flying scissors kick to down an opponent, you have to believe you can do it, or it will never work. Both optimistic and pessimistic thinking are energetic. Each transmits intention and begets like energy. Each energizes and creates the events of our lives, as well as those of others. People who feel positive about themselves don't cause problems for others, and the reverse is true as well. Indeed, it is the artist who constantly doubts himself who predictably causes the most injury to others in the dojo. This process is true in daily events, too. I recently listened to a friend explain that life won't let her out of the starting gate. She has come to believe this. The danger of such thinking is that it depresses the body and mind, which in turn dulls your awareness to windows of opportunity as life opens them for you. Pessimism is energetic sabotage. It's like that old anthem of seeing the glass half full or half empty. Be optimistic. Acknowledge your potential. It will guide you through.

EXERCISE

TELL YOURSELF FIRMLY that optimism creates a positive future. Pessimism creates the opposite—no matter how much you achieve. Whenever you catch yourself taking a pessimistic potshots, hit the brakes. Later ask yourself why you were thinking in a negative way. What is it that you want and have yet to acquire? Ask yourself why you want what you want. Look at it objectively. Will it really make you happier? Will getting the money for a new wardrobe really bring more fulfillment to your life? Lay out a logical plan to achieve your goal. See what happens.

331.

Don't Fear Imperfection

THERE IS NO place for fear of imperfection in the dojo. Most people can't just walk out on the mats and perform a perfect kata or riffle off a perfect roundhouse. Chances are you're going to be launching hundreds before you get it right. You'll also encounter a new circumstance that will require modifications, as well as new skills, and the process will begin again. People fear imperfection because they fear failure. Often the player who is afraid he can't do a kick challenges the effectiveness of the kick, becomes so fearful that he messes up, justifies not participating, gets sick on the day the kick is being trained, and drops out. The pattern, of course, leads to other difficulties. Everyday life is similar—for example, a community actor energetically trashes the media, saying they never give attention to local artists. In his rant he admits to needing such attention for his career. Ironically, he has justified *not* reaching his goals. *Everybody's been there.* Imperfection and failure, however, are just words. Remember, the martial Way is to participate in the process. You have to fall down a few times before you can walk. You have to walk before you can run.

EXERCISE

AT THE END of the day, list the major events and circumstances you encountered. Look at each of these as though they are parts of a map that lead to several destinations. Your first destination is a lesson you need to get you somewhere exciting. Seeking it and discovering where it will take you is the fun of being alive. Find your lesson. What skills does it incorporate? How can you better hone these skills? Excite yourself by considering some of the positive things for which life may be preparing you. Play with the notion that one of these may be your next destination. Sit back and wait to discover which it is! Look in the mirror and tell yourself you are still learning.

Don't Fear Success

THE DOJO TELLS you not to fear success. I love watching players receive their brown belts, because their black belts are now so close within reach. Their enthusiasm skyrockets overnight. They talk and move in a much more positive manner, and, of course, their confidence level is high. They can taste success. Their training intensifies. Their bodies bulk up. They beam. Once in a while, though, you see a player who starts sabotaging his or her imminent success: "Do you really think I can do it?" "Why do I need another belt?" "Aren't the other candidates so much more impressive than I am?" Some people fear success because of its demands. Brown belts have a lot of bodywork conditioning to do. In daily life, getting that new job you want may require telling your partner, leaving friends and family behind, as well as relocating. But if the job is your heart's desire, you must rise to the challenge. No matter how things work out, you will gain knowledge and skill that will float you forward. Flow with success. This is how you grow.

EXERCISE

THE NEXT TIME you find yourself resisting success, ask yourself if what you have been trying to achieve is something you really want deep in your heart. Visualize yourself not taking the action. How will you feel? Compare that to how you will feel if you do accomplish your goal. Are you saying one thing and feeling another in your heart? What part of the challenge has you so concerned? Look at the action objectively and ask if your concern is warranted. Is the action positive? Do you see it as a growth step? If so, follow up. Tell yourself you can only gain, no matter how things turn out.

333.

Feel Good

MARTIAL ARTS TEACH you to feel good—healthy and upbeat. The notion, however, also refers to feeling worthy—that is, perceiving yourself as a good person. It doesn't matter if you have ranked high in martial training, earned advanced college degrees, become rich or famous; you can still remain unable to find peace in life. Knowledge certainly helps make life goals possible, but it doesn't guarantee them. If you don't see yourself as worthy of goodness and abundance, you can still reject your goals every time they become available. Some people even punish themselves by doing things to counteract whatever good flows their way. Low self-worth transfers into energetically created conflict, both at work and at home. It fosters the attitude that what you have is never good enough. This notion often leads to overspending on material goods, as well as believing that pain or hard luck is life's constant, whereas goodness fizzles out. It's not uncommon, especially for seekers, to feel there is more we could be doing. But don't let this diminish who you are. Seek it because you are worth it!

EXERCISE

CONSCIOUSLY UPGRADE THE choices you make. Go for the best possible options. Flow through routines doing things the easiest way, because you are worthy of nothing less.

334.

Keep an Open Mind

DOJO EXPERIENCE ILLUMINATES the dangers of closed-mindedness. Your first lesson may be as simple as learning to breathe differently, see energy differently, or see cooperation as strength, not weakness. Remember, martial lessons are rooted in the physical realm. Repercussions of a closed mind are easy to spot. If, for example, you refuse to acknowledge the energy of focused Chi, it's unlikely that you'll ever develop the effortless power that all martial arts herald. Chi doesn't feel bad if you don't believe in it. You may, however, start wondering how the woman old enough to be your grandmother smashes through a block of wood like it's nothing and carries on in a robust and healthy manner, while the only thing you're trying to break is one cycle of sickness after another. Note: Keeping an open mind doesn't mean flip-flopping or doing something that is bad for you. It means using logic and intuition to panoramically identify your best life decisions. But there is a hidden meaning here. Whether on the mats or in daily routines, the mind must be open to embrace and utilize the fullest potential of spirit. Open-mindedness is a choice.

EXERCISE

FIND SOMEONE WHO is getting good results in an area you have been stressing over or are trying to improve. Ask that person how he or she has achieved such results. Keep an open mind. Identify a book that uses a radically different approach than you have employed to achieve results on a mutual interest. See what you can take from this approach. Follow up and give it a try. Check your newspaper for workshops or lectures that use very different approaches to goals you share. Attend one. Keep an open mind. Take whatever you can and follow up. See what happens.

Make Skill
a Matter of Spirituality

EVERYBODY HAS HIS or her own breakthroughs. You can practice martial theory for years or just months before these leaps forward begin. They do, however, follow a certain sequence. Everyone finds early techniques difficult and somewhat foreign. Then one day, though, you discover you can go through each movement with precision and even without thinking. Your next wave of breakthroughs is tapping into your internal energy system and using it to power your technique. Your sensitivity increases and you begin tapping into others' energy as well. All of this helps you move effectively and eases effort. Then you make the big leap and tap in to the energy of everything that surrounds you, using it to power up. And then you discover the Universal Body and energetically seek into it, centering mind and intentions (*Xin-Yi*) there and flowing this energy through all of your actions. At this level you begin to experience doing without doing. Here, skill and spirituality become one. You see the body as energy, movement as energy, thought as energy, memory as energy, spirit as energy, the world as energy, and universe as energy. Like the aikidoist, your job is to luxuriate in the playful flow of this energy. Your power of intention is technique enough. You feel that you have entered a level of deep spiritual experience. You feel this way because you truly have entered such a level.

EXERCISE

PICK A CIRCUMSTANCE today and navigate your movements using only your power of intention. Relax. Ask your heart what it desires. Use your power of heart-mind to plant your intention. As gently as possible (like the aikidoist), become sensitive to how things unravel. Stay in harmony, checking often to see what you desire. Wait for opportunities to arise and take each until you reach your destination.

336.

Don't Be Concerned
with Escaping

SOME MARTIAL INSTRUCTORS videotape novices to measure their improvement. These videos can be quite humorous in that there is more running going on than martial arts. As time goes on, however, you see more of a willingness to stay in the action. Part of the reason is that when you first head out onto the mats, you don't have many techniques at your disposal. They, of course, accrue with experience, and so does your confidence. In your earlier stages, you just want to escape any way possible; thus, *any* action, martial or otherwise, looks good. But later you discover that running opens targets. It can make you more vulnerable, not less. What's more, you still don't know how to respond effectively, sustaining your future vulnerability. Your concern over escaping hasn't gotten you far. Later you become more fixed on dealing with the problem, testing and sharpening your skills, growing into them, especially for future deployment. Rather than running from things, you face them. You wait for contact, face problems, stay with them, and rechannel to better directions if necessary. This experience teaches a good lesson. Rarely will running be to your advantage.

EXERCISE

THE NEXT TIME you're in a low-risk situation from which you want to escape, tell yourself to stay with it. This is the time to stay in the game and put your skills to the test. If you cannot improve the situation, let go, change the game, and commit to staying in that direction.

Liberate Others
by Liberating Yourself

IN THE DOJO, the more liberated you become, the more you liberate others. But as soon as you try to restrict and control another person, you immediately restrict your own movement. If I want to keep you in trapping range, for example, I have to give up entering other ranges myself. On the other hand, I can liberate myself of the need to be in any specific range by augmenting my training and working toward becoming competent in all ranges. By eliminating my fear of being caught in territories where I have no expertise, I eliminate my need to control you. I can now focus on harmonizing with you, thus eliminating stress and conflict. In daily life, if I want to force a student who has missed an assignment to meet me at my office at a certain time, then I am stuck having to be there as well. I can create a more harmonious situation by strategizing an alternate assignment that frees us both. This energetically reduces stressors. It sends positive energy and gathers the same. The more you liberate yourself, the more you liberate those around you, and the more liberated you become. The process is synergistic.

EXERCISE

THINK OVER SOME of the events in your past week. Consider those times when you labored to control someone or a situation. Ask yourself why you felt such a need to control. What were your specific concerns? Keep an open mind. Consider what skills you could enhance or acquire that would relinquish such concerns and, with them, your need to control. Strategize a plan to achieve the skills you need. As soon as you admit that the answer is within you, rather than somewhere outside of you, you immediately liberate yourself. Do this often.

338.

Keep a Joyful Spirit

THIS IS ONE of the greatest martial secrets. Your spirit can be high, quick, and radiant, or it can be dull. Your job is to make it as bright as any sun. As life energetically flows through you subatomically, what you turn on and let energize you is a conscious choice or triggered by a mental or behavioral template—that is an already established pattern. You, however, can *always* override the pattern. This, however, isn't always easy. Bad things happen to everyone—at work, home, in families, relationships, and such. I am not suggesting being untrue to yourself or playing a game of make-believe and deception with others. When circumstances are dreadful, you have to feel them. It's difficult, but you ultimately can choose to process energy and release it positively or negatively. Remember, spiritual energy is what literally creates the events of your life. When it is dulled, *Yi* (the power of intention) weakens. When it is joyous, it is fully charged. This energy is necessary to lift you, vault you from harm, and into good. No matter how bad things get, you *can* still push the "on" button to life energy as it flows through you. Similarly, you or some pattern can turn it off—it's your call.

EXERCISE

PRACTICE JOY. THE mind can work like a video camera. The next time you are in a circumstance that is depressing you energetically, pull back and focus on something pleasant in your environment. Zoom in close and let its positive energy enter you. Try pulling way back and then zooming in on something in the world that is spectacular, or perhaps a special moment in your life, and let its energy enter you. Absorb as much positive energy as you can. Note: Such joy is flowing through you always. It's your choice to put your awareness there and energetically use it in times of need. Choose well.

339.

Keep a Warm Heart

SPIRIT IS THE energy that gets things done. Informed by the heart, it moves to create your deepest desires. Your job as a warrior is to focus on those things that energetically peak life's energy as it flows through you, and to unblock the heart's desires so that they can merge. When your heart is warm and loving things that make you happy come to you, rather than you going out with pit bull determination to force the world to do what you want it to do. You may not, however, always get what you want. Nevertheless, the Way teaches that *you are always where you are meant to be.* This is one of the most difficult concepts to grasp—for all of us. If we could just step back far enough and see the whole picture, so much fear, worry, and disgruntledness would vaporize in an instant. This is why we have to practice.

EXERCISE

PRACTICE WARMING THE heart. Pick a circumstance from your day. Look at it from a distance. See yourself objectively. Regardless of what happened, look at each detail as a necessary component of your Way. Remember, everything happens for a reason. See if you can discover the reason, the lesson in each detail. What if you could step back far enough and see your self planning for each of these experiences before you were even born? What if each was an energetic product of your spiritual will to get you to where you want to be in this lifetime and beyond? Consider how each of the details in the circumstance you've chosen to examine was meant to vault you to even higher ground and greater successes.

340.

Practice Feeling Arcs of Energy

THERE IS AN arc to all movement, a rise and fall. Increasing your sensitivity to this pattern will minimize stress and strengthen your actions. Martial arts teach you to see a target, summon your energy, and take your shot. That's the essential paradigm. Within this model, however, are a few hidden elements that deal with tuning in to the arc of energies within you as well as around you. All techniques require a certain amount of power to make them useful. They are effective because they synchronize with surrounding energies. In sparring, scanning your opponent's energy, as well as your own, helps you synchronize which technique to launch and when. If your opponent is fully charged, coming at you with his pedal to the metal, you're in a good position to rechannel his energy (soft against hard). When his energy arcs downward and yours arcs upward, you are energetically posed for an effective counter. This principle works well in daily circumstances. Here's how you can apply it.

EXERCISE

PRACTICE FEELING ARCS of energy. Focus your attention on how you feel energy-wise just before you take any actions. Estimate the amount of energy required to successfully launch techniques and complete your strategy. Stay tuned to your energy as it rises and falls, as well as to the energies around you. Try making your move when your energy is peaking and when that of others is on the decline.

Keep the Little Stuff
from Taking Over

IN SPARRING IT is common for opponents to throw a bunch of little stuff like jabs, annoyance kicks, and arm movements. These can discombobulate your ability to effectively organize patterns of action and can unbalance your energy system. When opponents get the reaction they're looking for, they come at you with the real stuff. So you train to phase out the little stuff completely or use the smallest effort possible to remove it. If you have to react, you may not even bother with a serious block. Patting the annoyance out of the way is enough. This principle also works off the mats. By reacting full bore to annoyances, you risk walking into a much more serious situation. "Don't sweat the small stuff," says writer Richard Carlson. The more we shift toward living our process, the more we trust the Way, the more we learn to desire what is; indeed, the more we see: "It's all small stuff."

EXERCISE

AT THE END of your day, make a list of as many situations and actions as you can remember that elicited reactions from you. Which could you have simply ignored? Which would you have been better off ignoring? What can you learn from these events? Use this knowledge tomorrow.

342.

Become Your Own Fuel

NO MATTER WHAT kind of martial art you practice, you can't always rely on the energy of others to get you through. You have to tap your own internal energy to some capacity in order to efficiently execute any technique. To this end, martial arts teach you to become your own fuel to use your internal energy (Chi) to make more. As you proceed from one series of actions to another, you sensitize to your energy as it arcs downward. You shift your attention from external tasks to your internal energy centers, tapping their ability to make more energy. You can do this anywhere.

EXERCISE

REMEMBER, LIFE'S ENERGY is flowing through you at the speed of light. Envision a river of bright, white light running through each of your energy centers. Make yourself sensitive to your internal energy arcs. When you tap in to them, replenish them with more fuel.

343.

Remove Doubt

DO YOU EVER picture yourself doing something moments before actually doing it and suddenly everything turns out just as you envisioned? On the mats it happens like this. You're sparring. But before you actually do anything, you can see yourself firing off a punch, your opponent blocking, and you swinging his arm into an armlock that transforms into a throw. There is absolutely no doubt in your mind that things will turn out this way. The visual image happens in a split second, but the next thing you know, you've launched the techniques and everything is happening just as you visualized. Sometimes you see yourself collapsing under an opponent's attack, and of course, that happens. Martial arts teach that you have the power to shape your life by way of the intentions and images you let flow through your mind. Every moment offers opportunity. You can fill it with transmissions of confidence or doubt. Life will open accordingly.

EXERCISE

BEFORE HEADING INTO your daily tasks, rid yourself of self-defeating thoughts and images. If you have time, write them out or say them out loud to yourself. Tell yourself that they are destructive and that you will not be steered by them any longer. Reinforce your intentions with positive visuals. Tell yourself, "I *can* get this done." Say this several times. See yourself successfully accomplishing your goals before you do anything. Have faith that wherever you go is exactly where you need to be as you work your way to greater goods.

Solve Problems, Don't Fight Them

IN THE DOJO, you learn not to fight problems, because doing so only weakens you and makes it easier for your opponent to defeat you. For example, your opponent maneuvers you into a joint lock. Resisting will only give him better positioning, or you will deplete your energy, making the lock even more effective. How many times have you fought over some issue with a partner, family member, or colleague and later wished you had avoided fighting at all costs? Your choice to argue only made things worse. What's more, you realize that you would have retained more power had you done nothing. Problems exist. Some are severe. The martial Way, however, is to think about the solution. Rather than fighting off adversity, you train thinking *technique, technique, technique.*

EXERCISE

THE NEXT TIME you find yourself steaming over a problem and getting ready to unleash a rant against it, put the brakes on. Conserve your good energy. Think *technique.* Ask yourself what concepts you can draw upon to resolve the issue. Balance your energies. Focus on the concepts you have identified. Visualize a positive outcome. Then use the technique you've identified to solve the problem.

345.

Don't Be a Martyr

MARTIAL ARTS EMPHASIZE that the warrior does not declare himself a martyr and throw his or her hands up against the challenges of life, simply giving in to the judgments of the world. The artist dances with the world to carry out change. Sacrifice is indeed part of the martial Way. But there is a difference between giving things up and giving up on a goal. You may give up an hour of television for an extra hour in the dojo. In the ring, you may give up a punch for a take-down. At a different level, when you learn to sacrifice the result for the activity itself—for example, performing kata takes precedence over earning rank, or sparring takes precedence over winning or losing—the whole activity is performed for its own sake. Activity, not survival, becomes the pinnacle of value, one given up for the other. This kind of sacrifice is natural and selfless—no ax to grind, nothing to prove—rather than self-flattering, and it is a far cry from mar-tyrdom. Martyrdom represses and gives up life. Sacrifice, on the other hand, helps us dance freely and paint masterpieces of our lives.

EXERCISE

ATTITUDE EQUALS LONGITUDE. The next time you are about to give something up begrudgingly, put the brakes on. Remember, with everything that you give up there is something gained. The trick is in gaining the right things. Identify what you stand to gain from the situation. Is this appropriate to your life needs? Do you feel safer, more secure, happier, more content, and more stable? Sacrifice is intended to sustain life. If you feel that an action is depleting your life, try to identify the ways it is doing so. If these concerns are reasonable, free yourself to reconsider alternative actions to your goal. If you discover ways you are benefiting from such actions, enjoy your gift.

346.

Create New Choices

THERE IS A place in martial training to explore possibilities with a "what if" attitude. You execute a technique just to see what will happen. You do this just to play, but also to grow. For example, your habit and training may be that whenever you lock up with someone, you push, shuffle back, and fire off a kick. So one day you ask your partner to humor you and lock up. This time, instead of pushing away, you hit the ground and roll into a scissor kick. You may hit pay dirt, as they say, or you might not. Either way, the action will open a whole new window of choices, and that's exactly what you're after. Following up on any of these choices will open even more options. Trying something different every now and then is healthy. It helps you grow.

EXERCISE

START WITH SOMETHING small. The next occasion you have to make a decision, look for new choices and try something completely different. For example, if it is your habit to celebrate by going out to dinner, try going out to a concert or a play and then out for dessert after. If you always wear a certain fashion, try something new or if every time you meet with a certain friend you discuss that same thing, try moving the conversation somewhere else. See what innovative skills new choices can generate.

Give Your Partner
a Pat on the Back

THE LANGUAGE OF touch is in many ways more organic than words. Often in the dojo, you can say more with a simple touch than you ever could in sentences. A simple pat on the back conveys feelings of goodwill, camaraderie, acceptance, understanding, welcome, and the like. Touch is instinctual and primal, and can sometimes get to places where words cannot. It of course precedes the development of verbal skill and is no less necessary. Touch is a basic human need, but one that must be used appropriately, especially within the perimeters of different interpersonal relationship. In daily life, touch is essential to couples. It communicates heartfelt closeness, comfort, and trust. Psychology says that couples who don't utilize touch enough become distant, because the partners feel unloved. Touch sends a message of care and safety. It is a split-second way to reveal to others what is in your heart.

EXERCISE

WHEN APPROPRIATE, GIVE someone a hug or a pat on the back, especially an intimate partner. Use your heart as your guide.

348.

Trust

DEVELOPING TRUST ISN'T about blindly believing or having faith in everyone you bump into, or thinking that people everywhere are going to "do you right." Martial trust is about trusting in the living intelligence of the universe. It is about seeing the totality of life as good, even through episodes of hardship. On the mats, you might wind up in a bind and you wonder where the trust in that is. Sometimes it's difficult to see the whole picture. That movement could lead to another that puts you in an advantage. But no matter what, there is no losing if you trust that you are right where you need to be. Perhaps you invent a new move as a result, and that affects you in a much bigger way. This kind of trust is inspirational and freeing.. It rounds off edges created by stress. It keeps you connected to Universal Energy, especially during difficult times. It helps you see windows of opportunity as they open. Trust is your choice.

EXERCISE

THE NEXT TIME you have to make a difficult decision, use all of your faculties—body, mind, and spirit. Use your intuition. Let your heart speak. Then follow through. Tell yourself that whatever you have chosen is right. Look for the lessons and follow them. Trust yourself. Trust the universe.

Let Everyone Know
They Contribute

IN THE DOJO, it is important for everyone to know that he or she is making a contribution. Perhaps you help set up, clean, take down apparatus, teach, or other helpful tasks. Whatever you do, your work is acknowledged appropriately. This not only fosters goodwill, but it also generates and sustains a healthy environment. It invigorates self-expression and strengthens the community. It fuels the notion of growth through cooperation and camaraderie. When everyone is working toward calmness, reliability, safety, and well-being, it becomes easier to behave in such a way yourself. This principle also holds in daily life. Too many institutions complain of low morale. But there isn't any trick. Appropriate acknowledgement of other people's efforts goes a long way. Remember, positivity begets positivity. By acknowledging others you strengthen yourself.

EXERCISE

WHETHER AT HOME, at work, or with friends, find a way to acknowledge the contributions of others. You can use a simple smile or compliment or a more celebratory activity. See what happens.

Develop a Sense of Kindness

MARTIAL ARTS EMPHASIZE acting in kindness wherever you go. Remember, we are all energetically related, right down to the cellular level. Indeed, the big picture leads us to the realization that the universe is us, and we are the universe. Thus, in being kind to others, we are in fact kind to ourselves, and vice versa. For this reason, the martial Way directs us to make peace with ourselves if we want to break the chain of pain. The warrior who has found peace does not wish to have conflict with others. So your first jobs are developing a benevolent and forgiving attitude toward yourself and then passing it on to others. This mind-set works in conjunction with the laws of internal and Universal energies. Remember, you can process and transmit energy in two ways: in positivity or in negativity, each of which sends and returns specific energies out into the environment. It's your choice. You can disapprove of others' behavior and battle to defeat them. Acting out of compassion, forgiveness, and harmony energetically gives you full access to your power. Resentment and hate only build stress and disempower you.

EXERCISE

PURIFY YOUR MIND by taking a mental inventory of all the anger, hate, resentment, and other negative feelings you harbor. Write these feelings into a list. Let yourself feel each one again. Consider anyone involved with each circumstance, and mentally pardon him or her for the grief they may have caused. If you are not ready to do that, make peace with yourself by pardoning yourself for not being able to forgive them. Feel the weight immediately lifting from your shoulders as you shift from carrying negative energy to positive.

351.

Create an Internal
Leveling Tool

MANY OCCUPATIONS USE some type of leveling tool to indicate imbalances and irregularities. Today most of these instruments are laser driven. However, you may have seen the older models, with the small glass portal, filled with what looked like fluid and an air bubble that moved from side to side, resting in the center when everything was lined up or balanced. In the dojo, you can talk about balance all you want, but you have to know what it is before you can maintain it. For example, if you struggle to execute a leg sweep but you always launch it from too close, you don't know what it feels like to execute it from too far away—or from a point of balance. The best way to learn is to do the technique way too big. This helps makes the center more apparent. Once you know what balance feels like, you can use this sensitivity like an internal leveling tool that will signal imbalances and help you locate the center. The same principle works in daily routine. Here's how.

EXERCISE

EVERYBODY TENDS TO get used to breathing shallow. The next thing you know, shallow breathing feels normal. Try breathing big—taking big in-breaths through your nose that go all the way to the bottom of your feet. Exhale through your mouth. Slow your breathing down to an extreme. Let your body feel that. Then regenerate a depth and rhythm of breath that feels more balanced and is located more centrally in your body's lower *Dan Tien*.

Alternate: If you feel you are spending too much and this is interfering with other goals, such as saving for a new house, a child's education, or whatever, try spending nothing at all except for the absolute necessities for a pay period. This will help you relocate balance between what spending is frivolous and what is necessary.

352.

Reinvent Yourself

ONE OF THE greatest satisfactions in the dojo can be found in watching practitioners reinvent themselves into stronger, happier, healthier, more positive and empowered people. This doesn't happen overnight. It happens in baby steps. In fact, many complex postures and techniques are initially broken down into smaller simple actions until proficiencies become more automatic. The road is filled with a lot of stumbling around, messing up, and getting frustrated. But you learn to dig in and conquer these obstacles. You celebrate. You go on. Looking back every now and then, you remember when you first entered the dojo, perhaps wondering what you'd gotten yourself into. But you keep going forward. You get the job done. You reach your goal and, with black belt in hand, you realize the road doesn't seem so long from this vantage point. It was all a small price to pay for how you now feel. From here you see the road, which has been with you all along, as one of life's most magnificent gifts.

EXERCISE

CHANGE CAN BE risky and difficult, and in many ways it is inevitable. Contemplate where you would like to be six years from now. Keep in mind that in this span of time you could earn an entirely new set of credentials. If you wish, you could change your life dramatically. Ask yourself, *Would you like to pursue a new career or relocate? What is your heart's dream?* Break the goal up into smaller, more manageable components. Create a plan. Focus on your plan. Move ahead.

353.

Take Your Best Shot

ASK MARTIAL ARTISTS, "What's your best shot," and if you press them, they'll tell you. Most, however, will probably say, "It depends on the circumstances." And it does. Your best shot might be a roundhouse kick. This is probably the most popular kick in martial arts. Most experienced players can easily defend against it. Also, what if your opponent is twice your weight and height? Is the roundhouse kick still the way to go? Who's faster? What skills do you both share? What is exclusive to each of you? The list can go on almost infinitely. There are times when even your least favorite shot is best and you have to go with it. In daily situations, a retailer's best approach changes as he or she moves from one customer to another, a lawyer's changes from one jury to the next, a teacher's changes from one classroom to the next, and so on. Indeed, sometimes sitting still is the best action. Best actions are a matter of circumstance, not habit.

EXERCISE

CONSIDER AN INTERPERSONAL circumstance that keeps recurring and that you want to resolve. Next time you meet this person, spend a few minutes gently trying some different techniques. Watch how the person reacts and when; for instance, does he or she dismantle your best shot? If so, how? What keeps you from seeing this counteraction coming? Notice the other person's patterns. Can these help forecast his or her responses? How can you use this telegraphing to better shape and time your own technique? Do his or her patterns show openings from which counters to your actions are more difficult? If so, consider taking your shot there. Then follow through, taking shots and rechanneling what you've noticed so far. Stay present to possible surprise offenses coming at you.

Surrender to Life
by Not Surrendering

SURRENDER IS NOT giving up. It is an act of complete participation. My book *Be Like Water* focuses on how to flow through life, fitting in wherever you go—softly yet powerfully. Noninterference with life stands to gain you the most whether you are in the dojo or the workplace, amid interpersonal relationships, or whatever. Resistance sucks power. Conversely, surrender empowers gracefully assertive, uninhibited movement. Whatever you do becomes smoother and easier. In judo, surrendering to the fall is what allows you to roll out of it. In sparring, surrendering to your opponent's moves allows you to turn them around to your advantage. For example, your opponent wants to grab you, so you let him; in fact, you pull him in even quicker and tighter, using his own momentum to trap him and put leverage on your side. Then you throw him. When a martial artist enters the ring, the first thing she does is to relax from head to toe. By surrendering to the moment, she energetically begins to tap all of life's forces. Stress eats energy. Don't stress. Relax. It's like fueling on fresh power.

EXERCISE

STOP WASTING ENERGY today. As soon as you find yourself about to stress over any circumstance, push your pause button. Tell yourself to surrender completely, like water entering a cup. Enter into whatever the situation is. The more you surrender, the more power you sustain. Surrender isn't about victory. Remember, in the big picture there is no losing. Note: Sometimes what's best is to let someone come to you. Energetically follow your heart's intuitive messages. Things may not work out the way you want at the moment, but they are working out in the larger scheme of things. Focus on the lesson.

355.

Surrender to Death

BRUCE LEE ONCE said that in order to live, the warrior must "learn how to die." This is akin to an ancient Samurai maxim that says, "Relinquish your fear of death." At first these notions of life and death seem contradictory. Traditional martial instruction tells you to open your focus so that your mind is clear and present everywhere. In a life-or-death situation, you can't be preoccupied by the notion of dying, because such a mind-set steals energy and vision. The paradox is that by surrendering to the idea of death, your focus is on what's happening in the present moment. You are free—free to do whatever is necessary, even if it's risky, to get the job done. Restricted, you may turn away from exactly what you need to be doing to protect your life and thus lose it. The warrior is relaxed, focused. She knows that clinging to something only increases the risk of its slipping away.

EXERCISE

LOOK IN THE mirror and tell yourself that, yes, death is around every corner and that your job is to fight for your survival. Thus, you will not ignore the concept of death, because this will only steal your power against it. Instead, you will surrender to it, accepting whatever happens. You are going to use all of your energy to live!

356.

Be Loyal

DICTIONARY DEFINITIONS FOR the word "loyal" include *allegiance, dedication,* and *faithfulness,* to people as well as to ideas. Loyalty is the foundation of all healthy relationships, whether they are physical, intellectual, emotional, or spiritual. It is the heart of morality—personal, denominational, or public. It means you don't create opportunity or escape from troubles through betrayal. Loyalty doesn't apply to only good and easy times, but also to times of hardship as well. It is essential to good living. It helps us be spontaneous when we must. It helps create community. Martial arts teach that loyalty powers your capacity for courageous action. For example, Japanese samurai were bound to the death to defend their lord. On the mats, the warrior doesn't quit until the match is over. You have a strategy. You commit. You go, go, go—allowing for change on the way, of course, but forging onward until you either reach your goal or hear someone hollering, "Stop!" Note: Whenever loyalty becomes detrimental or destructive, as in acts of exploitation, crime, terrorism, and such, it must be avoided. Loyalty energetically helps you activate and see your way through dim moments. This same principle applies to daily living.

EXERCISE

LIST TEN MARTIAL principles that have worked very well for you. Organize them in order of which work best. Make a bookmark or card from your list. Try making several copies. Put them in places where you will see them throughout the day. Make a point of reading the list once in the morning before heading out and again at night. Revise your list often.

Alternate: Consider how you feel when someone or some institution has been disloyal. What can be learned about treating others in honesty?

Be Courageous

MARTIAL ARTS TEACH that courage is acting on your utmost beliefs. It means pushing past fear and apprehension to do what is right. In the ring, you may be up against a hulk when someone starts yelling, "Stay back!" You know you must make contact, however, to effectively use your techniques. You hear it again, "Don't get too close!" Your thoughts rock on a wave of uncertainty. Your heart says, "Stick with what you know and do." You balance. You move in. You fire. You prevail. In everyday life, you may want to save for your child's education. A tight budget and vanquishing debt has always been your guiding principle. At the end of the year, you have some extra funds, more than you're used to. Your accountant says that the sooner you eliminate your mortgage and start saving, the more savings you can accrue. You're not sure. You'd love to have the extra money, but your heart says your accountant is right. This too is courage. It extends from loyalty and principles you trust. It shows what you're made of.

EXERCISE

MAKE A LIST of the ten things you fear the most. These can range from internal concerns to external; for instance, fears related to expressing yourself interpersonally and spiritually, as well as fears about money, career, health, and the like. Make a list of martial principles that can be applied to alleviate each of these fears. Write it out on a card, and carry it around with you. As you eliminate each fear, mark your progress on the card. Find a way to reward yourself as you push past each fear.

Be Free

FREEDOM IS GOING with the flow. This is the martial artist's Way—to live wholly in the moment, moving with what *is*. Here, Way and end become the same movement—to harmonize. Heart and mind become a single energy current. All learned martial form evolves into free form. You become spontaneous. You don't interfere with action, preferring instead to become part of it and allow things to take their natural course. You are like a mirror reflecting everything, lovely or dreadful, without allowing any of it to spoil your calm. You appear carefree. You are soft on the outside and invincible on the inside. Egoless, you are liberated of personal fear and deception and unshackled from those of others. There is no limit to what can be done once you combine Universal Energy and heart. Living is discovering this potential. Freedom is using it choice by choice to paint the canvas of your life. Be creative. Be at peace. Paint joy.

EXERCISE

WHENEVER YOU FEEL like you're getting boxed in during your daily routines, look to the right or left, glance into the distance even for a moment. Tell yourself that you are free to choose whatever direction the next moments bring. Consider your choices. Consider their effects. Go with what is best.

Alternate: Slow down your speech patterns. Consider what you are about to say next in terms of cause and effect. Ask yourself what you want from the situation. Choose the words and body language that will best take you there.

Alternate: Meditate. Let your heart speak. See what your desires are. Later compare this to what others want of you. Use this information to make better choices. Tell yourself it's your call.

359.

Feel the Brightness

ONE OF THE treasures of the dojo experience is the sheer pleasure of high-energy, bright days. You learn to take full advantage of these moments. When you feel on top of the world, you are energetically better connected. You take more risks, and stressors role off more easily. You more effectively manage trouble and pain and can even transform them into success. In the ring, when you're flying high, you can take hits you ordinarily couldn't. You feel indestructible and compared to how you feel on your lower days. The idea is to use these opportunities to open new and interesting choices. Remember, high times are lessons, too. If you stay tuned, you can learn a lot about your capabilities. Maybe you always wished you could throw a lightning-fast acrobatic spin kick. Well, this is the time. Maybe you always wanted to paint the house, start your own business, or write books. Life is bright, and it's laying out the carpet to help you reach your goals.

EXERCISE

RISE TO THE occasion. Next time you feel your energies running high and bright, use them as an opportunity to push your capabilities and learn something new about yourself. Pay attention to how you round off any stressors that cross your path. See what you do to get things done. Make a mental blueprint of those actions. Put it in your toolbox for future use. Feel the life force flowing through you. Remember what this feels like. Summon it during times of lower energy.

Feel the Murkiness

BOWING TO LIFE is more than just embracing life's highs. It's a push, but martial arts ask you to meet life's murkiness with positivity as well. Indeed, these are times we may wish we could simply avoid. In training, however, you get used to the idea that on some days the going is rough. On these days, it's sometimes difficult to see the point of your efforts. It seems that whatever can go wrong does—people are late, techniques are off, tiredness and boredom set in, injuries occur, and you can't wait for the session to end. Sometimes the problem is that you look for meaning too far down the line. This makes it difficult to see. Clearing the murkiness might just be a question of asking, *What does lateness (and such) have to do with the next hour, or the next few minutes, or the next second?* You keep dividing things until you're able to read the choices that life is offering. Working through murkiness can often open unexpected parts of you. You can discover strengths you didn't know you had. Even low-energy days contribute to a more successful future.

EXERCISE

RISE TO THE occasion. Next time you find yourself in murky times, accept the challenge. Be prepared to reach inside yourself and discover the skills that life is drawing out of you that will be useful. Ask yourself, *What is life attempting to show you? What do I need more of? Attention? Trust? Faith? Courage? The ability to lighten up?* If you can't see the connection to something big down the way, apply questions to the next few minutes or seconds. Feel your energy immediately rise. Base your decisions on life's message.

Follow Divine Bliss

I ONCE ASKED a senior master, "What do you think life is all about." He said, "It's about me, you, and everybody, everything, everywhere. But your journey is to discover that it's about you!" Life is more than it appears. Each episode is a Divine event, containing choice, lesson, and the power to awaken you to your life's mysteries. Each is orchestrated and energized from the center of the heart—your own *and* that of the Divine. Indeed, intention at this level is one and the same. Living your deepest desire is living what the universe wants of you in an intimate way. Bliss is the illuminating light. On the mats, possibilities constantly burst open through which you can shine. You can be attentive, dismissive, or oblivious. It's up to you. Daily events work the same. You can transform a lifetime with just a tiny shift of attention.

EXERCISE

THE NEXT TIME you are faced with a decision, put your hand over your heart. Feel its energy. It is your telephone line to the Divine. Feel your choices. Feel the answer. Don't miss its input. Look for the good within the event. Consider it a session in your Earth dojo that is intended to power you up to your next level.

Follow the Warrior's Way

THE WARRIOR'S WAY isn't immune to challenge or hardship. These conditions are part of the human experience. Everyone is vulnerable. Nobody has it cushy all the time. In the dojo, workouts, drills, and matches aren't always a breeze. You can't always stop obstacles, but you can stop yourself from becoming the obstacle. Indeed, you come to recognize that tough circumstances are part of the cycle. Just as the athlete realizes hard exercise often yields better performance, the warrior mind seeks wisdom in life's challenges and uses that information to help see and make better choices down the line. When you are wiser, you are blinded less frequently by ignorance or fear. You are less manipulated. You discover that within you is the power to heal pain and suffering. You become confident. You stop fearing life's bumps and bruises and look to use them as a springboard to better places. Not everyone, however, wishes to be a warrior. Even this is a choice. You can apathetically sit around watching life happen, or you can jump in and start creating yours. It's up to you.

EXERCISE

WRITE THE WORDS "trust, "kindness," "loyalty," and "courage" on an index card (try making a bookmark). Take out your card and contemplate these words before going into each of the day's events. Plant them like seeds in your field of awareness, and tell yourself to try to tangibly put a little more of each of these qualities into every circumstance. See what happens. See how you feel.

Love

LOVE IS THE strongest force in the universe. Contrary to the Hollywood image of martial arts, love, not combat, is the core concept of all martial training. Indeed, anyone who misses this point, practitioner or otherwise, misses everything. From their inception, martial arts tuned in to the body's internal energy system and its function. Millenniums of study traced this energy (Chi) through the body, through all of nature, into the heavens, and ultimately into the very heart of the universe. The operative word here is *heart,* and martial philosophy takes this concept literally. You can call it whatever you want—God, Divine, Infinite, or Universe—but the martial artist's job is to use all of his or her martial skill to reconnect with this presence. Martial arts are your bridge from where you are to where you want to be. Why go across the bridge? Because doing so provides you with the power that creates, gives life, empowers, protects, and nourishes everything in the universe, including, of course, you. All martial laws and movements are a map to this place. One day when you're feeling much more than you're thinking, you're relaxed, content, and happy— you connect. On that day, you discover there is really just one heart. On that day, you discover that *you* are the universe.

EXERCISE

YOU HAVE WALKED across the bridge. Look ahead. Tell yourself confidently that you have earned the skill to rechannel all destructive thoughts into the creative, nurturing, protective power of love. Tell yourself that you choose from now on to live in love, to use the energy of your heart to create all of your days ahead.

364.

Teach

HISTORY TELLS US the Shaolin Temple was burned three times over the ages and the practice of martial arts forbidden. Each time the monks fled, some to distant places like Korea and Japan, they brought their knowledge with them. If not for the persistence and courage of these early teachers, martial arts as we know them would not exist today. The present-day Shaolin Temple, rebuilt yet a third time, contains pieces of stone from its original foundation. This symbolizes the sustenance and progress of knowledge. In turn, all martial practitioners are called forth to carry within them a piece of this foundation. You are now in a different place than when you first began reading this book. You understand nuances that you didn't earlier on. Teaching another person what you have learned not only carries on tradition, but also advances your skills, as well as the art that has gotten us here. Like the white belt turning black belt, turning white, turning black again, and so on, your journey is never-ending. Your job is to "empty your cup," begin anew, revisit each principle, and experience it through new history. Like the Shaolin monks before you, keep the foundation of martial arts strong by passing on a piece of what you know.

EXERCISE

FIND SOMEONE CLOSE to you and share the martial principles you have learned. Remember that in teaching you give back, but you also receive. Keep the good energy flowing.

365.

Seek Oneness

WHO AMONG US can say all that a kitten's purr means? Yet our body and deep consciousness know exactly what it means. The same is true with oneness. When in rare moments you energetically experience absolute peace—one single consciousness that swirls deep into your heart and extends to the very core of all things; one body manifesting itself in the form of lovers, opponents, all history, infinite faces, patterns, cells, particles, subatomic particles, creating and re-creating over and over in an ever-present *now*—no words can possibly do the experience justice. Indeed, oneness is indescribable, but not beyond feeling. It is our deep experience with being—that which we were born into and that to which we all have the power to return. Your brain cannot comprehend the experience. You can, however, feel its truths deep inside your heart. One of the greatest gifts of martial arts is that they guide us to this level of spirituality. This has been their purpose from ancient times onward. Enlightenment is ever-present in your dojo, which by now you realize is everywhere—and without walls. Then one day it happens: you experience absolute peace and oneness. Stay present. Let the path brighten before you. Feel how you and the light are one.

EXERCISE

TRY THIS TWICE a day. Relax and regulate your breathing. Concentrate on your heart's energy center. Feel your breast fill with energy. Direct this energy outward to the environment. Ask the environment to bless you. Ask it to bless someone in your daily experiences. Ask it to bless the human family, all of us traveling this road together.

A Final Word

THE REALIZATION THAT you and the universe are one doesn't take away life's challenges, but it does change the way you live. There is ancient martial arts tale that explains this notion. A child of twelve was devotedly studying martial arts. His job each day was to sweep the dojo blindfolded. As he swept, his martial master would softly cross the room and place a chair in his path. At first, the boy kept tripping over the chair. Several times, he fell over. Then he began to move more slowly, but the master just walked with a lighter step, and the chair continued to be an obstacle. It became a game. One day, the boy slowed down and became present enough to gently tap against the chair without knocking himself or the chair over. That day he smiled.

As time went on, sometimes the chair was there and sometimes it wasn't. Every now and then the boy would trip up again. But he had already tasted the solution. Each time, he became even more attentive and sensitive. In time he became so much so, like a cat, that he could hear his master's lightest footsteps. The more the master lightened, the more the boy increased his sensitivity. Eventually the boy learned he could intuit the chair. One day he moved in synchronicity with the master. Every step the master took, he was there. When the master placed the chair before him, he simply walked around it. That day both master and student smiled.

The game had become a lesson. By the time the boy reached adulthood, his powers had blossomed. People marveled at how he could disarm opponents without using any attacks or counterattacks. "There is no need for me to hurt anyone," he would say. "Obstacles are only obstacles if you perceive them as such. Once anything or anyone breaks harmony, they break themselves if they go far enough. The best thing you can do is harmonize yourself and help people rebalance. That way everyone is safe." This is the martial Way. It is a path charged by skill, trust, loyalty, courage, love, and self-empowerment, not by waiting passively for things to improve like a Hollywood fantasy. But there is always choice.

When life is darkest, you can choose to feel only darkness, or you can reach into your heart and feel the love of the universe swirling throughout you. You can let your most primal heartfelt instincts take over and relax in the presence of Divine light as you flow back into the brightness. The next moment of creation is all yours. Bow to the Divine in all things. Bow to the Divine in you. Bow to life.

Glossary

aikido: a Japanese martial art founded by Morihei Ueshiba. Aikido, a nonaggressive art that relies on redirecting an opponent's energy, translates to "harmony spirit way."

attachment: adhesion.

black belt: expert rank in martial arts.

brown belt: precedes the rank of black belt in many martial arts systems.

black sash: equivalent to black belt.

capoeira: a Brazilian martial art characterized by its dancelike and acrobatic movements. Usually practiced or performed with musical accompaniment.

centering: finding and strengthening your core. Centering is an essential martial arts concept and technique that is necessary for the development and advancement of physical, emotional, and spiritual skill.

centerline: an imaginary line beginning at the center of the forehead and extending straight down the front of the body.

Chi: life-force power, spirit, or energy flowing within and through all things. Martial arts teach how to harness this power through physical and meditative techniques in order to achieve tremendous physical and spiritual strength.

Chi Kung: a Chinese holistic art that focuses on harnessing chi for purposes of health, as well as physical, emotional, and spiritual strength.

Chi-Yi: directed life-force energy or spirit.

cooperative energy: a term for combined and coordinated energies with and among partners. Such energy is synergistic.

Divine: a term relating to or proceeding from the Infinite, God, the Universe.

Divine energy: pertaining the Infinite, God, the Universe.

Divinity: a term for the Infinite, God, the Universe.

Dojo: the place where martial arts are learned and trained.

Dumog: a Filipino martial art similar to judo and jujitsu in that the practitioner attempts to throw the opponent to the ground using grappling techniques.

Earth dojo: anywhere and everywhere on the entire planet, daily life.

energy centers: seven major areas located along the spine where energy enters the body, is processed, and is sent out again.

energy pumps: another term for energy centers.

full-tension movement: moving with muscles fully tensed or tensed as far as possible.

heart-mind: Xin-Yi, a core concept in martial arts training which utilizes chi to invoke the desires of one's heart.

highline: the upper third of the body.

holding center: remaining centered and protecting one's centerline.

Infinite: the supreme consciousness and intelligence of the universe.

information energy: a quality of energy; that force which gives energy purpose; the flow of information at the subatomic level in and throughout everything in the Universe.

jing: Chinese for "concentrated life force energy."

judo: a Japanese martial art founded in 1882, by Jigoro Kano, that relies on redirecting an opponent's energy.

jujitsu: one of the oldest Japanese martial arts that employs quick grappling techniques and emphasizes redirection of an opponent's force.

kali: a Filipino martial art that utilizes sticks and swords to teach open hand or unarmed techniques and movement. Kali is sometimes referred to as Arnis or Escrima.

karma: the universal law of action and reaction often referred to as the law of cause and effect by which a person creates his own destiny through thoughts, words, and deeds.

kata: a term for martial techniques linked together and performed in a series.

karate: a martial art developed in Okinowa, from Chinese Kenpo and Kung Fu, while Japan was still the governance of China.

Kenpo karate: sometimes spelled Kempo and often classified as a style of karate, is a Shaolin Chinese martial art style of Kung Fu that originated in the Shaolin Temple, in China.

Ki: Japanese word for Chi.

Kimi: focused, explosive power.

kung fu: martial art style developed at the Shaolin Temple, in China.

life force energy: the supreme energy within all things, another term for Chi.

lower *Dan Tien*: the major location of Chi in your body.

martial way: in accordance with the guiding principles of martial arts.

Muay Thai: a form of kickboxing founded in Thailand.

prayer hands: positioning your palms to face each other and holding them together as if praying.

Prana: Sanskrit for Chi.

redirecting: rechanneling energy.

reference point: initial point of contact.

regulated breathing: inhaling through the nose and exhaling through the mouth.

rooting: a way to strengthen your ability to balance.

Shaolin martial arts: martial arts styles developed and practiced at the Shaolin Temple, in China.

Tae Kwon Do: a Korean martial art characterized by its vast array of spinning, jumping, and flying kicking techniques.

Tai: supreme ultimate.

Tai Chi: often spelled taiji, is a martial art that originated in the Shaolin Temple of China and is characterized by its deep explorations of chi and it applications to health and spirituality, as well as self defense. Of significance are the tai chi concepts of internal energy and yin-yang which form/share the basis for traditional Chinese medicine.

Tai Chi Chuan: a form of Tai Chi known for its stress-reducing benefits as well as its self-defense applications. Tai Chi Chuan is known as one of the best practices for physical and emotional well being.

Tao: Way.

Tao Te Ching: an ancient text providing the philosophical basis for a way of living known as Taoism.

tap out: to end or withdraw from a match.

telegraphing: forecasting, announcing.

template: blueprint for behavior and cell development.

Universal Body: the quantum level.

Universal Chi: energy of the Universe, another term for Universal Energy Field.

Universal Consciousness: consciousness of the Universe.

Universal dojo: anywhere and everywhere in the cosmos.

Universal Energy: another term for chi.

Universal Energy Field: the energy within everything in the universe.

visualization: a process by which you use your mind's eye to see yourself performing a technique successfully.

Way, the: Tao.

Wheel of Life: a metaphor for the continuous cycle of birth, life, and death.

white belt: beginning rank in martial arts.

Wing Chun kung fu: a martial art of the Shaolin Temple, China. Founded by Zen nun Ng Mui, wing chun translates to "beautiful spring" and has become one of the most fascinating and respected martial arts of our times.

Wu Chi: the practice of conscious stillness.

wu-shin: empty-mindedness.

Wushu: the current name given to all Chinese forms of kung fu in order to standardize them for the purpose of athletic as well as aesthetic performance and competitive sport.

wu-wei: non-striving.

Xin: heart consciousness.

Xin-Yi: heart-mind.

Yi: intention.

yin: female, or reproductive, energy; energy that comes at you.

yin-yang: harmonizing with whatever is around you.

yang: male, or productive, energy; energy that pulls away from you.

Zen: short for Zen-Buddhism.